PAYARD DESSERTS

THIS BOOK IS DEDICATED TO ALL OF THE CHEFS AND PEOPLE I HAVE HAD THE PLEASURE OF WORKING WITH THROUGHOUT MY CULINARY CAREER. WITHOUT YOUR INSPIRATION, DEDICATION, AND TALENT, I WOULDN'T BE WHERE I AM TODAY.

—François Payard

PAYARD DESSERTS

FRANÇOIS PAYARD with TISH BOYLE

Photography by ROGÉRIO VOLTAN

Houghton Mifflin Harcourt

Boston • New York • 2013

Published by Houghton Mifflin Harcourt.
Published simultaneously in Canada.

For information about permission to reproduce selections from this book, write to Permissions, Houghton Mifflin Harcourt Publishing Company, 215 Park Avenue South, New York, New York 10003.

www.hmhbooks.com

Design by Vertigo Design NYC

LIBRARY OF CONGRESS CATALOGING-IN-PUBLICATION DATA:

Payard, François.
 Payard Desserts/François Payard with Tish Boyle; photography by Rogério Voltan.
    pages cm
 Includes bibliographical references and index.
 ISBN 978-1-118-43589-2 (cloth); 978-0-544-18646-0 (ebk)
 1. Desserts. 2. Cooking, French. I. Boyle, Tish. II. Voltan, Rogério. III. Title.
 TX773.P358 2013
 641.860944—dc23   2012043885

Printed in China

TOP 10 9 8 7 6 5 4 3 2 1

CONTENTS

Introduction *1*

Ingredient Notes *5*

Equipment Notes *8*

FROZEN DESSERTS

VACHERIN À LA MINUTE WITH LICORICE AND
FARM STRAWBERRY SORBET *15*

FRIED BLUEBERRY ICE CREAM WITH
BLUEBERRY COULIS *17*

PEPPERMINT PARFAIT GLACÉ WITH
CHOCOLATE PASTRY CREAM TUILE *21*

FRUIT DESSERTS

MANGO CARPACCIO WITH GINGER SYRUP,
POACHED GINGER, AND GINGER ICE CREAM
WITH CANDIED LIME PEEL *40*

APRICOT CHARLOTTE WITH RUM-SOAKED
RAISINS, CHAMOMILE CRÈME ANGLAISE, AND
WHOLE MILK ICE CREAM *43*

APPLE SPIRAL TEMPURA WITH APPLE CIDER
REDUCTION *47*

STEAMED BABY PLUMS IN EXTRA-VIRGIN
OLIVE OIL, FLEUR DE SEL, AND CARDAMOM ICE
CREAM *49*

YOGURT CAKE WITH SAUTÉED CHERRIES AND

PEAR POACHED IN PASSION FRUIT CARAMEL, ARLETTE, AND HONEY AND NOUGAT ICE CREAM   73

BROWN BUTTER ROASTED PEAR WITH MAPLE SYRUP AND VANILLA-PRUNE ICE CREAM   77

ROASTED SUMMER APRICOTS WITH HONEY PAIN PERDU AND SAFFRON ICE CREAM   81

PINEAPPLE SEARED WITH THYME WITH TAPIOCA PARFAIT WRAPPED IN PINEAPPLE GELÉE AND COCONUT SORBET   85

QUINCE COOKED IN CARAMEL WITH CHOCOLATE-BANANA BEIGNET   88

TROMPE L'OEIL PHYLLO PEARS WITH WALNUT CREAM AND POIRE WILLIAM CRÈME ANGLAISE   91

PASTRIES, MERINGUES, & OTHER BAKED DESSERTS

BUTTERMILK SCONES WITH STRAWBERRY AND TOMATO JAM   97

ALMOND-PRUNE NAPOLEON WITH PRUNE-ARMAGNAC ICE CREAM   100

CHESTNUT ICE CREAM NAPOLEON WITH WHIPPED CREAM AND CHOCOLATE-GINGER SAUCE   105

FOUR-HOUR BAKED APPLE NAPOLEON WITH CARAMEL CHANTILLY AND CARAMEL SAUCE   109

RED CURRANT NAPOLEON WITH PEPPERED NOUGATINE   112

BLUEBERRY PAVLOVA WITH WARM BLUEBERRY COULIS   115

RHUBARB NAPOLEON FILLED WITH BRAISED RHUBARB   119

WHITE CHOCOLATE ROSE WATER NAPOLEON WITH LYCHEE CRÈME GLACÉ   123

FEUILLE DE BRICK FILLED WITH SAUTÉED APPLES, PAIN D'ÉPICES, AND CARAMEL SAUCE   127

SOUFFLÉ OF PUFF PASTRY WITH ORANGE-SCENTED PASTRY CREAM, CANDIED PECANS, AND CARAMEL BUTTER SAUCE   129

PEANUT BUTTER AND MILK CHOCOLATE CRISPY NAPOLEON   133

CASSIS JAPONAIS WITH JAPONAIS NOODLES AND CASSIS PORT SAUCE   137

CUSTARDS, MOUSSES, & OTHER CREAMY DESSERTS

BEET AND MINT CRÈME BRÛLÉE—A MARKET INSPIRATION   142

PUMPKIN CRÈME BRÛLÉE WITH VANILLA CHANTILLY, CRISPY MERINGUE, AND CHESTNUT PURÉE   145

SHOT OF BUTTERMILK PANNA COTTA WITH TARRAGON-SCENTED MANGO   147

RECONSTRUCTION OF CAFÉ LIÉGEOIS WITH CACAO NIB–ESPRESSO TUILE AND MERINGUE STICKS   151

CRANBERRY GELÉE FILLED WITH PEAR BAVARIAN, NOUGATINE, AND POACHED PEAR   153

DULCE DE LECHE COULANT WITH AVOCADO PURÉE AND CHOCOLATE SORBET   156

DECONSTRUCTION OF CREMA CATALANA: BLOOD ORANGE GELÉE, FOAMED CRÈME BRÛLÉE, AND CINNAMON ICE CREAM   159

RICE PUDDING WITH SZECHUAN PEPPERCORN ANGLAISE AND CARAMEL BALSAMIC SAUCE   163

BANANA LEAF BOAT WITH LEMONGRASS CHIBOUST AND CITRUS SAUCE   167

HAZELNUT PRALINE DOME WITH GANACHE CITRON AND HONEYED PHYLLO LEAVES   171

RICE CRISPIES WITH MILK CHOCOLATE AND CRISPY CHOCOLATE PHYLLO 175

LEMONGRASS CHIBOUST WITH POMEGRANATE PINEAPPLE 179

STEAMED MERINGUE AND RHUBARB CREAM WITH BERRIES IN VANILLA BEAN SYRUP 183

BIG PALET D'OR FILLED WITH HAZELNUT WAFER AND MANJARI MOUSSE 186

CARRÉ PAYARD WITH CARAMEL ANGLAISE, FLEUR DE SEL, AND CARAMEL ICE CREAM 191

DUO OF COFFEE AND CHOCOLATE WITH A MASCARPONE-ESPRESSO SHOT 195

PYRAMID OF GIANDUJA WITH HIBISCUS BERRY GELÉE AND HIBISCUS SAUCE 198

CHOCOLATE DOME WITH VANILLA CRÈME BRÛLÉE AND HAZELNUT DACQUOISE 203

MILK CHOCOLATE CUBE FILLED WITH EARL GREY TEA MOUSSE AND GRAPEFRUIT AND ORANGE GELÉE 206

TARTS

APPLE CROUSTADE 213

WARM LEMON TART WITH FRESH RASPBERRIES, LEMON-BASIL SHERBET, AND BASIL OIL 215

LUCAS CARTON FIG TART WITH CARAMELIZED FIGS 218

BANANA TART WITH WHITE CHOCOLATE CREAM AND PASSION FRUIT SAUCE 221

CARROT CAKE TART WITH CREAM CHEESE ICE CREAM, HONEY-CARROT EMULSION, ORANGE BLOSSOM MERINGUE, AND FRIED CARROTS 225

FROMAGE BLANC SOUFFLÉ TART WITH BLUEBERRY MARMALADE AND FROMAGE BLANC SORBET WITH CUMIN 228

MASCARPONE TART WITH ROASTED FIGS AND MASCARPONE ICE CREAM 231

MEDITERRANEAN FENNEL TART FILLED WITH ANISE CREAM AND CANDIED FENNEL 235

CARAMELIZED PINEAPPLE-PECAN TART WITH BROWN BUTTER ICE CREAM 239

WARM CHOCOLATE TART WITH RASPBERRIES, CACAO NIB CRUNCH, AND GIANDUJA ICE CREAM 243

PEACH STREUSEL UPSIDE-DOWN TART WITH LEMON THYME ICE CREAM 247

WARM HONEY TART WITH CANDIED ORANGE AND HONEY-NOUGAT ICE CREAM 250

TRADITIONAL APPLE TARTE TATIN WITH BANANA CHIPS AND BANANA-RUM RAISIN ICE CREAM 254

RED WINE TART WITH SANGRIA PRUNES AND POACHED PEAR IN VANILLA SYRUP 257

COLD DESSERT SOUPS, CRÊPES, SOUFFLÉS, & OTHER DESSERTS

PEACH SOUP WITH APRICOT SORBET AND CRYSTALLIZED LAVENDER 263

CRÊPE PURSE FILLED WITH SAUTÉED BANANAS AND PASSION FRUIT WITH CHOCOLATE-PASSION FRUIT SAUCE 265

DARK CHOCOLATE SOUFFLÉ WITH PISTACHIO ICE CREAM 268

PLUM SODA WITH VANILLA ICE CREAM STICK AND ALMOND FINANCIER 271

EARL GREY TEA SOUP WITH TAPIOCA AND ORANGE SORBET 275

FARM STRAWBERRY-BASIL SOUP WITH LEMON-ELDERFLOWER SHERBET AND STRAWBERRY TUILE 277

RED BERRY AND TOMATO GAZPACHO WITH TOMATO CHIPS 281

CITRUS TERRINE WITH ELDERFLOWER-PERRIER SOUP AND TANGERINE SORBET 283

SPICY KUMQUAT SOUP WITH KUMQUAT-

BRIOCHE PANINI WITH RASPBERRY JAM AND PEANUT BUTTER CRUNCH ICE CREAM 289

CHOCOLATE BEIGNETS WITH ORANGE BLOSSOM CRÈME ANGLAISE 292

WATERMELON AND VODKA SOUP WITH A "LIMESICLE" AND LIME SYRUP 295

ORANGE TUILE RING FILLED WITH MARSHMALLOW AND ORANGE BLOSSOM ICE CREAM 298

THE CHEESE COURSE: SAVORY DESSERTS

BLACK OLIVE MACARON WITH GORGONZOLA ICE CREAM 304

APPLE TATIN WITH AGED WHITE CHEDDAR CHEESE, FRISÉE SALAD, AND TOASTED WALNUTS 307

WARM RICOTTA TART WITH CITRUS-MINT SALAD 311

POACHED SECKEL PEAR WITH POMEGRANATE, CABRALES CHEESE, AND SZECHUAN PEPPER ICE CREAM 313

BUTTERMILK PANNA COTTA WITH CITRUS TERRINE, MÂCHE SALAD, AND PARMESAN TUILE 317

FETA CHEESECAKE WITH RED WINE–POACHED DATES AND WHITE PEPPER ICE CREAM 321

PLUM TOMATO NAPOLEON WITH ROSEMARY DIPLOMAT CREAM AND TOMATO-BASIL SORBET 324

WARM BARTLETT PEAR WITH CHÈVRE CHEESECAKE, WALNUT CAKE, AND FRIED SAGE LEAVES 327

BASIC RECIPES

BASIC SWEET TART DOUGH 332

CHOCOLATE TART DOUGH 333

SABLÉ BRETON DOUGH 333

CHOCOLATE SAUCE 334

CARAMEL SAUCE 334

CRÈME ANGLAISE 335

CARAMEL CRÈME ANGLAISE 335

CARAMEL GARNISHES 336

CHOCOLATE MOUSSE 337

FRUIT TUILES 338

VANILLA TUILES 338

ORANGE TUILES 339

SIMPLE SYRUP 339

VANILLA ICE CREAM 340

ALMOND CREAM 341

PASTRY CREAM 341

STREUSEL 342

BRIOCHE 342

PUFF PASTRY 345

NOUGATINE 345

PINEAPPLE CHIPS 345

TOASTED NUTS 346

FRIED HERBS 347

TEMPERED CHOCOLATE 348

CLARIFIED BUTTER AND BEURRE NOISETTE 348

CITRUS SUPRÊMES 348

INTRODUCTION

WHAT MAKES A GREAT DESSERT?

This book is a collection of my favorite plated dessert recipes, from my years as a young pastry chef in Paris to my current role as a pastry entrepreneur in New York City. Though my style has evolved over the years, all the desserts in this book have one thing in common—they were all inspired by ingredients and flavor.

My philosophy of what makes a great dessert is a simple one: To capture great flavor, you must use ingredients as they come into season. Every great pastry chef works with the seasons, just like every great culinary chef. This means that you need to use a certain fruit when it's at its peak, not just because it happens to be available. And if you work within the seasons, your job will be a lot easier, because the flavor is already there—you just need to make the most of it by matching it with complementary flavors, ideally in a presentation that combines a variety of textures and temperatures.

I keep my presentation simple. I want food to look like food, and I want my ingredients to taste as good as they possibly can. A great plated dessert, in my view, begins by marrying simple presentation with incredible flavor. This philosophy, along with lots of hard work, has been the key to my success as a pastry chef.

When creating a dessert, I believe in using only as many ingredients as are necessary and no more, and that is why most of my desserts are relatively simple. If I am making a pear dessert, I make it all about the pear. The pear should be the star of the plate. For my Brown Butter–Roasted Pear with Maple Syrup and Vanilla-Prune Ice Cream, for example, the secret is to find the juiciest, most flavorful pear in the world from the market and try to represent its flavor in the best way possible, accenting it by roasting it in brown butter and maple syrup, then serving it with a round of baked almond cream, crunchy puff pastry, and a creamy vanilla-prune ice cream made with sangria prunes. Though there are other elements on the plate, this dessert works because it is still all about the pear.

Sometimes I see pastry chefs loading up the plate with lots of flashy elements, but they tend to forget about how the flavors work together and whether or not they add to the overall theme—too much showbiz, and not enough substance. What makes a great dessert? For me it is the subtle interplay of flavor, texture, and temperature, along with a streamlined presentation that conceals its complexity—that's what makes a great dessert.

DESSERT DU JOUR

Like fashion, pastry trends change from year to year, and sometimes even from season to season. This change in style is clear in the look of plated desserts, particularly those served at high-end restaurants, where talented pastry chefs can show off their imagination and skills every day to appreciative customers. Trends come and go, and plated desserts that were once cutting edge inevitably become tired looking and dated.

In the 1980s, for example, small portions and minimalism ruled, as the nouvelle cuisine produced a clean, pared-down style of desserts. In the early 1990s, architectural desserts became all the rage—probably as a backlash to the minimalist movement—and pastry chefs piled various elements skyward into towering creations that today seem extreme and just a little ridiculous. Then, in the latter part of the 1990s, comfort food became stylish, and classic recipes and simpler presentations were in vogue. With the new millennium came the pastry world's obsession with extreme dark chocolate and desserts made with the highest percentage chocolate available. Then came the molecular gastronomy craze. During this period, which continues today, pastry chefs started making liquid nitrogen ice cream and fruit "caviar" and garnishing their desserts with flavored foams.

While I appreciate the techniques of molecular gastronomy, I don't really use them. To my eye, desserts made with molecular techniques don't look like food anymore. I prefer to look at a dessert and know what I'm looking at and about to eat, and to be able to anticipate the flavors. Some chefs know how to execute molecular gastronomy techniques very well; they will combine French techniques with some molecular technique. That's fine, but other chefs take it too far. Why would I want to make a liquid nitrogen ice cream that is icy when I can have an incredibly creamy ice cream made with a standard ice cream machine? But now, because it sounds fun and new, people love it. I may be more conservative in that respect, but I prefer ice cream that has been prepared classically and has a creamy texture to a gimmick that produces an inferior product.

THE EVOLUTION OF A PASTRY CHEF

In this book, you will see various styles of desserts from different periods in my career. When you're a pastry chef, you always have to please the market, please your clientele, and, above all, please the chef you are working for, so you must adapt your style or you will not succeed. This is probably the biggest reason that my desserts evolved.

Each dessert was influenced by the style of the restaurant and standards of the chef I was working for at the time. The desserts I created in France at La Tour d'Argent and for Lucas Carton, for example, were mostly classics that required time-consuming presentations. The desserts were complicated because the patrons expected something amazing; an experience, something a little avant-garde. At these restaurants we never served more than 80 covers a night, and we had a large staff, so making labor-intensive desserts was not a problem. Then, in 1990, I came to New York to work for Gilbert Le Coze at Le Bernardin. The biggest challenge I faced then was to make desserts of the same quality as I had in Paris for sixty to eighty people a night in restaurants that now served desserts to 200 people a night. To do this, I had to eliminate some steps in their preparation, without sacrificing quality or having the very worldly customers be aware of the cut corners. The quality and execution needed to be the same, but I had to produce three times the volume with the same number of staff. My solution was to serve desserts that did not require a lot of à la minute, or last-minute, preparation. My Lucas Carton Fig Tart with Caramelized Figs, for example, needed to be carefully brûléed right before serving, and this took time and attention, so I decided not to put it on my menu at Le Bernardin. I was forced to streamline my recipes, choosing desserts that could be made in advance with limited labor required for plating.

At Restaurant Daniel, where I was the pastry chef from 1993 to 1996, my style changed again under Daniel Boulud's influence. Daniel encouraged me to make my desserts a little more playful, a little more showy. He understood that dining at Daniel was a special experience, and dessert was the diner's final memory of a meal there, so it had to be exceptional. My work area at Daniel was relatively small, so I was forced to adapt my recipes to accommodate my surroundings by preparing as much as possible ahead and trying to avoid à la minute desserts.

When I opened Payard Patisserie and Bistro in 1997, I had to adapt my style yet again. The kitchen was small, so the garde manger chef was making the cold appetizers and salads as well as plating the desserts. Because of the size of the bistro and its fast pace, we had to streamline the production of the desserts. Instead of making desserts requiring four or five steps, we chose desserts that had only three steps so that the garde manger chef could execute them without too much trouble, preferably in less than two minutes per plate. My Pyramid of Gianduja with Hibiscus Berry Gelée and Hibiscus Sauce, for example, was a time-consuming recipe, but it worked at Payard because everything could be prepared in advance: the dacquoise, the hibiscus gelée, the gianduja mousse pyramid, and the chocolate triangles for garnish. For plating, I only needed to add some sauce, the chocolate triangles, and a little gold leaf for garnish, and it was ready to go.

My Carré Payard is another example of a dessert that could be prepared in advance and plated quickly. The mousse cubes, with their salted caramel centers, were unmolded and waiting in the reach-in refrigerator for plating. To plate, they were simply set on a square of baked chocolate sablé breton and served with a spoonful of caramel crème anglaise and a quenelle of caramel ice cream. A piece of gold leaf was the finishing touch, and the dessert was ready to be served. My Roasted Summer Apricots with Honey Pain Perdu (French toast) and Saffron Ice Cream was another elegant presentation that could be prepared quickly with proper planning. The apricots were roasted an hour in advance, then warmed up right before serving and arranged on the warm pain perdu, with some sauce drizzled on top. A quenelle of saffron ice cream and a sugared vanilla bean completed the dessert in less than three minutes.

Twenty-five years ago, plated desserts did not even exist at high-end restaurants. Desserts—slices of cake and tarts and mousses scooped from a large bowl—were served from a cart that the waiter rolled to each table. But little by little, pastry chefs began serving individual plates from the kitchen, and it's really amazing just how far we've come in the past quarter century. I wrote this book to share the pastry knowledge I have acquired over the course of my career. I hope you will look at it not just as a collection of recipes, but as a resource for ideas and a source of inspiration, whether you're a working pastry chef, an aspiring culinary student, or a home cook with a passion for desserts. If you want to improve your craft, you must keep learning and keep your mind open, no matter how long you've been in this business or how good you think you are. After all, once we stop learning, we might as well just retire.

A Note on the Recipes

The recipes in this book were all tested in a conventional home oven. Some of the elements in the desserts—puff pastry, tart shells, cakes—however, will benefit from being baked in a convection oven. If you do this, simply reduce the oven temperature by 25 degrees F.

Cooking times will vary from oven to oven and from stove to stove, which is why I always give a range of time. Times may also vary depending on whether you use a gas or electric stovetop—electric burners take longer to react to temperature adjustments, so take this into account. You know the nuances of your oven and stove best, so use the cooking times in my recipes as a guideline and be sure to carefully check whatever is being cooked or baked.

These recipes were designed to be served in a restaurant, so they are not simple; most have multiple components. While none of the components are difficult to make, it does take time to make a complete recipe. For guidance, I've given each recipe a difficulty rating ranging from one to three whisks. One whisk means the recipe is relatively simple, without a lot of components, while three whisks means the recipe has multiple elements and will take several hours to complete.

A Note on the Wine and Drink Pairings

I asked Olivier Flosse, the talented sommelier and wine director of A Voce restaurants in New York, to pair each dessert with a specific wine or drink. Olivier carefully matched each dessert with a wine, liqueur, beer, or cocktail, and his brilliant recommendations are at the end of each recipe.

INGREDIENT NOTES

Using the best-quality ingredients possible is an important first step in making a great dessert. Here are my notes on some of the most frequently used ingredients in the recipes in this book.

ARMAGNAC. This brandy comes from the Armagnac region of southwest France, and it is aged for a long time in oak barrels made from local trees. It has a very sophisticated taste, subtle yet forceful, and I like to use it in desserts that feature winter fruits, particularly prunes and pears.

BUTTER. Always use unsalted butter, the best you can get. I only use Plugra brand, which is a European-style butter with a fat content of 86 percent. Because it has a low moisture content, it is creamier than regular table butter, and will make flakier pastry and richer sauces.

CACAO NIBS. These crunchy bits of roasted cacao bean add a nice crunch and intense cocoa flavor to everything from tuiles to ice cream.

CHESTNUTS. I use whole chestnuts and chestnut paste in my Chestnut Ice Cream Napoleon with Whipped Cream and Chocolate Ginger Sauce (page 105). The only brand I use is Sabaton from France, because it's the best. You can order Sabaton chestnut paste and whole chestnuts online from a number of sources (including www.qourmetfoodstore.com; see Sources, page 350).

CHOCOLATE. Though I use a few brands of chocolate in my shop, my preferred brand is Valrhona, because it is simply the best. Pay attention to the cacao percentages mentioned in each recipe, as using the wrong percentage can sometimes cause problems.

CHOCOLATE CIGARETTES. I use these as a garnish for a few desserts in this book. Though you can make your own, you can easily buy them from a number of sources (including www.pastrychef.com; see Sources, page 349), which is a great time saver and will allow you to spend more time making the actual dessert.

COCOA POWDER. I always use Valrhona cocoa powder, which is the best. It is a Dutch process (alkalized) cocoa powder and has a dark brown color and deep flavor. Cacao Barry and Guittard also make excellent cocoa powders.

COCOA BUTTER. To give a dessert a velvet finish (also known as *flocage*), melt together equal parts cocoa butter and dark chocolate and spray the mixture through a chocolate or paint sprayer. Always buy unflavored cocoa butter.

COCONUT. I always use unsweetened desiccated coconut in my desserts. It is available at many supermarkets and bulk or natural food stores.

CREAM. For most of my recipes, I use pasteurized cream with 38 percent butterfat. The exception is for ganache, where I use cream with 33 percent butterfat because of the high cocoa butter content of couverture. Try not to use ultrapasteurized cream—it lacks the flavor of pasteurized cream.

CRÈME FRAÎCHE. This is made by adding a bacterial culture to cream that has about 28 percent butterfat. I love its tangy flavor, which contrasts nicely with sweet elements, and I use it frequently in my desserts.

FEUILLES DE BRICK. This ultrathin, flaky dough is similar to phyllo, but it's lighter and a little more delicate. I love to use it to add texture to a dessert. When using it, you must work quickly, as it tends to absorb liquid and can soften and disintegrate. Get your pastry into the oven as soon as possible after assembling it.

FEUILLETINE. These are small, crispy flakes of baked crêpe that are ideal for adding crunch and texture to a dessert. I like to add them to chocolate along with some praline paste and use the mixture as a crunchy layer in desserts.

FLEUR DE SEL. This salt, which means "flower of the sea," is great as a finishing salt, for sprinkling on top of things before serving. It complements the flavor of sweet things, especially caramel, and it also adds a nice texture.

FLOUR. Most of my recipes call for all-purpose flour, and for that you should always use unbleached flour. One or two of my recipes call for pastry flour, which is available online (www.kingarthurflour.com; see Sources, page 350).

FONDANT. Poured fondant (not to be confused with rolled fondant) is an ingredient in the nougatine layers in my Red Currant Napoleon with Orange Zest Nougatine (page 112). Caullet is my preferred brand, because I like its consistency. Some brands of fondant are so thick that you practically break the spoon trying to get it out of the bucket.

FRUIT PURÉES. I use quite a few fruit purées in my recipes. The benefit of using a prepared fruit purée is that you get a consistent product. Fruit purées generally have 10 percent added sugar. My favorite brands are Ravifruit, Capfruit and Boiron, which are all available online (see Sources, page 349).

GELATIN. All the recipes in this book that include gelatin call for silver-grade gelatin sheets, which have a bloom strength of 160. If you prefer to use powdered gelatin (which has a bloom strength of 225), simply divide the weight of the gelatin leaves by 1.19. This will yield the weight of the powdered gelatin to use. For example, if the recipe calls for 3 sheets (0.21 oz/6 g) gelatin, you would divide 6 g by 1.19, which equals 5 grams of powdered gelatin. One teaspoon of powdered gelatin weighs 2.8 grams, so you would use just under 2 teaspoons of powdered gelatin as a substitute for the leaves in this case. Powdered gelatin needs to be sprinkled evenly over liquid (preferably cold water) and allowed to soften for 5 minutes before dissolving over gentle heat.

GLUCOSE SYRUP. Made through the conversion of starch into sugar, glucose syrup is mostly used as an ingredient in ice creams and sauces. Though you can order it easily online, you can also substitute light corn syrup for it.

ICE CREAM AND SORBET STABILIZERS. These emulsifiers reduce iciness and extend the shelf life of ice cream and sorbet. If you want to make ice cream or sorbet and keep it for a week, you must use a stabilizer. But, if you work in a restaurant and spin your ice cream and sorbet every day, it's not necessary.

INVERT SUGAR. Also known as Trimoline, invert sugar is a syrup derived from sucrose that has been split into glucose and fructose, and is manufactured by adding an acid to sucrose. Products made with invert sugar, such as sorbet, are less prone to crystallization than those made with standard sugar. Invert sugar is available from a number of sources (including www.pastrychef.com; see Sources, page 349).

LEMONGRASS. This long stalk has a lemony scent and is used frequently in Thai cooking. I love to use it in my desserts, because it pairs so well with fruits.

NUT FLOURS. These flours, which are nuts that have been ground to a fine powder, are a staple in my pastry kitchen, and I use them frequently in my desserts. They are available at natural food stores and a variety of sources online (including Bob's Red Mill; see Sources, page 349).

PRALINE PASTE. This is smooth paste made from hazelnuts and/or almonds and sugar. Use a European brand if possible, with 60 percent nut paste and 40 percent sugar. Available from www.lepicerie.com and other sources.

ORANGE BLOSSOM WATER. This is distilled water that contains the essential oils of the orange blossom. I love to use this Middle Eastern ingredient because it has a very subtle flavor and adds a hint of citrus to fruit soups, pastry cream, and many other components. Available at Middle Eastern groceries or online at www.chefswarehouse.com.

PHYLLO DOUGH. This is great for plated desserts, especially as an alternative to puff pastry. You always want to add some texture to desserts, something flaky, and you don't always have the room to make your own puff pastry.

ROSE WATER. This flowery ingredient has a very distinctive flavor, so it is important that you don't use too much, or it will overwhelm your dessert. Available at Middle Eastern grocers or online.

RUM. I use dark rum in my desserts, preferably Myers's brand, which is excellent.

VANILLA BEANS. Most of my recipes call for using whole vanilla beans as opposed to extract; whole beans give you a much fuller flavor. I like Mexican and Bourbon beans, but sometimes I mix them because they have different perfumes. Available from a number of sources, including www.amadeusvanillabeans.com.

EQUIPMENT NOTES

If you're serious about making desserts, you need the proper equipment, and if you've bought this book, no doubt you already have much of it. I think of the pastry chef as the MacGyver of the kitchen—the ultimate problem solver who can make a pastry comb or a tuile template out of a plastic lid, or fashion a tool from an item purchased at a home improvement store. But it's a real pleasure if you have the right tool for the right task on hand. Here are my notes on the equipment that is essential in a well-equipped pastry kitchen.

ELECTRICAL EQUIPMENT

BLENDER. A standard blender is a good alternative to a food processor or immersion blender, and works well for making a very smooth purée for a number of components, from sauces to sorbets.

ELECTRIC JUICER. A juicer is a great appliance to make fresh juice to infuse flavor into your desserts. I like to use fresh apple juice, for example, in place of purée to make apple sorbet. Fresh ginger juice also has an incredible spicy flavor that you won't get from a simple infusion or the addition of grated ginger. A juicer is also necessary for the fresh beet juice in the Beet and Mint Crème Brûlée (page 142), and for the carrot juice used in the Honey-Carrot Emulsion (page 226).

ELECTRIC SLICER. Nothing works better than an electric slicer for cutting ultrathin slices of fruit for chips and carpaccio.

FOOD PROCESSOR. This is a great tool for many tasks in the pastry kitchen, including making purées and grinding hard nougatine and other elements to a powder.

HEAVY-DUTY STAND MIXER. Don't try to cut corners by using a handheld mixer; you need a sturdy, well-built stand mixer that has a least a 5-quart capacity for these recipes. I recommend KitchenAid or Breville mixers.

IMMERSION BLENDER. I love this tool, because it's so convenient. It's great for emulsifying ganache, puréeing things right in the saucepan, or fixing a sauce that has "broken."

PACOJET OR STANDARD ICE CREAM MACHINE. The Pacojet machine, which "micro-purées" deep-frozen food such as ice cream and sorbet bases and mousses, is ideal for a small restaurant where the pastry chef needs to make small batches of several different ice creams and sorbets for service. I prefer the product made by a standard ice cream machine, however, so that's what I recommend.

BAKEWARE

SHEET PANS. These rimmed aluminum baking pans come in quarter, half, and full sizes. Most of the recipes in this book call for half sheet pans, which will fit in any oven. For best results, make sure your pans are perfectly flat and not warped.

SILICONE BAKING MATS. Used for lining sheet pans, these sturdy mats are made of fiberglass and silicone and can withstand oven temperatures up to 500°F (260°C). They are one of the best innovations in the pastry kitchen in the past fifteen years. Don't put them in the oven to dry—this just shortens their lifespan.

SILICONE MOLDS. I use these wonderful molds, which come in a variety of shapes and sizes, for many of the desserts in this book, from pyramids to domes to savarin shapes and financiers. They are great because it's so easy to unmold things from them, and they can be reused so many times. I often prefer to shape things by hand, into quenelles, for example, rather than use a mold, but these molds are great for banquets where you need to make 600 to 1,000 desserts.

TARTLET RINGS AND PANS. You have the option of either using 3-inch tartlet rings or pans for the tartlet recipes in this book. The only difference is that tartlet pans are easier to move around, because they have bottoms, while tartlet rings do not.

TUILE TEMPLATES. Most pastry chefs make their own tuile templates from large plastic lids, such as the one from a fish box, but you can use a plastic ice cream lid or a plastic folder. You can also purchase high-quality templates in a huge variety of shapes from www.tuiletime.com (see Sources, page 349).

COOKWARE

SAUCEPANS AND SAUTÉ PANS. A good selection of saucepans and sauté pans in assorted sizes are necessary for a number of tasks in the pastry kitchen. Choose heavy-bottomed, high-quality pans for your collection.

CRÊPE PAN. You'll need a good nonstick 6- or 8-inch crêpe pan to make crêpes for a few of my recipes.

HOTEL PANS. These deep, rectangular pans are ideal for baking custards, making granités, or chilling down mousses and other fillings quickly. For home use, I recommend a half-hotel pan.

MEASURING EQUIPMENT

DIGITAL SCALE. If there's one piece of equipment that you must have in the pastry kitchen, it's a good digital scale. Baking is a precise art, so it's very important to weigh ingredients. Get one that converts from metric to imperial measurements.

TIMER. A good timer is essential in the pastry kitchen, particularly when you are preparing multiple components of a dessert. Get one that can be programmed for multiple time settings, if possible.

INSTANT-READ THERMOMETER. It's necessary to have a good digital instant-read thermometer for cooking sugar, making crème anglaise, and many other tasks. A laser thermometer, an infrared thermometer that measures the electromagnetic radiation coming from the surface of a sauce (or whatever it's aimed at), is more expensive, but in my opinion is the best.

SMALL TOOLS AND SUPPLIES

ACETATE. These clear sheets are required for achieving a shiny finish on chocolate work. They are available in craft or art supply stores.

APPLE CORER AND PEELER. This hand-cranked tool peels, cores, and slices apples for pies or tarts incredibly fast. It makes slices that are all the same size and shape, which is important, because then they will all cook at the same rate. It will also turn an apple into a long, elegant spiral that can be coated and deep-fried, as in the Apple Spiral Tempura with Apple Cider Reduction (page 47).

BAMBOO SKEWERS. I use these all the time—they have many uses, such as serving fruit kebabs or as a tool for making caramelized nuts and chestnuts (see Hazelnut Praline Dome with Ganache Citron and Honeyed Phyllo Leaves, page 171, and Chestnut Ice Cream Napoleon with Whipped Cream and Chocolate-Ginger Sauce, page 105), or deep-frying delicate items (see Apple Spiral Tempura with Apple Cider Reduction, page 47).

BLOWTORCH. A propane or butane blowtorch is handy for caramelizing sugar on crème brûlées and tarts or on meringue. It is also ideal for warming the sides of ring molds before unmolding.

CHOCOLATE SPRAYER. This tool allows you to coat a dessert with a fine spray of chocolate and cocoa butter for a velvety finish. It is particularly useful for high-volume production of plated desserts.

DOUGH DOCKER. This spiked roller is used to prick doughs like puff pastry and pâte sucrée, which prevents them from rising too much during baking. Though it will take longer, you can also use the tines of a fork to do this.

FINE-MESH SIEVE OR CHINOIS. This simple tool is so important in the pastry kitchen. Use it for sifting dry ingredients and straining sauces, ice cream and sorbet bases, and infusions.

MANDOLINE OR BENRINER. If you don't have an electric slicer, this is a good, relatively inexpensive tool to use for slicing fruit for decorative chips or carpaccio.

MICROPLANE ZESTER. I love this tool. It is a long, extra-sharp rasp, which is essential for grating citrus zest, chocolate, and nuts.

PARCHMENT PAPER. Used for everything from lining pans to making small decorating cornets, this versatile paper is an essential supply for the pastry kitchen.

PASTRY BAGS AND TIPS. Select 18- or 20-inch disposable pastry bags, which are perfect for most piping jobs in the pastry kitchen. You should also have pastry tips, both plain and star, in a variety of sizes on hand. The higher the number of the tip, the larger the opening.

PASTRY BRUSHES. Available with natural, nylon, or silicone bristles, pastry brushes are used for jobs such as applying egg wash and prepping cake pans. If you are using a brush with natural or nylon bristles, be careful not to put it into hot liquids, as this will cause the bristles to loosen and fall out.

PASTRY COMBS. Also known as cake combs, these tools are made from plastic or metal and have serrated edges (either pointed or squared off) for making decorative designs on cakes, tuiles, and chocolate.

PASTRY CUTTERS. A set of round pastry cutters is essential for making plated desserts. Buy a set of cutters in graduated sizes ranging from 7/8 inch to 4 7/16 inch.

REGULAR AND OFFSET METAL SPATULAS. You should have both types of metal spatulas in large and small sizes for tasks such as leveling cake batter, spreading mousse, and spreading out tuile batter.

RING MOLDS. I use these stainless steel rings a lot for my desserts, particularly the 3-inch-diameter size. They are available in a variety of diameters and heights and allow you to unmold desserts easily.

ROLLING PIN. Though they are available in a variety of types and sizes, my favorite rolling pin is the simple dowel or "French" rolling pin, because I find it gives you more control than the ball-bearing pins.

SPATULAS AND SCRAPERS. You should have an assortment of rubber and silicone spatulas for folding, stirring, and scraping sauces, mousses, and other mixtures. Silicone spatulas are great for stirring sauces over the stove, as they are heat resistant up to 500°F (260°C), but they do have a finite lifespan and will eventually dry out, at which point they should be replaced. A plastic bowl scraper is great for transferring batters, mousses, etc., and smoothing the tops of things.

VEGETABLE PEELER. You will need a good, sharp peeler to peel fruit for many of the recipes in this book. My favorite peeler is made by OXO.

WHIPPED CREAM CANISTER WITH N$_2$O CHARGERS. This is one of the only molecular gastronomy tools I will use, occasionally, as I do in the Deconstruction of Crema Catalana (page 159). You can also use them to make flavored foams, which I like to see from time to time (but not on every dessert!).

FROZEN DESSERTS

FROZEN DESSERTS CAN TAKE MANY FORMS, and can be made from ice cream, sorbet, and an egg yolk pâte à bombe, among other bases. The beauty of these desserts is that they are all prepared in advance—in fact, they must be—and generally can be assembled and plated very quickly. In this chapter, sorbet is featured in an elegant fashion in my Vacherin à la Minute with Licorice and Farm Strawberry Sorbet, and as the filling for a thin chocolate shell meant to look like a coconut in my Chocolate Shell filled with Coconut Sorbet and Star Anise Sabayon. It's also the interior of the crispiest napoleon you'll ever eat in my Croustine filled with Fromage Blanc Sorbet and Blackberry Sauce. In three of the desserts in this chapter, a French parfait, made with eggs, sugar syrup, and cream, is molded and served with crunchy elements like caramelized nuts and tuiles to counterbalance its smooth texture. And finally, a fresh Blueberry Ice Cream is dipped in a fritter batter and refrozen multiple times before being deep-fried and served with a vibrant Blueberry Coulis, for a refined take on a Chinese restaurant classic.

VACHERIN À LA MINUTE with LICORICE and FARM STRAWBERRY SORBET

I CALL THIS RECIPE A NON-DESSERT, because each spoonful is like a puff of sweet air. This was a dessert I created for the ladies who lunched at Daniel, and it's made of a thin, licorice-scented meringue round filled with fresh strawberry sorbet. Licorice and strawberry is an excellent flavor pairing, though it's one you don't see very often. Diet-conscious diners love this dessert because it is much more interesting than eating a bowlful of plain sorbet, but doesn't have many more calories. Licorice powder is available online from L'Épicerie (see Sources, page 349) or from spice shops or Indian grocers.

MAKES 8 SERVINGS

COMPONENTS

STRAWBERRY SORBET
LICORICE MERINGUE ROUNDS
STRAWBERRY SAUCE

SPECIAL EQUIPMENT | ice cream machine; medium plain pastry tip (Ateco #5); 3-inch-diameter by 1½-inch-high tart rings

PERFECT MATCH | 2008 Zind-Humbrecht Riesling Brand Alsace Grand Cru, France

STRAWBERRY SORBET

8 cups (1 kg/2.2 lb) fresh, local farm strawberries, washed and hulled

Juice of 2 lemons

3 cups (700 g/24.7 oz) Simple Syrup (page 339)

3 cups (680 g/24 oz) water

1. Place the strawberries in a blender with the lemon juice. Blend until completely puréed and smooth.

2. In a medium bowl, combine the strawberry purée with the Simple Syrup and water. Cover and chill the sorbet base for at least 4 hours, or overnight.

3. Process in an ice cream machine according to the manufacturer's instructions. Transfer the sorbet to an airtight container and freeze until ready to serve.

LICORICE MERINGUE ROUNDS

1 tsp (3 g/0.1 oz) licorice powder

¾ cup (80 g/2.82 oz) confectioners' sugar, sifted

3 large (90 g/3.17 oz) egg whites, at room temperature

⅓ cup plus 2 Tbsp (90 g/3.17 oz) granulated sugar

1. Preheat the oven to 175°F (79°C). Line a half-sheet pan with a silicone baking mat.

2. In a small bowl, combine the licorice powder with the confectioners' sugar and set aside.

3. In the bowl of a stand mixer fitted with the whisk attachment, whip the egg whites on medium speed until soft peaks begin to form. Gradually add the granulated sugar and whip on high speed until the meringue forms stiff peaks. Remove the bowl from the mixer stand and gently fold in the confectioners' sugar mixture. Transfer the meringue to a pastry bag fitted with a medium, plain tip and pipe out eight 3-inch rounds and eight 2¾-inch rounds onto the sheet pan, spiraling the meringue from the center out. Bake the rounds for 2 hours, or until they are dry and crisp. Turn the oven off and leave the meringues in the oven for another hour. Cool completely.

STRAWBERRY SAUCE

   ¼ cup plus 1 Tbsp (62 g/2.18 oz) granulated sugar

   1 Tbsp (25 g/0.88 oz) glucose syrup

   1 cup (250 g/8.8 oz) strawberry purée

   1 vanilla bean, split lengthwise and seeds scraped

   ¼ cup (60 g/2.1 oz) water

1. In a small, heavy-bottomed saucepan, combine the sugar and glucose and heat over medium-high heat, occasionally washing down the sides of the pan with a wet pastry brush to prevent crystals from forming, and watching carefully, until the sugar caramelizes and turns a pale amber color, 3 to 5 minutes.

Stir in ½ cup (125 g/4.4 oz) of the strawberry purée and the vanilla bean pod and seeds and continue to cook, stirring, until any hardened lumps of sugar are dissolved, about 2 minutes. Remove the pan from the heat and stir in the remaining ½ cup (125 g/4.4 oz) strawberry purée and the water. Strain the sauce through a fine-mesh sieve and set aside to cool.

2. Cover the sauce and refrigerate until ready to serve.

ASSEMBLY

   8 small strawberries

Stir the frozen sorbet with a spoon to soften it. Place a 2¾-inch Licorice Meringue Round on a plate and place a 3-inch-diameter by 1½-inch-high ring mold around it. Spread the softened sorbet in the ring and use a spatula to level the top. Top with a 3-inch meringue round. Remove the ring. Garnish the top with a strawberry and spoon some Strawberry Sauce on the plate.

FRIED BLUEBERRY ICE CREAM with BLUEBERRY COULIS

CRAIG HARZEWSKI, one of my sous-chefs at Payard, and I improvised this recipe one September day as a way to use the beautiful blueberries that had just arrived. It was Craig's idea to make an ice cream from the berries, coat it in fritter batter, and then deep-fry it as the Chinese do. The dessert is a little time-consuming, as the ice cream needs four coats of batter to insulate it from the hot oil during frying. It took us a few tries to get it just right, but in the end we created a late-summer dessert that is fun, refreshing, and a little bit out of the ordinary.

MAKES 8 SERVINGS

COMPONENTS

FRIED BLUEBERRY ICE CREAM
BLUEBERRY COULIS

SPECIAL EQUIPMENT   ice cream machine; eight 2½-inch tart rings; bamboo skewers; Styrofoam block

PERFECT MATCH   Massenez Kirschwasser, Villé, France

BLUEBERRY ICE CREAM

2⅔ cups (320 g/11.26 oz) fresh blueberries

½ cup (120 g/4.2 oz) Simple Syrup (page 339)

1 cup (250 g/8.8 oz) whole milk

1 cup (250 g/8.8 oz) heavy cream

1 vanilla bean, split lengthwise and seeds scraped

6 large (112 g/4 oz) egg yolks

½ cup plus 2 Tbsp (125 g/4.4 oz) granulated sugar

1.   Set aside 24 of the blueberries. In a small saucepan, combine the remaining blueberries with the Simple Syrup and cook over medium heat, stirring occasionally, until the berries have softened, about 5 minutes. Remove from the heat and let the berries cool for 5 minutes.

2.   Transfer the blueberries and syrup to a blender and blend until smooth. Strain through a fine-mesh sieve. Place in a covered container and refrigerate until ready to use.

3.   In a medium saucepan, combine the milk, cream, and vanilla bean pod and seeds and bring to a gentle boil over medium heat.

4.   In a medium bowl, whisk together the egg yolks and sugar until pale. Whisk about half of the hot milk mixture into the yolks, then return this mixture to the remaining milk mixture in the saucepan and cook over medium heat, stirring constantly with a wooden spoon, until it thickens enough to coat the back of the spoon and reaches 175°F (79°C) on an instant-read thermometer; do not let the mixture boil, or the egg yolks will curdle. Remove the pot from the heat and strain the ice cream base immediately into a bowl. Set the bowl in an ice bath and stir frequently until cold. Stir in the reserved blueberry purée.

5. Transfer the ice cream base to an airtight container and refrigerate for at least 4 hours, or overnight.

6. Process the base in an ice cream machine according to the manufacturer's instructions. (Be careful not to overchurn the ice cream or it will become grainy.)

7. Arrange eight 2½-inch tart rings on a parchment paper–lined half-sheet pan. Scrape the ice cream into the rings, spreading the top level with a small, offset metal spatula. Insert 3 blueberries into the ice cream in each ring and smooth it with a spatula. Freeze the ice cream rings for at least 2 hours, or until firm.

8. Unmold the ice cream rounds and poke a bamboo skewer into the side of each round, as if it were a lollipop. Loosely cover the rounds with plastic wrap and freeze for at least 4 hours, or until hard.

BLUEBERRY COULIS

8⅓ cups (1 kg/2 lb, 3.27 oz) fresh blueberries

¼ cup (60 g/2.11 oz) crème de cassis liqueur

1. Place the blueberries in a medium saucepan over medium-low heat. Cook, stirring occasionally, until the berries are completely soft, about 8 minutes. Remove from the heat and let cool for 5 minutes.

2. Place the berries in a blender and purée until smooth. Add the liqueur and pulse just until blended. Strain the mixture through a fine-mesh sieve. Place in a covered container and refrigerate until ready to serve.

FRIED ICE CREAM

3½ cups (450 g/15.8 oz) all-purpose flour

1¼ tsp (8 g/0.28 oz) salt

½ cup plus 1 Tbsp (125 g/4.4 oz) olive oil

2⅔ cups (625 g/22.04 oz) water

4 large (120 g/4.23 oz) egg whites

Blueberry Ice Cream rounds (page 18)

4 cups (858 g/30.26 oz) vegetable oil

1. In a medium bowl, combine the flour and salt. In another bowl, combine the olive oil and water and slowly whisk it into the flour mixture.

2. In the bowl of a stand mixer fitted with the whisk attachment, whip the egg whites on medium speed until frothy. Increase the speed to high and whip to medium peaks. Fold the whites into the batter.

3. Dip the Blueberry Ice Cream rounds into the fritter batter once and stick the skewers into a Styrofoam block in the freezer to hold them up. Freeze for at least 30 minutes. Repeat until the ice cream rounds have been coated with batter 4 times. Keep frozen until ready to fry the ice cream.

4. In a deep, straight-sided saucepan or deep fryer, heat the oil to 400°F (204°C). Line a half-sheet pan with paper towels. Carefully slip the coated ice cream rounds into the oil, a few at a time, turning them frequently so that they color evenly. The rounds should expand and turn golden brown. Drain on the paper towels.

ASSEMBLY

Remove the skewers from the Fried Ice Cream and serve immediately with the Blueberry Coulis.

PEPPERMINT PARFAIT GLACÉ with CHOCOLATE PASTRY CREAM TUILE

FRESH PEPPERMINT HAS A VERY DISTINCTIVE, FRESH FLAVOR that can be described as both peppery and green. It goes really well with chocolate, so in this dessert I top a chocolate chiffon cake with a frozen peppermint parfait. The delicate chocolate tuile on the plate is unusual because it's made with a chocolate pastry cream that is baked and shaped into a fan while hot. A rich chocolate sauce stands up to the strong mint flavor of the parfait in this refreshing dessert.

MAKES 10 SERVINGS

COMPONENTS

CHOCOLATE CHIFFON CAKE
PEPPERMINT PARFAIT
CHOCOLATE PASTRY CREAM TUILE
CRYSTALLIZED MINT LEAVES
CHOCOLATE SAUCE

SPECIAL EQUIPMENT | 9 by 13-inch baking pan; 2¼-inch round pastry cutter; candy thermometer; medium, plain pastry tip (Ateco #6); ten 3-inch-diameter by 1-inch-high ring molds

PERFECT MATCH | 2009 Domaine Ramonet Bourgogne Blanc, France

CHOCOLATE CHIFFON CAKE

½ cup (53 g/1.86 oz) cake flour

½ cup (48 g/1.7 oz) unsweetened alkalized cocoa powder

½ tsp plus ⅛ tsp (2.6 g/0.09 oz) baking powder

Pinch of salt

3 large (56 g/2 oz) egg yolks

¼ cup plus 3 Tbsp (86 g/3 oz) granulated sugar

⅓ cup (60 g/2.1 oz) vegetable oil

3 large (90 g/3.1 oz) egg whites

1. Preheat the oven to 350°F (177°C). Coat the bottom and sides of a 9 by 13-inch baking pan with nonstick cooking spray and line the pan with parchment paper.

2. In a medium bowl, sift together the cake flour, cocoa powder, baking powder, and salt; whisk to blend and set aside.

3. In the bowl of a stand mixer fitted with the whisk attachment, whip the egg yolks with half of the sugar on high speed for 5 minutes, or until the mixture is pale and thick. Reduce the speed to medium and gradually beat in the vegetable oil. Remove the bowl from the mixer stand and fold in the dry ingredients.

4. In a clean mixer bowl, using a clean whisk attachment, whip the egg whites on medium speed until soft peaks begin to form. Gradually add the remaining sugar and whip on high speed until the whites form stiff peaks. Gently fold the whites into the batter.

5. Spread the batter into the prepared pan and bake for about 10 minutes, or until a toothpick inserted into the center of the cake comes out clean. Cool the cake in the pan, set on a wire rack.

6. Unmold the cake and, using a 2¼-inch pastry cutter, cut out 10 rounds from the cake.

PEPPERMINT PARFAIT

½ cup (100 g/3.5 oz) granulated sugar

¼ cup plus 2 Tbsp (90 g/3.17 oz) water

5 sprigs fresh peppermint

4½ large (87 g/3 oz) egg yolks

1 cup plus 1¼ Tbsp (250 g/8.8 oz) heavy cream

3 or 4 drops green food coloring

½ Tbsp (7 g/0.24 oz) peppermint schnapps

1. In a small saucepan, combine the sugar and water and bring to a boil over medium-high heat, stirring, just until the sugar has dissolved. Remove the pan from the heat, add the mint sprigs, cover, and allow to infuse for 15 minutes.

2. In the bowl of a stand mixer fitted with the whisk attachment, begin beating the egg yolks on medium speed. Strain the syrup, return it to the saucepan, and place over high heat. Heat the syrup until it registers 248°F (120°C) on a candy thermometer. Slowly pour half of the hot syrup into the whipping yolks (discard the remaining half, or refrigerate, covered, for up to 1 week for another use). Increase the speed to high and whip until the yolks are completely cool, about 5 minutes.

3. In another mixer bowl, using the whisk attachment, beat the cream on high speed to medium peaks. Gently fold the whipped cream, food coloring (just enough to make the mixture a pale green), and schnapps into the yolk mixture. Transfer the parfait to a pastry bag fitted with a medium, plain tip.

4. Place ten 3-inch ring molds on a half-sheet pan and pipe the parfait around the bottom interior edge of each mold. Place a cake round into each mold, pressing it into the bottom of the mold. Pipe the parfait on top of the cake in each mold, filling the molds. Use a metal spatula to level the top of each parfait and freeze the desserts until firm, at least 3 hours.

CHOCOLATE PASTRY CREAM TUILE

1 cup (250 g/8.8 oz) whole milk

¼ cup (50 g/1.76 oz) vegetable oil

⅔ cup (130 g/4.6 oz) granulated sugar

3½ large (180 g/6.3 oz) eggs

⅓ cup (40 g/1.4 oz) all-purpose flour

2½ Tbsp (20 g/0.7 oz) cornstarch

8.8 oz (250 g) 72% bittersweet chocolate, melted

1. In a small saucepan, combine the milk, oil, and ⅓ cup (65 g/2.3 oz) of the sugar and bring to a boil over medium-high heat, stirring, just until the sugar is dissolved. Remove the pan from the heat.

2. In a medium bowl, whisk the eggs until blended. Add the flour, cornstarch, and the remaining ⅓ cup (65 g/2.3 oz) sugar and

whisk until light and pale. Whisk about half of the hot milk mixture into the egg mixture, then return this mixture to the remaining milk mixture in the saucepan and cook over medium-high heat, whisking constantly, until the mixture comes to a boil and thickens. Remove the pan from the heat and stir in the melted chocolate until blended. Mix the batter with an immersion blender to emulsify the oil. Scrape the pastry cream through a fine-mesh sieve into a stainless steel bowl, set the bowl in an ice bath, and stir frequently until cold. Chill the batter for at least 30 minutes.

3.   Preheat the oven to 375°F (191°C). Line a half-sheet pan with a silicone baking mat.

4.   Using an offset metal spatula, spread the batter in a relatively thin layer onto the prepared sheet pan into two 4 by 10-inch rectangles. Bake for 3 to 5 minutes, or just until the tuiles are no longer shiny. Run a spatula under the entire length of each tuile rectangle to release it from the baking mat. Allow the tuile to cool long enough that it is firm enough to shape, but still warm (the tuiles are extremely delicate and break very easily). Curve the tuile into a loose-shaped fan. Repeat to make a total of 10 tuiles. Store the tuiles in an airtight container until ready to serve.

CRYSTALLIZED MINT LEAVES

⅓ cup (66 g/2.3 oz) granulated sugar

1 large (30 g/1 oz) egg white

12 fresh mint leaves

Put the sugar in a small bowl and set aside. Put the egg white in a second small bowl and whisk it a little to loosen it. Place a mint leaf on a piece of parchment paper or wax paper and gently brush both sides with the egg white. Toss the leaf in the sugar and place it on a plate. Repeat with the remaining mint leaves. Let the sugar-coated leaves dry for at least 8 hours, or overnight.

ASSEMBLY

Chocolate Sauce (page 334)

Unmold the frozen Peppermint Parfaits by placing each on an inverted cup and warming the sides of the ring mold with a blowtorch or a hot, damp towel. Slide the mold in a downward motion off the dessert. Place a Chocolate Pastry Cream Tuile on a plate and lean one edge of a Peppermint Parfait on top of it. Garnish with a Crystallized Mint Leaf and a drizzle of Chocolate Sauce.

CHOCOLATE SHELL filled with COCONUT SORBET and STAR ANISE SABAYON

THE TROMPE L'OEIL PRESENTATION OF THIS DESSERT, which looks just like a split coconut shell, hints at its tropical flavors. The shell is made by dipping a blown-up balloon in chocolate, allowing it to set, and filling it with a layer of Coconut Sorbet. The shell is then filled with a Star Anise Sabayon and served on a bed of Pineapple Carpaccio. The sorbet and pineapple are very refreshing, but the chocolate and sabayon are rich enough to make this dessert seem indulgent.

MAKES 8 SERVINGS

COMPONENTS

COCONUT SORBET
CHOCOLATE COCONUT SHELL
STAR ANISE SABAYON
PINEAPPLE CARPACCIO

SPECIAL EQUIPMENT | ice cream machine; 10 balloons; candy thermometer; mandoline or electric slicer; blowtorch

PERFECT MATCH | M. Chapoutier Ermitage Vin de Paille, Rhône, France

COCONUT SORBET

2¾ cups (660 g/23.28 oz) coconut milk

2 cups (500 g/17.6 oz) whole milk

1⅔ cups (330 g/11.6 oz) granulated sugar

1 cup (90 g/3.2 oz) unsweetened desiccated coconut

1.   In a medium saucepan, combine the coconut milk, milk, and sugar and bring to a boil over medium-high heat, stirring occasionally to dissolve the sugar. Remove the pan from the heat and stir in the coconut. Transfer the sorbet base to a medium bowl and place the bowl in an ice bath. Let stand, stirring occasionally, until completely cool. Transfer the sorbet base to an airtight container and refrigerate for at least 4 hours, or overnight.

2.   Process the base in an ice cream machine according to the manufacturer's instructions. Transfer the sorbet to an airtight container and freeze until ready to use.

CHOCOLATE COCONUT SHELL

1 lb (454 g) bittersweet chocolate, tempered (see Tempered Chocolate, page 347)

Coconut Sorbet (left)

Shredded coconut, for sprinkling

1.   Line a half-sheet pan with a piece of parchment paper. Blow up 10 small (11-in/ 28-cm) balloons. Dip one in the tempered chocolate, dipping it deep enough so that the

chocolate forms a bowl shape around the balloon. Set the dipped balloon, chocolate side down, on the prepared sheet pan. Repeat with the remaining balloons and chocolate. Let the chocolate set at room temperature until hardened, about 1 hour.

2.   Gently release the air from the balloons and remove them from the shells. Remove the Coconut Sorbet from the freezer and let it soften for about 10 minutes.

3.   Spoon some softened sorbet into a chocolate shell and smooth it with a spoon to cover the interior of the chocolate. It should look like a coconut shell. Sprinkle a little shredded coconut on the sorbet. Freeze until ready to serve.

STAR ANISE SABAYON

½ cup plus 1½ Tbsp (120 g/4.2 oz) granulated sugar

¼ cup (60 g/2.1 oz) water

2 pieces star anise

5 large (93 g/3.3 oz) egg yolks

¼ cup (60 g/2.1 oz) white wine

1.   In a small saucepan, combine the sugar, water, and star anise pieces and bring to a boil over medium-high heat, stirring, just until the sugar has dissolved. Remove the pan from the heat, cover, and allow to infuse for 10 minutes.

2.   Fill a pot halfway with water and bring the water to a boil over high heat. Reduce the heat to medium-low, so that the water is just at a bare simmer. In a medium stainless steel bowl, whisk together the egg yolks and white wine. When the sugar syrup has infused,

strain it and return it to the saucepan. Place over medium-high heat and cook, occasionally washing down the sides of the pan with a wet pastry brush to prevent crystals from forming, and watching carefully, until it registers 248°F (120°C) on a candy thermometer. Whisk the hot syrup into the yolk mixture and place the bowl over the simmering water. Heat, whisking constantly, until the mixture just begins to thicken (take care not to overheat this, or the egg yolks will curdle), about 2 minutes. Remove the bowl and whisk the mixture by hand until cool, about 5 minutes.

PINEAPPLE CARPACCIO

¼ pineapple, peeled and cored

Cut the pineapple in half lengthwise and slice it as thinly as possible on a mandoline or using an electric slicer.

ASSEMBLY

Granulated sugar, for sprinkling

Arrange 3 slices of Pineapple Carpaccio on each dessert plate. Place a frozen Chocolate Coconut Shell off center on the plate. Spoon some Star Anise Sabayon onto the plate, on top of the pineapple, with a portion of the sauce coming off of the coconut. Sprinkle some sugar onto the sabayon and use a propane or butane blowtorch to caramelize the top, taking care not to melt the chocolate. Serve immediately.

MAPLE SYRUP NOUGAT GLACÉ with ALMOND and PISTACHIO, and PISTACHIO CRÈME ANGLAISE

THIS FROZEN DESSERT was on my lunch menu at Daniel. Diners, especially women, prefer to eat light desserts at lunch, and this Maple Syrup Nougat Glacé, which is made with an Italian meringue, is refreshing and not at all heavy. It's also not too sweet—I don't like overly sweet desserts—because it's sweetened with maple syrup, not sugar. The chocolate and vanilla tuile loops have a pattern on one side, adding some drama to the presentation. A Pistachio Crème Anglaise and chopped pistachio nuts are a good match for this nut-studded glacé.

MAKES 8 SERVINGS

COMPONENTS

MAPLE SYRUP NOUGAT GLACÉ
PATTERNED TUILE LOOPS
PISTACHIO CRÈME ANGLAISE
CARAMEL STICKS

SPECIAL EQUIPMENT | metal or plastic decorative screen; 2½-inch-diameter by 1½-inch-high ring molds; candy thermometer; 3-inch ring molds; blowtorch

PERFECT MATCH | Brasserie Saint-Germain Page 24 Triple Beer, Aix-Noulette, France

MAPLE SYRUP NOUGAT GLACÉ

½ cup (125 g/4.4 oz) heavy cream

2 tsp (10 g/0.35 oz) Grand Marnier

2 large (60 g/2.1 oz) egg whites

¼ cup (75 g/2.6 oz) maple syrup

3 Tbsp (60 g/2.1 oz) glucose syrup

1 Tbsp (25 g/0.9 oz) diced candied orange peel

½ cup plus 1 Tbsp (50 g/1.76 oz) sliced almonds, toasted and chopped (see Toasted Nuts, page 346)

⅓ cup (50 g/1.76 oz) pistachios, toasted and chopped (see Toasted Nuts, page 346)

1. Line a half-sheet pan with a silicone baking mat and arrange eight 2½-inch-diameter by 1½-inch-high ring molds on it.

2. In the bowl of a stand mixer fitted with the whisk attachment, whip the heavy cream and the Grand Marnier to medium peaks. Cover the bowl and refrigerate the cream until ready to use.

3. In a clean mixer bowl, using a clean whisk attachment, begin whipping the egg whites on low speed. Meanwhile, in a small saucepan, combine the maple syrup and glucose and cook over high heat, occasionally brushing down the sides of the pan with a wet pastry brush to prevent crystals from forming, and watching carefully, until the syrup reaches 248°F (120°C) on a candy thermometer. Slowly pour the hot syrup into the whipping egg whites in a steady stream and whip on high speed until they are completely cool. Gently fold in the candied orange peel and nuts. Fold

in the whipped cream. Scrape the mixture into a pastry bag with no tip and pipe the mixture into each of the ring molds, filling them all the way. Level the tops with a metal spatula and freeze for at least 3 hours, or until firm.

4. Warm the sides of the rings with a propane blowtorch or a hot, damp towel, and unmold the Maple Syrup Nougat Glacés by pushing them up from the bottom. Loosely cover and freeze until ready to serve.

PATTERNED TUILE LOOPS

Vanilla Tuile batter (page 338)

2 Tbsp plus 2 tsp (15 g/0.5 oz) unsweetened alkalized cocoa powder, sifted

1. Place half the tuile batter in a medium bowl. Stir in the cocoa powder until blended. Place a silicone baking mat on a sheet pan. Place a metal or plastic decorative screen on the mat and spread some of the chocolate tuile batter over the screen, covering it in a thin, even layer. Lift off the screen and freeze the tuile batter for at least 2 hours, until firm.

2. Preheat the oven to 350°F (177°C). Remove the baking mat from the freezer and immediately, before the cocoa batter softens, spread a thin, even layer of plain Tuile Batter on top of the cocoa tuile design. Bake just until the tuile sheet is set, but not colored, about 5 minutes. Remove the pan from the oven and invert the baking mat onto a cutting board. Peel the mat off the tuile sheet and place it back on the sheet pan. Using a pastry wheel, cut out eight long strips, each 1½ inches wide in the center, that have tapered, pointed ends (see photograph opposite). Return the strips to the lined sheet pan and bake until the plain tuile batter is golden, about 4 minutes. While the strips are still warm, wrap each around one of the 3-inch ring molds or a 3-inch canister, forming a looped shape. (Rewarm the strips in the oven for a minute or two before molding them if they have cooled down too much and are no longer pliable.) Cool the tuiles, remove the molds, and store the tuile loops in an airtight container until ready to serve.

PISTACHIO CRÈME ANGLAISE (page 335)

CARAMEL STICKS

Caramel Garnishes (page 336)

1. Follow the instructions for the Caramel Garnish through step 2. Dip a thick wooden spoon in the caramel and move the spoon back and forth over the silicone baking mat, drizzling the caramel in solid, even lines. Allow the caramel to harden.

2. When the caramel lines have hardened, cut them with a knife so that they are about 6 inches long. Store the sticks in an airtight container at room temperature.

ASSEMBLY

8 shelled pistachios

Finely chopped pistachio nuts, for sprinkling on the plate

Using a long skewer, poke a hole through the center of each Maple Syrup Nougat Glacé. Place a nougat glacé round on its side inside one of the Patterned Tuile Loops, and place the dessert on a plate. Push a Caramel Stick through the center hole so that it comes out the other side. Top with a pistachio nut. Garnish the plate with a drizzle of Pistachio Crème Anglaise and a sprinkling of chopped pistachio nuts.

KUGELHOPF CARAMEL GLACÉ with RUM-RAISIN PARFAIT, CARAMEL CRÈME ANGLAISE, and CHOCOLATE SAUCE

YEARS AGO, this frozen dessert was a best seller at my dad's pastry shop in Nice, and I started making it at Daniel when I became their first pastry chef in 1993. It's not made in a kugelhopf mold, but the idea is the same—there's a caramel ice cream on the outside and a beautiful rum-raisin parfait inside. People love it because it's refreshing and relatively light—the perfect way to end a big meal. I serve it with caramel and chocolate sauces and a delicate tuile. The presentation might look a little dated, but it really is delicious!

MAKES 10 SERVINGS

COMPONENTS

CARAMEL PARFAITS
   CARAMEL ICE CREAM
   RUM-RAISIN PARFAIT CENTERS
TUILE OVALS
CARAMEL STICKS
CARAMEL CRÈME ANGLAISE
CHOCOLATE SAUCE

SPECIAL EQUIPMENT | ice cream machine; eight 3-inch-diameter dome molds; 5-inch-long, oval-shaped stencil for tuiles; small, plain pastry tip (Ateco #3)

PERFECT MATCH | Dönnhoff Ice Wine, Nahe, Germany

CARAMEL ICE CREAM

4 cups plus 2 Tbsp (1 kg g/35.27 oz) whole milk

2¼ cups (450 g/16 oz) granulated sugar

¼ cup (59 g/2 oz) water

Pinch of sea salt

¼ cup plus 1 Tbsp (100 g/2.1 oz) glucose or light corn syrup

14 large (250 g/8.8 oz) egg yolks

1.   In a small saucepan, heat the milk over medium heat until hot. Reduce the heat to low to keep the milk warm.

2.   In a small, heavy bottomed saucepan, combine 1¼ cups (250 g/8.8 oz) of the sugar with the water, salt, and glucose and cook over medium-high heat, occasionally washing down the sides of the pan with a wet pastry brush to prevent crystals from forming, until the sugar caramelizes and turns a medium amber color. Remove the pan from the heat and gradually stir in the warm milk (be careful—the mixture will bubble up as you add the milk). Return the pan to the heat and stir until any hardened bits of caramel are dissolved. Remove the pan from the heat.

3.   In a medium bowl, whisk together the egg yolks and the remaining 1 cup (200 g/7 oz) sugar until pale. Whisk about ½ cup of the hot caramel mixture into the yolks, then return this mixture to the remaining caramel mixture in the saucepan. Cook over medium heat, stirring constantly, until the mixture thickens enough to coat the back of a spoon and reaches 175°F (79°C) on an instant-read thermometer; do not let the mixture boil, or the egg yolks will curdle. Remove the pot from the heat and strain the ice cream base through a fine-mesh sieve into a bowl. Set the bowl in an ice bath and stir frequently until completely cool. Transfer the ice cream base to an airtight container and refrigerate for at least 4 hours, or overnight.

4.   Process the base in an ice cream machine according to the manufacturer's instructions. (Be careful not to overchurn the ice cream or it will become grainy.)

5.   Fill eight 3-inch-diameter dome molds halfway with the soft ice cream, and using a spoon, spread the ice cream up the sides of each mold, all the way to the top, creating an indentation in the center. Place the molds in the freezer for at least 4 hours, or until firm.

RUM-RAISIN PARFAIT CENTERS

¼ cup (40 g/1.4 oz) golden raisins (if they are hard, soak them in hot water for an hour and drain before using)

1½ Tbsp (20 g/0.7 oz) Meyers's dark rum

¾ cup plus 1½ Tbsp (200 g/7 oz) water

1 cup (200 g/7 oz) granulated sugar

1 cup plus 2 Tbsp (100 g/3.5 oz) sliced almonds

2 large (100 g/3.5 oz) eggs

¾ cup (175 g/6.17 oz) heavy cream, whipped to soft peaks

Caramel Ice Cream (page 31)

1.   In a small container, combine the raisins and rum. Cover and let soak overnight.

2.   Preheat the oven to 350°F (177°C). In a small saucepan, combine the water and sugar and bring to a boil, stirring, just until the sugar has dissolved. Remove from the heat and cool.

3.   Set aside ¾ cup (200 g/7 oz) of the syrup. In a medium bowl, combine the almonds with enough of the remaining syrup to coat them well, tossing to coat evenly. Spread the nuts out on a half-sheet pan and bake for about 10 minutes, tossing once or twice during baking, until golden brown. Cool completely.

4.   In the bowl of a stand mixer fitted with the whisk attachment, whip the eggs on medium speed. Meanwhile, reheat the reserved sugar syrup in a small saucepan until it registers 240°F (116°C) on a candy thermometer. Gradually add the hot syrup to the whipping eggs, then increase the speed to high and whip until the eggs are completely cool, about 5 minutes. Remove half of the whipped eggs and gently fold the whipped cream, toasted

almonds, and rum-soaked raisins (and any leftover rum) into the remaining half (you will not use the other half of the egg mixture, but it is too difficult to whip up a smaller amount of eggs and syrup than this; discard it or use it as a topping for berries).

5. Remove the Caramel Ice Cream Parfaits from the freezer and spoon the rum-raisin mixture into the indentations. Freeze until firm, at least 4 hours.

TUILE OVALS

Vanilla Tuile batter (page 338)

Preheat the oven to 350°F (177°C). Line a half-sheet pan with a silicone baking mat. Using an offset metal spatula, spread a thin layer of tuile batter over a 5-inch-long, oval-shaped stencil onto the baking mat. Form 3 more tuile ovals on the mat. Bake the tuiles for about 8 minutes, or until golden brown. Remove the pan from the oven and, while the tuiles are still hot, use a small, plain pastry tip to make a hole at the short ends of each tuile. Return the tuiles to the oven for about a minute to rewarm, then curve each tuile around a rolling pin. Allow to cool. Repeat this process to make 4 more Tuile Ovals. Store the tuiles in an airtight container until ready to serve.

CARAMEL STICKS

Caramel Garnishes (page 336)

1. Follow the instructions for the Caramel Garnish through step 2. Dip a thick wooden spoon in the caramel and move the spoon back and forth over the silicone baking mat, drizzling the caramel in solid, even lines. Allow the caramel to harden.

2. When the caramel lines have hardened, cut them to the desired size with a knife. Store the sticks in an airtight container at room temperature.

CARAMEL CRÈME ANGLAISE
(page 335)

CHOCOLATE SAUCE (page 334)

ASSEMBLY

Cocoa powder, for dusting

Spoon some Caramel Crème Anglaise in a circle on a plate. Draw a circle with the Chocolate Sauce on the inside perimeter of the caramel sauce. Using a toothpick in a circular motion, make a design through the sauces. Unmold the Caramel Parfaits. Lightly dust the dome with cocoa powder and place the frozen dessert in the center of the plate. Thread a Caramel Stick through the two holes of a Tuile Oval and press it into the dome. (Make sure to push a hole into the parfait with a skewer before inserting the stick, or the stick will break.) The tuile should rest on top of the dome like a sail, with the stick pointing straight up.

CROUSTINE filled with FROMAGE BLANC SORBET and BLACKBERRY SAUCE

A FEW YEARS AGO, I was looking through an old French pastry book and came across a recipe for a croustine, which is similar to a baked nougatine. That inspired me to create this dessert, which is composed of ultrathin, crispy croustine rounds layered with a tangy Fromage Blanc Sorbet, fresh blackberry slices, and a sweet-tart Blackberry Sauce. The dessert is crowned with crescents of baked phyllo dough that have been lightly dusted with confectioners' sugar for a dramatic presentation. Make this one in late summer, when blackberries are at their peak.

MAKES 8 SERVINGS

COMPONENTS

CROUSTINE TUILE ROUNDS
FROMAGE BLANC SORBET
PHYLLO CRESCENTS
BLACKBERRY SAUCE

SPECIAL EQUIPMENT | ice cream machine; 2¾-inch round pastry cutter: 2-inch round pastry cutter; 3-inch round pastry cutter

PERFECT MATCH | Brasseries Kronenbourg Wel Scotch Beer, Strasbourg, France

CROUSTINE TUILE ROUNDS

2⅔ cups (300 g/10.6 oz) confectioners' sugar

⅔ cup (80 g/2.8 oz) all-purpose flour

3½ cups (300 g/10.6 oz) sliced almonds

⅓ cup (120 g/4.2 oz) honey

14 Tbsp (200 g/7 oz) unsalted butter, cut into tablespoon-size pieces

1. Line two half-sheet pans with silicone baking mats. In a medium bowl, stir together the confectioners' sugar, flour, and sliced almonds.

2. Place the honey and butter in a medium saucepan over medium heat. Cook, stirring occasionally, until the butter has melted. Stir the mixture into the dry ingredients until

blended. Using an offset metal spatula, spread half of the batter onto each of the prepared sheet pans, smoothing it into an even layer. Refrigerate the batter on the pans for 1 hour.

3. Preheat the oven to 350°F (177°C). Bake the batter, one sheet pan at a time, for 18 to 20 minutes, or until the tuile sheets are caramelized and dark brown. Let cool for 5 minutes.

4. While the tuile sheet is still warm and pliable, run a metal spatula underneath it and carefully transfer it to a cutting board. Using a 2¾-inch round pastry cutter, cut out 24 rounds from the sheet (if necessary, return the tuile sheet to the oven for a minute or two to soften it). Transfer the rounds to a flat sheet pan and cool completely. Store in an airtight container until ready to serve.

FROMAGE BLANC SORBET

¼ cup plus 2¾ Tbsp (100 g/3.5 oz) water

⅔ cup (130 g/4.6 oz) granulated sugar

Finely grated zest of 1 orange

Finely grated zest of ½ lime

¾ cup plus 1 Tbsp (200 g/7 oz) fromage blanc

½ cup (125 g/4.4 oz) sour cream

⅓ cup plus 1 Tbsp (100 g/3.5 oz) yogurt

1.   In a small saucepan, combine the water, sugar, and citrus zests. Bring to a boil over high heat, stirring occasionally, just until the sugar is dissolved. Remove from the heat.

2.   In a large mixing bowl, use an immersion blender to combine the fromage blanc, sour cream, and yogurt. Add the sugar syrup and blend well. Cover the bowl and refrigerate for at least 4 hours.

3.   Line a half-sheet pan with a piece of parchment paper. Process the sorbet base in an ice cream machine according to the manufacturer's instructions. Spread the sorbet onto the prepared sheet pan in an even layer. Cover with plastic wrap and freeze until firm, at least 3 hours.

4.   Using a 2-inch round pastry cutter, cut out 16 rounds of sorbet from the sheet. Reserve the remaining sorbet in an airtight container in the freezer. Place the rounds on a half-sheet pan, cover with plastic wrap, and freeze until ready to use.

PHYLLO CRESCENTS

4 (13 by 18-inch) sheets phyllo dough

16 Tbsp (226 g/8 oz) unsalted butter, melted

Confectioners' sugar, as needed

1.   Position a rack in the center of the oven and preheat the oven to 350°F (177°C). Line a half-sheet pan with a silicone baking mat and set aside.

2.   Place a sheet of the phyllo dough on a piece of parchment paper and brush it with the melted butter. Dust the sheet with confectioners' sugar. Repeat the layering process until you have used 4 phyllo sheets. Brush the top sheet with butter and dust with confectioners' sugar. Refrigerate the phyllo layers for 30 minutes, or until the butter has firmed up.

3.   Transfer the layers to a cutting board and, using a 3-inch round cutter, cut out a round from the stack. Remove the round and move the cutter about ½ inch into the uncut phyllo and cut out a crescent shape. Place the crescent on the prepared sheet pan and repeat to make a total of 8 crescents. Bake for 10 minutes, or until the crescents are crisp. Place the sheet pan on a wire rack and cool completely.

BLACKBERRY SAUCE

¾ cup (250 g/8.8 oz) blackberry purée

¼ cup plus 1 Tbsp (62 g/2.2 oz) granulated sugar

3 Tbsp (48 g/1.7 oz) crème de cassis liqueur

Finely grated zest of 1 lime

In a small saucepan, combine the blackberry purée, sugar, and liqueur. Cook over medium heat, stirring constantly, for 5 minutes, or until all of the sugar has dissolved. Remove from the heat and stir in the lime zest. Cool completely.

ASSEMBLY

2½ cups (283 g/10 oz) fresh blackberries, sliced

Put a Croustine Tuile Round in the center of a plate. Place a frozen Fromage Blanc Sorbet disk in the center of the tuile. Arrange the blackberry slices around the outside portion of the sorbet, with the cut side facing out. Place a second Croustine Tuile Round on top and repeat. Top with a third round. Place a small scoop of the reserved Fromage Blanc Sorbet in the center of the round. Cut a Phyllo Crescent crosswise in thirds, and stick each part into the sorbet, with the tips pointing outward. Place one blackberry slice between each Phyllo Crescent. Pour some Blackberry Sauce over the scoop of sorbet onto the dessert.

FRUIT
DESSERTS

I HAVE TO CREDIT DANIEL BOULUD for inspiring me to create so many fruit desserts. Daniel loves fruit, and when I worked for him, I really focused on using the best fruit the market had to offer during its peak season. In my opinion, a pastry chef should think more like savory chefs do in terms of produce. That is, they should decide what to make once they see what is available, then select the best fruits or berries that will become the prime ingredient of a memorable dessert.

The fruits used in the recipes in this chapter represent all seasons, from the lush berries and stone fruits of summer to the pears, quinces, and apples of fall, and the citrus fruits of winter to the delicate pink rhubarb of spring. Whatever the season, make sure you use the best possible produce available, as nothing will compensate for the lack of flavor of poor-quality, out-of-season, or unripe fruit.

MANGO CARPACCIO with GINGER SYRUP, POACHED GINGER, and GINGER ICE CREAM with CANDIED LIME PEEL

THE INSPIRATION FOR THIS DESSERT came from my friend Pierre Hermé, who makes something very similar, a mango carpaccio topped with crystallized cilantro. Instead of cilantro, my version uses ginger as a spicy complement to the sweet mango. I drizzle a Ginger Syrup on top, add some pieces of Poached Ginger, and then a quenelle of Ginger Ice Cream. The subtle acidity of Candied Lime Peel tempers the sweetness of the fruit. To me, it's the perfect summer dessert: light, simple, and so refreshing.

MAKES 6 SERVINGS

COMPONENTS

GINGER SYRUP
POACHED GINGER
GINGER ICE CREAM
CANDIED LIME PEEL
MANGO CARPACCIO

SPECIAL EQUIPMENT |
cheesecloth; ice cream machine; saucepan; fine-mesh sieve; electric slicer or mandoline

PERFECT MATCH | S. A. Prüm "Essence" Riesling, Mosel, Germany

GINGER SYRUP

1 (2½-inch) piece (75 g/2.6 oz) fresh ginger, peeled and grated

1 cup (236 g/8.3 oz) water

1½ cups (300 g/10.5 oz) granulated sugar

1.   Place the ginger in a double-layered square of cheesecloth and gather the cheesecloth around it to form a purse. Squeeze the ginger, letting the juice trickle into a bowl, until all its juice has been extracted. You should have about ¼ cup (56 ml/2 fl oz) ginger juice.

2.   In a small saucepan, combine the water and sugar and bring to a boil over medium-high heat, stirring, just until the sugar has

dissolved. Remove the pan from the heat and stir in the ginger juice. Set aside to cool.

3.   Refrigerate the Ginger Syrup in a covered container for at least 24 hours.

4.   Strain through a fine-mesh sieve before using.

POACHED GINGER

1 (2½-inch) piece (75 g/2.6 oz) fresh ginger

1 cup (250 g/8.8 oz) Simple Syrup (page 339)

1.   Peel the ginger and slice it into very thin slices on a mandoline. Place the slices in a

small saucepan with the Simple Syrup and bring to a boil over medium heat. Reduce the heat to medium-low and simmer until the ginger is translucent, about 10 minutes. Set aside to cool.

2. Reserve about 3 tablespoons (28 g/1 oz) of the poached ginger slices to use in the Ginger Ice Cream. Place the remaining ginger and syrup together in a covered container in the refrigerator until ready to serve.

GINGER ICE CREAM

1 cup (250 g/8.8 oz) whole milk

1 cup (250 g/8.8 oz) heavy cream

1 (2½-inch) piece (75 g/2.6 oz) fresh ginger, peeled and chopped

6 large (112 g/4 oz) egg yolks

½ cup plus 2 Tbsp (125 g/4.4 oz) granulated sugar

Reserved Poached Ginger slices (page 40), chopped

1.   In a medium saucepan, combine the milk, cream, and the chopped fresh ginger and bring to a gentle boil over medium heat. Remove the pan from the heat, cover, and allow to infuse for 20 minutes.

2.   Return the pan to medium heat and bring to a boil. In a medium bowl, whisk together the egg yolks and sugar until pale. Whisk about half of the hot milk mixture into the yolks, then return this mixture to the remaining milk mixture in the saucepan and cook over medium heat, stirring constantly with a wooden spoon, until it thickens enough to coat the back of the spoon and reaches 175°F (79°C) on an instant-read thermometer; do not let the mixture boil, or the egg yolks will curdle. Remove the pot from the heat and strain the ice cream base immediately into a bowl. Set the bowl in an ice bath and stir frequently until cold.

3.   Transfer the ice cream base to an airtight container and refrigerate for at least 4 hours, or overnight.

4.   Process the base in an ice cream machine according to the manufacturer's instructions, adding the 3 tablespoons (28 g/1 oz) reserved, chopped Poached Ginger during the final minute of churning. (Be careful not to over-churn the ice cream or it will become grainy.)

Transfer the ice cream to an airtight container and freeze until ready to serve.

CANDIED LIME PEEL

1 lime

1 cup (250 g/8.8 oz) Simple Syrup (page 339)

1.   Peel the lime with a vegetable peeler and remove the white pith from the peel with a paring knife. Cut the peel into long, thin strips.

2.   Fill a small saucepan halfway with water and add the lime peel. Bring to a boil and boil for 3 minutes. Strain through a fine-mesh sieve. Place the Simple Syrup and the blanched peel into the saucepan and bring to a boil over high heat. Reduce the heat to medium-low and simmer until the peel is translucent, about 10 minutes. Set the peel aside in the syrup and cool.

MANGO CARPACCIO

5 ripe but firm mangoes

Peel the mangoes with a vegetable peeler. Using an electric slicer (best choice) or mandoline (second-best choice), cut the mangoes into very thin sheets and divide them equally among 6 plates. Set aside, covered, in the refrigerator.

ASSEMBLY

Drizzle some Ginger Syrup on the Mango Carpaccio slices. Place some Poached Ginger slices and Candied Lime Peel on top. Place a quenelle of Ginger Ice Cream in the center of each plate. Garnish with additional lime peel.

APRICOT CHARLOTTE with RUM-SOAKED RAISINS, CHAMOMILE CRÈME ANGLAISE, and WHOLE MILK ICE CREAM

THIS DESSERT CELEBRATES the sweet-tart flavor of fresh apricots, one of my favorite summer fruits. Though its form resembles a French charlotte, it's really more like a baked American bread pudding that's made with day-old brioche, cubes of fresh apricot, and rum-soaked raisins. I serve it with a fragrant Chamomile Crème Anglaise, which has a sweet, floral flavor that complements the bright tartness of the apricots, and a simple Whole Milk Ice Cream. If you can't get brioche, you can use challah or even plain white bread instead.

MAKES 8 SERVINGS

COMPONENTS

CHAMOMILE CRÈME ANGLAISE
ORANGE-ALMOND TUILES
WHOLE MILK ICE CREAM
APRICOT CHARLOTTE
   CUSTARD BASE
   RUM-SOAKED RAISINS

SPECIAL EQUIPMENT | ice cream machine; eight 2½-inch-diameter by 2½-inch-high ring molds

PERFECT MATCH | Di Majo Norante Moscato del Molise Apianae, Italy

CHAMOMILE CRÈME ANGLAISE

1 cup (250 g/8.8 oz) whole milk

1 cup (250 g/8.8 oz) heavy cream

3½ Tbsp (10 g/0.35 oz) chamomile tea

6 large (112 g/4 oz) egg yolks

¼ cup plus 2 Tbsp (75 g/2.6 oz) granulated sugar

1. In a medium saucepan, combine the milk and cream and bring to a gentle boil over medium heat. Remove the pan from the heat, stir in the chamomile tea, cover, and allow to infuse for 30 minutes.

2. Strain the milk mixture through a fine-mesh sieve, discarding the tea leaves, and return it to the saucepan. Reheat the mixture until it just begins to boil. Remove from the heat.

3. In a medium bowl, whisk together the egg yolks and sugar until pale. Whisk about half of the hot milk mixture into the yolks, then return this mixture to the remaining milk mixture in the saucepan and cook over medium heat, stirring constantly with a wooden spoon, until it thickens enough to coat the back of the spoon and reaches 175°F (79°C) on an instant-read thermometer; do not let the mixture boil, or the egg yolks will curdle. Remove the pot from the heat and strain the mixture immediately into a bowl. Set the bowl in an ice bath and stir frequently until cold.

4. Transfer the sauce to an airtight container and refrigerate until ready to serve.

ORANGE-ALMOND TUILES

(page 339)

1.   Preheat the oven to 350°F (177°C). Line a half-sheet pan with a silicone baking mat. Using a small, offset metal spatula, spread a layer of the tuile batter (about ½ cup or 155 g/5.4 oz) over the mat. Bake for about 8 minutes, or until just beginning to turn golden in spots. Cool completely.

2.   Break the cooled tuile rectangle into shards and reserve for garnish.

WHOLE MILK ICE CREAM

(page 340)

CUSTARD BASE

4 large (74 g/2.6 oz) egg yolks

½ cup (100 g/3.5 oz) granulated sugar

2 cups (464 g/16.36 oz) heavy cream

In a bowl, whisk together the yolks and sugar until blended. Add the cream. Cover and set aside in the refrigerator until ready to use for the Apricot Charlotte.

RUM-SOAKED RAISINS

⅓ cup (100 g/3.5 oz) golden raisins

1 cup (236 g/8.3 oz) boiling water

⅓ cup (85 g/3 oz) Simple Syrup (page 339)

2 Tbsp (30 g/1.05 oz) Myers's dark rum

1.   Place the raisins in a heatproof bowl and pour the boiling water over them. Let the raisins soak for 15 minutes.

2.   Drain the raisins and return them to the bowl. Pour the Simple Syrup on top and stir in the rum. Allow to macerate for 8 hours, or overnight, before using in the Apricot Charlotte.

APRICOT CHARLOTTE

6 (650 g/23 oz) fresh apricots

3 Tbsp (60 g/2.1 oz) honey

1 Brioche loaf (page 342), preferably 1 or 2 days old

1.   Preheat the oven to 375°F (191°C). Cut out eight 3-inch squares of aluminum foil. Brush each square with butter, then dust with granulated sugar and set aside. Brush the insides of eight 2½-inch ring molds with butter and dust with granulated sugar. Set aside. Line a half-sheet pan with a silicone baking mat.

2.   Cut the apricots in half and remove the stones. Cut each half in half again, then cut the quarters into ½-inch cubes.

3.   Pour the honey into a sauté pan over medium heat and heat until warm. Add the apricot cubes and sauté gently for 1 to 2 minutes. Remove from the heat.

4.   Wrap a prepared foil square around the bottom of each of the prepared ring molds and arrange them on the prepared sheet pan. Using a serrated knife, trim the crust off each brioche and discard. Cut the loaf lengthwise into ½-inch strips and then cut the strips into half cubes. You will need about 7 cups (245 g/8.6 oz). Reserve 1 cup (35 g/1.2 oz) of the brioche cubes to place on the top of the desserts. Put the remaining brioche cubes in a medium

bowl with the apricot cubes and Rum-Soaked Raisins and toss to combine. Add just enough of the Custard Base to moisten the brioche, but not enough to make it soggy. Line the bottom of each ring mold with some of the moistened brioche cubes, packing them down firmly. Do not overstuff the molds, however, as that will yield a thick, dry base. Fill each ring mold almost to the top with the remaining brioche and fruit mixture. Top each charlotte with a few of the reserved unsoaked brioche cubes. Bake the charlottes for about 10 minutes, or until

they are just set and have the texture of bread pudding. Run a knife around each charlotte to help release it from the ring. Serve the charlottes warm.

ASSEMBLY

Place a warm Apricot Charlotte on a plate and spoon some Chamomile Crème Anglaise on the plate. Top the charlotte with a quenelle of Whole Milk Ice Cream, and insert an Orange-Almond Tuile in the ice cream. Serve immediately.

APPLE SPIRAL TEMPURA with APPLE CIDER REDUCTION

I CAME UP WITH THIS DESSERT as a result of playing in the kitchen one day. I was working at Daniel, and we used a machine that peeled and cored apples, turning each one into a beautiful, long accordion spiral. I decided I wanted to deep-fry this apple spiral and tried many different things, including coating it with a beignet batter. But the batter was a little too thick, and it took too long to cook. After much trial and error, I discovered the perfect solution: tempura batter. Because it cooks quickly, the apple stays juicy and retains its cylindrical shape. This dessert reminds me of the delicious *beignets chichi*—apples fried in a beer batter and topped with brown sugar and cinnamon—that are sold at the beach in the South of France every summer. So simple, but so delicious.

MAKES 6 SERVINGS

COMPONENTS

APPLE CIDER SAUCE
APPLE TEMPURA SPIRAL

SPECIAL EQUIPMENT
mechanical apple peeler/slicer;
12 bamboo skewers

PERFECT MATCH | Étienne Dupont Organic Cidre Bouché Brut de Normandie, Victot-Pontfol, France

APPLE CIDER SAUCE

¼ cup (50 g/1.76 oz) granulated sugar

1 Tbsp (8 g/0.28 oz) cornstarch

1½ cups (350 g/12.3 oz) apple cider

½ stick cinnamon

3 Tbsp (45 g/1.6 oz) freshly squeezed lemon juice

5½ Tbsp (80 g/2.82 oz) unsalted butter, cut into tablespoon-size pieces

1.   In a medium bowl, combine the sugar with the cornstarch and ½ cup (116 g/4.1 oz) of the apple cider until smooth. Set aside.

2.   In a small saucepan, combine the remaining 1 cup (233 g/8.2 oz) cider with the cinnamon stick and lemon juice and bring to a boil over high heat. Continue to boil until the cider is reduced by half, about 4 minutes. Whisk in the cornstarch mixture and bring to a boil, whisking constantly. Boil for 1 minute, then remove from the heat and whisk in the butter. Continue to whisk until it has melted. Strain the sauce through a fine-mesh sieve, and keep warm until ready to serve.

APPLE SPIRALS

6 apples (such as McCoy, Fuji, or La Reine de Reinette)

Use an apple peeling machine to peel, core, and slice an apple into a spiral. Thread a long skewer through the apple on one side of the hole. Gently stretch the apple spiral layers and thread another skewer through the apple on the opposite side of the hole. Lift the skewered apple by the ends so that its slices are kept separate and place it in a shallow pan. Repeat with the remaining apples.

TEMPURA APPLE SPIRALS

9 cups (2 kg/4.4 lb) vegetable oil

1 large (50 g/1.76 oz) egg

¾ cup (180 g/6.3 oz) ice cold water

1 cup plus 1 tsp (130 g/4.6 oz) all-purpose flour, sifted

Pinch of salt

1. In a deep, straight-sided saucepan or deep fryer, begin heating the oil to 375°F (191°C). Line a half-sheet pan with paper towels.

2. Meanwhile, make the tempura batter. In a medium bowl, whisk the egg until smooth. Add the cold water and whisk until blended. Whisk in the flour and salt until the batter is very smooth, about 1 minute; do not overmix.

3. Drizzle the batter over one of the apple spirals, turning the skewer until the apples are completely covered. Lift the spiral and, very carefully, place it in the hot oil. Fry the apple spiral until it is crisp and begins to color, about 1 minute. Transfer the fried apple spiral to the prepared sheet pan to drain. Repeat with the remaining apples and batter.

ASSEMBLY

Place a hot Tempura Apple Spiral on a dessert plate and serve with the warm Apple Cider Sauce.

STEAMED BABY PLUMS in EXTRA-VIRGIN OLIVE OIL, FLEUR DE SEL, and CARDAMOM ICE CREAM

❄ HERE'S A DESSERT that was created by my former sous-chef, Eric Estrella. Eric wanted to use baby plums at the peak of their perfection, which is a very short window in the summer, just 2 or 3 weeks. Because baby plums are so flavorful, he kept things simple, steaming the plums with olive oil and serving them with a light cream, Cardamom Ice Cream, and a sprinkling of fleur de sel. A plum tuile is a pretty garnish for this very fresh, delicious summer dessert. You can find baby plums at farmers' markets throughout July and August.

MAKES 8 SERVINGS

COMPONENTS

CARDAMOM ICE CREAM
CRÈME FRAÎCHE CREAM
PLUM TUILES
STEAMED BABY PLUMS
STREUSEL

SPECIAL EQUIPMENT ice cream machine; 8-inch round cake pan; food steamer (or steamer basket insert for a pot); 2-inch round pastry cutter

PERFECT MATCH Chartreuse Verte, V.E.P., France

CARDAMOM ICE CREAM

1 cup (250 g/8.8 oz) whole milk

1 cup (250 g/8.8 oz) heavy cream

6 large (112 g/4 oz) egg yolks

½ cup plus 2 Tbsp (125 g/4.4 oz) granulated sugar

1½ tsp (3 g/0.1 oz) ground cardamom

1.   In a medium saucepan, combine the milk and cream and bring to a gentle boil over medium heat.

2.   In a medium bowl, whisk together the egg yolks and sugar until pale. Whisk about half of the hot milk mixture into the yolks, then return this mixture to the remaining milk mixture in the saucepan and cook over medium heat, stirring constantly with a wooden spoon, until it thickens enough to coat the back of the spoon and reaches 175°F (79°C) on an instant-read thermometer; do not let the mixture boil, or the egg yolks will curdle. Remove the pot from the heat and strain the ice cream base immediately through a fine-mesh sieve into a bowl. Stir in the ground cardamom. Set the bowl in an ice bath and stir frequently until cold.

3.   Transfer the ice cream base to an airtight container and refrigerate for at least 4 hours, or overnight.

4. Process the base in an ice cream machine according to the manufacturer's instructions. (Be careful not to overchurn the ice cream or it will become grainy.) Transfer the ice cream to an airtight container and freeze until ready to serve.

CRÈME FRAÎCHE CREAM

2 sheets (4 g/0.14 oz) gelatin (silver grade)

1½ cups (350 g/12.3 oz) heavy cream

1 cup (250 g/8.8 oz) crème fraîche

¼ cup (60 g/2.1 oz) mascarpone cheese

⅓ cup plus 1 tsp (70 g/2.5 oz) granulated sugar

½ vanilla bean, split lengthwise and seeds scraped

Juice of 1 lemon

1. Line an 8-inch round pan with plastic wrap. Fill a medium bowl one-third of the way with ice-cold water and add the gelatin sheets.

2. In a medium stainless steel bowl, combine the cream, crème fraîche, mascarpone, sugar, and vanilla bean pod and seeds and place the bowl over a pot half full of simmering water. Heat, stirring constantly, until the crème fraîche and mascarpone are melted and the mixture is smooth. Drain the gelatin, squeezing out the excess water, and add it to the mixture, stirring until the gelatin has dissolved. Stir in the lemon juice. Pour the mixture into the prepared pan and remove the vanilla bean pod. Cover and freeze until firm, at least 3 hours.

3. Unmold the cream and cut out at least 8 rounds using a 2-inch round pastry cutter. Freeze the rounds, loosely covered, until ready to serve.

PLUM TUILES (see Fruit Tuiles, page 338)

Prepare the Fruit Tuiles as directed, using strained plum purée.

STEAMED BABY PLUMS

40 baby plums, halved and stones removed

3 Tbsp (40 g/1.4 oz) extra-virgin olive oil

1. In a large bowl, toss the plums in the olive oil.

2. Place a steamer insert in a pot and pour water in the pot to just below the bottom of the steamer. Bring the water to a simmer over medium heat and add the plum halves to the steamer. Cover and steam for 1 to 2 minutes, or until the plums are tender. Remove the pot from the heat and remove the steamer insert. Set the plums aside to cool for 5 minutes.

3. Gently peel off the skins of the plums.

STREUSEL, BAKED (page 342)

ASSEMBLY

Extra-virgin olive oil, for drizzling

Fleur de sel, for sprinkling

Place a Crème Fraîche Cream round in the center of a plate and allow to defrost for 10 minutes. Sprinkle the top of the cream with Streusel. Place the Steamed Baby Plums (about 10 halves) around the cream and drizzle with olive oil. Sprinkle with some fleur de sel. Place a quenelle of Cardamom Ice Cream on top of the streusel and garnish it with a Plum Tuile.

LEMON–POPPY SEED CAKE filled with RED WINE–POACHED CHERRIES and CLOTTED CREAM

A TENDER, HOME-STYLE LEMON POPPY SEED CAKE gets a makeover in this elegant dessert. The cake is made with butter and margarine, which makes it extra moist. I top the savarin-shaped cake with cherries that have been poached in red wine and spices, and serve it with a whipped clotted cream and a tuile spiral. Clotted cream is now readily available from a number of sources online, but you can substitute whipped crème fraîche or ice cream for it if you prefer.

MAKES 8 SERVINGS

COMPONENTS

POACHED CHERRIES
LEMON–POPPY SEED CAKE
WHIPPED CLOTTED CREAM
TUILE GARNISH

SPECIAL EQUIPMENT | Eight 3½-inch savarin molds; medium, plain pastry tip (Ateco #6); 1 by 8-inch rectangular stencil; 2 wooden dowels or wooden spoons

PERFECT MATCH | Jorge Ordóñez & Co. Passito, Málaga, Spain

POACHED CHERRIES

4 cups (960 g/33.8 oz) red wine (any kind)

½ cup (100 g/3.5 oz) granulated sugar

Peel of 2 oranges, white pith removed

Peel of 1 lemon, white pith removed

1 whole clove

½ stick cinnamon

4 cups (500 g/17.6 oz) cherries, pitted, but kept whole

1.   In a medium saucepan, bring the red wine to a boil over medium-high heat. Add the sugar and continue to boil until the liquid has reduced to about one-third of its original volume. Add the orange and lemon peels, clove, and cinnamon stick and bring to a boil. Boil for 2 minutes more. Remove from the heat.

2.   Place the cherries in a large saucepan and strain the red wine mixture over them. Bring to a boil over high heat, then remove from the heat and set aside to cool.

LEMON–POPPY SEED CAKE

1⅓ cups (170 g/6 oz) all-purpose flour

½ tsp plus ⅛ tsp (3.25 g/0.1 oz) baking powder

⅛ tsp plus 1/16 tsp (0.8 g/0.02 oz) baking soda

4 Tbsp (56 g/2 oz) unsalted butter, softened

½ cup (100 g/3.5 oz) granulated sugar

4 Tbsp (56 g/2 oz) margarine

1 large (50 g/1.76 oz) egg

2 Tbsp plus 2 tsp (16 g/0.56 oz) finely grated lemon zest

2 Tbsp plus 2 tsp (40 g/1.4 oz) buttermilk

2 Tbsp plus 2 tsp (41 g/1.5 oz) freshly squeezed lemon juice

¼ tsp (1 g/0.03 oz) vanilla extract

1¼ Tbsp (11 g/0.38 oz) poppy seeds

1.   Preheat the oven to 350°F (177°C). Coat eight 3½-inch savarin molds with nonstick cooking spray and place them on a half-sheet pan.

2.   In a medium bowl, sift together the flour, baking powder, and baking soda.

3. In the bowl of a stand mixer fitted with the paddle attachment, beat the butter on medium speed until creamy, about 2 minutes. Gradually add the sugar and beat on high speed until light, about 2 minutes. Add the margarine and beat on medium speed until blended. Add the egg, mixing well and scraping down the sides of the bowl with a rubber spatula as necessary. Beat in the lemon zest. Reduce the speed to low and add the dry ingredients in three additions, alternating with the buttermilk, lemon juice, and vanilla in two additions and mixing just until blended. Remove the bowl from the mixer stand and fold in the poppy seeds.

4. Transfer the batter to a large pastry bag fitted with a medium, plain pastry tip and pipe it into the savarin molds, smoothing the tops so that they are even. Bake the cakes for about 15 minutes, or until a toothpick inserted into the cakes comes out clean. Cool the cakes in the molds on a wire rack for 5 minutes, then invert them onto the rack, remove the molds, and cool completely.

WHIPPED CLOTTED CREAM

1 cup (232 g/8.18 oz) clotted cream
(see Sources, page 349)

Place the clotted cream in a medium bowl and whisk it by hand just until it starts to hold its shape. Refrigerate, covered, until ready to serve.

TUILE GARNISH

Vanilla Tuiles (page 338)

Preheat the oven to 350°F (177°C). Line a half-sheet pan with a silicone baking mat. Have 2 wooden dowels or wooden spoons ready. Place a 1 by 8-inch rectangular stencil on the mat and, using a small, offset metal spatula, spread some of the tuile batter over it. Repeat to form another tuile. Bake the tuiles for about 6 minutes, or until golden brown around the edges. While the tuiles are still warm, wrap them around the wooden dowels or spoon handles to form corkscrew shapes. Cool, then slip the tuiles off and store in an airtight container. Repeat to form at least 8 tuiles.

ASSEMBLY

Place a Lemon Poppy Seed Cake in the center of a plate. Drain some of the Poached Cherries and arrange them in the center of the cake. Pour some of the poaching liquid onto the cherries. Place a dollop of the Whipped Clotted Cream on the cherries and garnish with a corkscrew Tuile Garnish.

BANANA RAVIOLI with EXOTIC SORBET and PASSION FRUIT

RAVIOLI IS TRADITIONALLY A SAVORY DISH, but this ravioli conceals a sweet filling of sautéed bananas. I use a chef's shortcut by using wonton wrappers in place of pasta dough for the ravioli—they're paper-thin and work wonderfully for this dessert. The crispy Passion Fruit Tuiles and Exotic Sorbet add a tropical note to the musky banana filling.

MAKES 8 SERVINGS

COMPONENTS

EXOTIC SORBET
PASSION FRUIT TUILES
BANANA RAVIOLI
    SAUTÉED BANANA FILLING

SPECIAL EQUIPMENT | ice cream machine; 2¾-inch fluted, round pastry cutter

PERFECT MATCH | Rhum J.M. VSOP, Martinique

EXOTIC SORBET

¾ cup (180 g/6.3 oz) water

½ cup plus 1½ Tbsp (120 g/4.2 oz) granulated sugar

2 tsp (10 g/0.35 oz) freshly squeezed lemon juice

1 cup (250 g/8.8 oz) passion fruit purée

⅔ cup (160 g/5.6 oz) banana purée

1.   In a small saucepan, combine the water and sugar and bring to a boil, stirring, just until the sugar has dissolved. Remove from the heat and stir in the remaining ingredients.

2.   Transfer the sorbet base to a medium bowl. Place the bowl in an ice bath and stir frequently until completely cool. Cover the bowl and refrigerate the sorbet base for at least 4 hours, or overnight.

3.   Process the base in an ice cream machine according to the manufacturer's instructions. Transfer the sorbet to an airtight container and freeze until ready to serve.

PASSION FRUIT TUILES

½ cup lightly packed (100 g/3.5 oz) light brown sugar

½ cup (100 g/3.5 oz) granulated sugar

¾ cup (100 g/3.5 oz) all-purpose flour

½ cup (100 g/3.5 oz) passion fruit purée

7 Tbsp (100 g/3.5 oz) unsalted butter, at room temperature

1.   Place the dry ingredients in a food processor fitted with the blade attachment. With the machine running, gradually add the passion fruit purée and process until well blended.

Turn off the machine and add the butter. Process the batter just until the butter is incorporated and there are no large lumps. Transfer to a covered container and chill the batter for at least 6 hours, or overnight.

2.   Preheat the oven to 350°F (177°C). Line a half-sheet pan with a silicone baking mat. Spread some of the chilled batter over the entire mat in a thin, even layer. Bake for about 5 to 7 minutes, or until golden and lacy. Remove from the oven and, while the tuile sheet is still warm, cut it into at least eight 4-inch-long by 1½-inch-wide triangles. While they are warm, curl the tuiles around a large can to make them curved. Cool completely and store in an airtight container until ready to serve.

SAUTÉED BANANA FILLING

> 3½ Tbsp (50 g/1.76 oz) unsalted butter, cut into chunks
>
> 6 medium, ripe bananas, sliced ¼ inch thick
>
> 1½ Tbsp (20 g/0.7 oz) granulated sugar
>
> 2 Tbsp (30 g/1 oz) Myers's dark rum
>
> ½ cup (125 g/4.4 oz) passion fruit purée

Melt the butter in a sauté pan over high heat. Add the banana slices and sauté as you gradually add the sugar, about 1 minute. Add the rum and, using a flame igniter, very carefully flambé the liquid, and cook until the flame dies out. Stir in the passion fruit purée, remove the pan from the heat, and cool.

BANANA RAVIOLI

> 48 (3-in/8-cm) square wonton wrappers (a 12-oz package)
>
> 2 large (60 g/2.1 oz) egg whites, lightly whisked with a fork
>
> 1 qt (944 g/33.3 oz) water
>
> 3¾ cups (750 g/26.4 oz) granulated sugar
>
> 1 cup (250 g/8.8 oz) freshly squeezed orange juice

1.   Place a wonton wrapper on a cutting board and arrange 2 or 3 sautéed banana slices in the center of the square. Brush some egg white around the edges and top with another wonton wrapper, pressing down the edges (while eliminating as much air as possible) to seal them. Using a 2¾-inch round fluted pastry cutter, cut the ravioli into a round. Repeat to make a total of 24 ravioli.

2.   In a medium saucepan, combine the water, sugar, and orange juice and bring to a boil over medium-high heat, stirring to dissolve the sugar. Reduce the heat slightly so that the mixture is at a gentle boil, and add 6 ravioli to the pot. Cook for about 3 minutes, or until the wrappers are tender. Remove the ravioli from the pan with a slotted spoon or spider and place in a shallow container. Repeat until all the ravioli are cooked.

ASSEMBLY:

> 2 fresh passion fruit, halved

Place 3 Banana Ravioli on a plate and sprinkle with some pulp from the fresh passion fruit. Arrange a quenelle of Exotic Sorbet in the center of the ravioli and top the sorbet with a Passion Fruit Tuile.

FRICASSÉE of CHERRIES with HYSSOP, PISTACHIO CRUMBLE, and PISTACHIO ICE CREAM

I LOVE TO SERVE THIS COMFORTING DESSERT, which is similar to a crisp, when cherries are at their peak in June. Hyssop is an herb that you don't see too often, but it lends an interesting flavor— a slightly bitter, minty one– to the sautéed cherries. Pistachio is a great flavor complement to cherries, so I serve a sprinkling of Pistachio Crumble and a quenelle of Pistachio Ice Cream on top. It's a simple summer dessert that's not too heavy on the palate.

MAKES 8 SERVINGS

COMPONENTS

PISTACHIO ICE CREAM
PISTACHIO CRUMBLE
CANDIED PISTACHIOS
CHERRIES IN HYSSOP

SPECIAL EQUIPMENT | ice cream machine

PERFECT MATCH | Massenez Eau de Vie de Framboise Sauvage, Villé, France

PISTACHIO ICE CREAM

1 cup (250 g/8.8 oz) whole milk

1 cup (250 g/8.8 oz) heavy cream

6 large (112 g/4 oz) egg yolks

½ cup plus 2 Tbsp (125 g/4.4 oz) granulated sugar

2 Tbsp plus 1 tsp (45 g/1.58 oz) pistachio paste

1.   In a medium saucepan, combine the milk and cream and bring to a gentle boil over medium heat.

2.   In a medium bowl, whisk together the egg yolks and sugar until pale. Whisk about half of the hot milk mixture into the yolks, then return this mixture to the remaining milk mixture in the saucepan and cook over medium heat, stirring constantly with a wooden spoon, until it thickens enough to coat the back of the spoon and reaches 175°F (79°C) on an instant-read thermometer; do not let the mixture boil, or the egg yolks will curdle. Remove the pan from the heat and whisk in the pistachio paste. Strain the ice cream base through a fine-mesh sieve into a medium bowl. Set the bowl in an ice bath and stir frequently until cold.

3.   Transfer the ice cream base to an airtight container and refrigerate for at least 4 hours, or overnight.

4.   Process the base in an ice cream machine according to the manufacturer's instructions. (Be careful not to overchurn the ice cream or it will become grainy.) Transfer the ice cream to an airtight container and freeze until ready to serve.

PISTACHIO CRUMBLE

4 Tbsp (57 g/2 oz) unsalted butter

⅓ cup (62 g/2.2 oz) granulated sugar

½ cup (60 g/2.1 oz) all-purpose flour

⅔ cup (58 g/2 oz) finely chopped pistachio nuts

1.   In the bowl of a stand mixer fitted with the paddle attachment, mix the butter and sugar together on medium-low speed until smooth. Add the flour and pistachios and mix until blended. Shape the dough into a disk, wrap in plastic wrap, and refrigerate until firm, about 1 hour.

2.   Preheat the oven to 375°F (191°C). Line a half-sheet pan with a silicone baking mat. Unwrap the dough and crumble it into large chunks onto the prepared pan. Bake for 10 minutes, or until golden brown. Cool completely.

CANDIED PISTACHIOS

¾ cup (114 g/4 oz) shelled pistachio nuts

½ large (15 g/0.5 oz) egg white

1 Tbsp (12 g/0.42 oz) granulated sugar

1.   Preheat the oven to 350°F (177°C). Line a half-sheet pan with a silicone baking mat.

2.   Place the egg white in a medium bowl, add the pistachios, and stir to coat the nuts evenly. Sprinkle over the sugar and toss the nuts to coat them evenly with the sugar. Spread the nuts in an even layer on the lined sheet pan. Bake, tossing the nuts twice, for 8 minutes, or until lightly browned. Cool

completely. (This recipe will yield more Candied Pistachios than you will need. Store the extra nuts in an airtight container at room temperature for later use.)

CHERRIES IN HYSSOP

2 Tbsp (30 g/1 oz) unsalted butter

2 Tbsp plus ¾ tsp (30 g/1 oz) light brown sugar

6½ cups (1 kg/2.2 lb) cherries, pitted, but kept whole

Juice of 1 lemon

2 sprigs fresh hyssop, julienned

Prepare the cherries right before serving. Melt the butter over medium-high heat in a skillet. Add the sugar and cherries and sauté until the cherries are tender, about 3 minutes. Remove from the heat and add the lemon juice and hyssop.

ASSEMBLY

8 hyssop sprigs

Spoon the hot Cherries in Hyssop onto a serving plate. Sprinkle some Pistachio Crumble on top of the cherries and top with a quenelle of Pistachio Ice Cream. Garnish with some Candied Pistachios and a hyssop sprig.

POACHED PEAR in PORT and BLACK CURRANT with JULIENNED BLACK TRUFFLE and SZECHUAN PEPPER ICE CREAM

I CREATED THIS SUMPTUOUS DESSERT for a dinner honoring Alain Ducasse in Miami. It may not be the most elegant-looking dessert, but the flavors—pear, port, black currant, and black truffles—are incredible. The pears are poached in a cassis-flavored syrup, and served with a garnet red port sauce and a julienne of black truffle. A Szechuan Pepper Ice Cream, which has a little bite to it, goes very well with this luxurious dessert.

MAKES 8 SERVINGS

COMPONENTS

SZECHUAN PEPPER ICE CREAM
POACHED PEARS
TRUFFLE GARNISH
PORT SAUCE
STREUSEL

SPECIAL EQUIPMENT | pepper mill; ice cream machine; apple corer

PERFECT MATCH | La Coume du Roy Maury Tradition, Languedoc-Roussillon, France

---

SZECHUAN PEPPER ICE CREAM

Vanilla Ice Cream (page 340), prepared through step 2

Szechuan peppercorns in a pepper mill

Add 3 to 5 turns of freshly crushed Szechuan pepper to the ice cream base, then proceed with the recipe on page 340 as directed. Transfer the ice cream to an airtight container and freeze until ready to serve.

POACHED PEARS

8 Anjou pears, peeled

1½ cups (350 g/12.3 oz) cassis purée

1 qt (944 g/33.3 oz) water

2 cups (400 g/14.1 oz) granulated sugar

1. Slice off the bottom of each pear so that it is flat. Cut off the tip of each pear about an inch from the top and reserve the stems. Use an apple corer to make a hole through each pear starting from the top and through the base.

2. In a large saucepan, combine the cassis purée with the water and sugar and bring to a boil over medium-high heat. Reduce the heat to a simmer, stand the pears in the pan, and add the tops. Poach the pears until they are tender, about 30 minutes. Set the pears aside to cool for 3 hours in the poaching liquid.

TRUFFLE GARNISH

2 small (60 g/2.1 oz) black truffles

1. Clean the truffles under cold water using a soft brush to remove any sand. Dry them well with paper towels.

2. Cut the truffles into julienne strips and set aside.

PORT SAUCE

½ cup (100 g/3.5 oz) granulated sugar

2 cups plus 2 Tbsp (500 g/17.6 oz) water

1 qt (960 g/33.8 oz) port wine

1 vanilla bean, split lengthwise

Juice of 1 lemon

3½ Tbsp (200 g/7 oz) unsalted butter

In a medium saucepan, combine the sugar with 2 tablespoons (30 g/1 oz) of the water and cook over medium-high heat, occasionally brushing down the sides of the pan with a wet pastry brush to prevent crystals from forming, and watching carefully, until the sugar caramelizes and turns light amber, 3 to 5 minutes. Gradually add the remaining 2 cups (470 g/16.5 oz) water and return to a boil, stirring occasionally, until any hardened bits of caramel are dissolved, about 2 minutes. Add the port wine, vanilla bean pod, and lemon juice and bring to a boil. Very carefully touch a flame igniter to the liquid and flambé to allow the alcohol in the port to burn off. Reduce the heat to a simmer and add the truffles from the Truffle Garnish. Poach the truffles in the liquid for 5 minutes. Remove the truffles with a slotted spoon and dry them off; set aside for

the garnish. Increase the heat to high and boil the port mixture until it has reduced by half, about 20 minutes. Remove the pan from the heat and whisk in the butter until emulsified. Strain the sauce through a fine-mesh sieve and keep it warm.

STREUSEL, BAKED (page 342)

ASSEMBLY

Freshly ground black pepper

Place a Poached Pear in the middle of a plate. Sprinkle some Streusel in a mound on the plate and place a quenelle of Szechuan Pepper Ice Cream on the mound and garnish with some freshly ground black pepper. Pour some Port Sauce into the pear's hollow core. Sprinkle some Truffle Garnish onto the pear. Place the top back on the pear.

FRICASSÉE of WINTER FRUITS with VANILLA ICE CREAM

✳ I FIRST MADE THIS COMFORTING WINTER FRUIT MEDLEY to serve for dessert at the end of a twelve-course wine dinner at Daniel. After that many courses and that much wine, diners want something sweet, but not too sweet, and nothing over the top. The fruits—pears, apples, apricots, oranges, and prunes—are sautéed with a little Armagnac, which adds a warm, sophisticated flavor that is a good match for many wines.

MAKES 6 SERVINGS

COMPONENTS

VANILLA ICE CREAM
WINTER FRUIT MEDLEY

SPECIAL EQUIPMENT | ice cream machine

PERFECT MATCH | 2005 Zind-Humbrecht Gewürztraminer Clos Windsbuhl, Alsace, France

VANILLA ICE CREAM
(page 340)

WINTER FRUIT MEDLEY

1 orange

1 lemon

2 cups plus 2 Tbsp (500 g/17.6 oz) water

2 cups (400 g/14.1 oz) granulated sugar

3 dried apricots, halved

3 prunes, halved

1 vanilla bean, split lengthwise

3 pears (Bartlett or Bosc)

3 apples (Macoun or Fuji)

1. Using a vegetable peeler, remove the peel in strips from the orange and lemon. With a paring knife, cut off any of the white pith from the strips. Using a chef's knife, cut the peel into thin strips.

2. Cut the remaining white pith off from the exterior of the orange. Using a paring knife, cut out each segment and set aside (see page 348). Juice the remaining lemon and reserve the juice.

3. In a medium saucepan, combine the water and sugar and bring to a boil over medium-high heat. Add the orange and lemon peel strips and boil for 10 minutes. Remove the pan from the heat and add the apricots, prunes, and vanilla bean. Set aside to cool to room temperature.

4. Peel and core the pears and apples and cut them each into 8 wedges. Place them into a large bowl and toss them with the reserved lemon juice.

5. Strain the candied citrus zest and dried fruit and set aside.

ASSEMBLY

2 Tbsp (30 g/1 oz) unsalted butter

1 vanilla bean, split lengthwise and seeds scraped

2½ Tbsp (30 g/1 oz) granulated sugar

¼ cup (60 g/2.1 oz) Armagnac or brandy

In a large sauté pan over high heat, melt the butter with the vanilla bean pod and seeds. Add the pear and apple slices and cook, stirring or tossing frequently, until they are tender, about 5 minutes. Add the strained citrus zest and dried fruit and the sugar and cook for another 2 to 3 minutes, or until the sugar begins to caramelize. Add the orange segments and Armagnac and cook for 2 minutes, tossing frequently. Remove the vanilla bean pods, divide the fricassée equally among 6 shallow bowls, and serve each with a scoop of Vanilla Ice Cream.

ROSEMARY-SCENTED CHEESECAKE with OVEN-ROASTED STRAWBERRIES and ROSEMARY ICE CREAM

THE CLASSIC STRAWBERRY-TOPPED CHEESECAKE gets a serious makeover in this recipe. The cake itself is subtly flavored with rosemary, giving it a woodsy character that works so well with sweet strawberries. The strawberries are dusted with sugar and briefly roasted in the oven, which concentrates their flavor and makes them really juicy. I serve the cake on a tender baked sablé with a scoop of Rosemary Ice Cream. Make this dessert in the summer, when strawberries are at their peak.

MAKES 12 SERVINGS

COMPONENTS

ROSEMARY-SCENTED CHEESECAKE

OVEN-ROASTED STRAWBERRIES

ROSEMARY ICE CREAM

STREUSEL

SABLÉ BRETON BASE

SPECIAL EQUIPMENT | 9-inch square baking pan; ice cream machine

PERFECT MATCH | 2004 Duché de Longueville Cidre Gros Oeillet, Normandy, France

ROSEMARY-SCENTED CHEESECAKE

1 sprig fresh rosemary

⅓ cup (72 g/2.5 oz) heavy cream

Softened butter, for greasing the pan

¼ cup (36 g/1.3 oz) graham cracker crumbs

3¾ cups (850 g/1 lb, 14 oz) cream cheese, at room temperature

1 cup (200 g/7 oz) granulated sugar

2 Tbsp (15 g/0.5 oz) all-purpose flour

3 large (150 g/5.3 oz) whole eggs

2 large (37 g/1.3 oz) egg yolks

1. Remove the rosemary leaves from the stem and chop them. Place the cream in a 1-cup glass measure and microwave on high power until the cream comes to a gentle boil, about 1 minute. Add the rosemary to the hot cream, stir to combine, then cover the container and allow to infuse for 15 minutes.

2. Position a rack in the center of the oven and preheat the oven to 300°F (149°C). Butter the bottom and sides of a 9-inch square baking pan and dust it with the graham cracker crumbs. Tap out the excess crumbs.

3. Strain the infused heavy cream and discard the rosemary leaves. Place the cream cheese in the bowl of a stand mixer fitted with the paddle attachment and beat it on low speed until smooth, about 1 minute. Add the sugar

PEAR POACHED in PASSION FRUIT CARAMEL, ARLETTE, and HONEY AND NOUGAT ICE CREAM

I developed this wonderful dessert at Payard, and it features an *arlette*, the famous thin caramelized puff pastry wafer. It's very French, made with Poached Pears that are macerated overnight in a Passion Fruit Caramel, which gives them a great flavor. I serve it with a crunchy Honey and Nougat Ice Cream, but it would also work with many other ice cream or sorbet flavors. The only really important thing here is that you use ripe, flavorful pears. If you can't get them, substitute the best Poire William (available in either a jar or can) you can find.

MAKES 8 SERVINGS

COMPONENTS

POACHED PEARS
PASSION FRUIT CARAMEL
HONEY AND NOUGAT ICE CREAM
ARLETTE

SPECIAL EQUIPMENT   ice cream machine

PERFECT MATCH   Kanu Chenin Blanc, Stellenbosch, South Africa

POACHED PEARS

8 ripe pears (Bartlett or Bosc)

2 cups (472 g/16.6 oz) water

2 cups (400 g/14.1 oz) granulated sugar

3 vanilla beans, split lengthwise and seeds scraped

1.   Peel the pears, cut them in half lengthwise, and core them. Place the pears in a medium saucepan with the water, sugar, and vanilla bean seeds and pods. Bring the liquid to a boil over medium-high heat, then reduce to a simmer. Simmer the pears, stirring occasionally, until they are tender, about 15 minutes. Transfer the pears and their poaching liquid to a medium bowl and allow to cool.

2.   Cut the cooled pears in half again and return them to the poaching liquid.

PASSION FRUIT CARAMEL

1⅓ cups (350 g/12.3 oz) passion fruit purée

3½ cups (812 g/28.64 oz) heavy cream

2¼ cups (450 g/15.9 oz) sugar

1.   In a medium saucepan, combine the purée and cream and bring to a boil over medium heat. Reduce the heat to low while you cook the sugar.

BROWN BUTTER ROASTED PEAR with MAPLE SYRUP and VANILLA-PRUNE ICE CREAM

A CRISP ROUND OF PUFF PASTRY and baked almond cream—both made with a healthy amount of butter—serve as the base for this beautiful maple-glazed roasted pear. A flavorful Vanilla-Prune Ice Cream makes a simple, yet sophisticated, accompaniment. Be sure to use firm, yet ripe, pears in this dessert, so that they hold their shape during roasting.

MAKES 8 SERVINGS

COMPONENTS

SANGRIA PRUNES
VANILLA-PRUNE ICE CREAM
PUFF PASTRY ROUNDS
ALMOND ROUNDS
ROASTED PEAR AND SAUCE
STREUSEL

SPECIAL EQUIPMENT
cheesecloth; kitchen twine; ice cream machine; 2¾-inch round pastry cutter; 9-inch square baking pan; 2½-inch round pastry cutter; 1-inch round pastry cutter

PERFECT MATCH | 1995 Domaine Huët Vouvray Cuvée Constance Moelleux, Loire, France

SANGRIA PRUNES

1 vanilla bean, split lengthwise and seeds scraped

1 stick cinnamon

Zest of 1 grapefruit

Zest of 1 lemon

Zest of 1 orange

1 whole clove

1 cup (250 g/8.8 oz) red wine

1 cup (250 g/8.8 oz) white wine

¼ cup (50 g/1.76 oz) granulated sugar

1 cup (142 g/5 oz) prunes

1. Place the vanilla bean, cinnamon stick, citrus zest, and clove in the center of a square of cheesecloth and form the cloth into a pouch. Tie the ends with a piece of string and set aside.

2. Combine the red and white wine in a medium saucepan and bring to a boil. Add the spice pouch, sugar, and prunes and bring to a simmer. Cover the pan and simmer until the prunes are soft, about 12 minutes. Remove from the heat and cool the prunes in the liquid.

3. Remove the prunes from the syrup and coarsely chop them. Discard the spice pouch and liquid. Place the prunes in a bowl, cover, and refrigerate until ready to use.

VANILLA-PRUNE ICE CREAM

3 cups (696 g/16.3 oz) half-and-half

1 vanilla bean, split lengthwise and seeds scraped

9 large (167 g/6 oz) egg yolks

1 cup (200 g/7 oz) granulated sugar

Sangria Prunes (page 77)

1.   Place the half-and-half and the vanilla bean pod and seeds in a saucepan and bring to a boil. Remove the pan from the heat, cover, and allow to infuse for 10 minutes.

2.   Place the egg yolks and sugar in a medium bowl and whisk together until thickened and pale. Continuing to whisk, drizzle in half of the warm half-and-half. Return this mixture to the pan with the remaining warm half-and-half and whisk to combine. Place the pan over medium heat and cook, stirring constantly with a wooden spoon, until the mixture thickens slightly and reaches 175°F (79°C) on an instant-read thermometer. This should take about 4 minutes; do not let the mixture boil, or the egg yolks will curdle. Remove the pan from the heat and immediately strain the ice cream base through a fine-mesh sieve into a medium bowl. Set the bowl of custard into a bowl of ice water and stir occasionally until it is cold. (At this point the custard base can be stored, covered, in the refrigerator for up to 1 day before freezing in the ice cream machine.)

3.   Process the base in an ice cream maker according to the manufacturer's instructions, adding the chopped Sangria Prunes during the final minute of churning. Transfer the ice cream to an airtight container and freeze for at least 4 hours before serving.

PUFF PASTRY ROUNDS

8 oz (227 g) Puff Pastry (page 343) or store-bought puff pastry

1 egg, whisked with a fork with a small amount of water, for egg wash

1.   Preheat the oven to 375°F (191°C). Line a half-sheet pan with a silicone mat.

2.   On a lightly floured work surface, roll the puff pastry out to a thickness of ⅛ inch. Using a 2¾-inch round pastry cutter, cut out 8 rounds from the dough. Refrigerate the rounds for 15 minutes. Place the chilled rounds on the prepared sheet pan and brush them with the egg wash. Bake for 16 to 18 minutes, or until the rounds are golden brown and crispy. Transfer to a wire rack and cool completely. Leave the oven on at 375°F (191°C).

ALMOND ROUNDS

8¾ Tbsp (125 g/4.4 oz) unsalted butter

½ cup plus 2 Tbsp (125 g/4.4 oz) granulated sugar

1⅓ cups (125 g/4.4 oz) almond flour

2 large eggs

1 Tbsp plus 1 tsp (10 g/0.35 oz) all-purpose flour

1.   Coat the bottom and sides of a 9-inch square baking pan with nonstick cooking spray. In the bowl of a stand mixer fitted with the paddle attachment, mix together the butter and sugar on medium speed until creamy and well blended, about 2 minutes. Add the almond flour and mix until blended. Reduce the mixer speed to medium-low and add the eggs, one at a time, mixing well after each

addition and scraping down the sides of the bowl as necessary. Add the flour and mix until blended. Scrape the almond mixture into the prepared pan, smoothing it into an even layer. Bake for 18 to 22 minutes, or until golden brown. Place the pan on a wire rack and cool completely. Leave the oven on, but raise the temperature to 400°F (204°C) to bake the pears.

2.   Using a 2½-inch round pastry cutter, cut out 8 rounds of baked almond cream. Using a 1-inch round cutter or the wide end of a pastry tip, cut out a 1-inch hole in the center of each round.

ROASTED PEAR AND SAUCE

4 ripe, firm Bosc pears

Juice of 1 lemon

5½ Tbsp (78 g/2.75 oz) unsalted butter

1 vanilla bean, split lengthwise and seeds scraped

¾ cup (198 g/7 oz) maple syrup

1.   Peel the pears, cut them in half (keeping the stems intact, if possible), and remove the cores. Rub the cut pears with lemon juice to prevent browning.

2.   Melt 3½ tablespoons (50 g/1.75 oz) of the butter in a large ovenproof sauté pan. Add the vanilla bean pod and seeds and the pear halves, cut side down. Cook the pears until the butter browns and the pears turn brown around the edges, about 3 minutes on each side. Add the maple syrup and place the pan in the oven for 15 minutes, with the pears cut side down, basting them with the syrup twice

during roasting, until they are tender when pierced with a skewer. Carefully transfer the pears to a plate.

3.   Return the pan to the stovetop over medium-high heat and bring the maple syrup mixture to a boil. Whisk in the remaining 2 tablespoons (28 g/1 oz) butter until melted. Carefully strain the sauce through a fine-mesh sieve into a microwave-safe container and set aside until you are ready to serve the pears. Warm the sauce in the microwave right before serving.

STREUSEL, BAKED (page 342)

ASSEMBLY

Place an Almond Round on top of a Puff Pastry Round and arrange them off center on a plate. Place a warmed Roasted Pear half on the round, using the hole to balance it. Sprinkle some Streusel on the plate and place a quenelle of Vanilla-Prune Ice Cream on top of it. Drizzle the pear with the reserved warm pear sauce.

ROASTED SUMMER APRICOTS with HONEY PAIN PERDU and SAFFRON ICE CREAM

THIS SUMMER DESSERT IS SO SIMPLE, SO fresh. Apricots can be very tart, probably because most are picked before they are completely ripe to minimize shipping damage. But when they're roasted, as they are here, their flavor brightens and takes on a beautiful sweet-tart character. I serve them on a piece of Honey Pain Perdu (French toast) with an earthy Saffron Ice Cream. For something so simple, it's an amazingly good combination of flavors.

MAKES 8 SERVINGS

COMPONENTS

SAFFRON ICE CREAM
APRICOT SAUCE
ROASTED APRICOTS
VANILLA BEAN GARNISH
STREUSEL
HONEY PAIN PERDU

SPECIAL EQUIPMENT   ice cream machine

PERFECT MATCH   Di Majo Norante Moscato del Molise Apianae, Italy

SAFFRON ICE CREAM

1 cup (250 g/8.8 oz) whole milk

1 cup (250 g/8.8 oz) heavy cream

⅛ tsp (0.05 g/0.0017 oz) saffron threads

1 vanilla bean, split lengthwise and seeds scraped

6 large (112 g/4 oz) egg yolks

½ cup plus 2 Tbsp (125 g/4.4 oz) granulated sugar

1. In a medium saucepan, combine the milk, cream, saffron threads, and vanilla bean pod and seeds and bring to a gentle boil over medium heat. Remove the pan from the heat, cover, and allow to infuse for 20 minutes. Strain, return the milk mixture to the saucepan, and bring back to a gentle boil. Remove from the heat.

2. In a medium bowl, whisk together the egg yolks and sugar until pale. Whisk about half of the hot milk mixture into the yolks, then return this mixture to the remaining milk mixture in the saucepan and cook over medium heat, stirring constantly with a wooden spoon, until it thickens enough to coat the back of the spoon and reaches 175°F (79°C) on an instant-read thermometer; do not let the mixture boil, or the egg yolks will curdle. Remove the pot from the heat and strain the ice cream base immediately into a bowl. Set the bowl in an ice bath and stir frequently until cold.

3. Transfer the ice cream base to an airtight container and refrigerate for at least 4 hours, or overnight.

4. Process the base in an ice cream machine according to the manufacturer's instructions. (Be careful not to overchurn the ice cream or it will become grainy.) Transfer the ice cream to an airtight container and freeze until ready to serve.

PINEAPPLE SEARED with THYME with TAPIOCA PARFAIT WRAPPED in PINEAPPLE GELÉE and COCONUT SORBET

THIS VERY REFRESHING DESSERT was inspired by both Asian and Middle Eastern flavors. A pineapple square is dusted with a mixture of spices that includes thyme, sumac, and sesame seeds (in the Middle East, *za'atar*, as this spice combination is called, is used to flavor a variety of dishes), and then pan-seared, which gives it a succulent, buttery flavor. It's topped with a light Tapioca Parfait that has been shaped into logs and wrapped in thin sheets of Pineapple Gelée. A Coconut Sorbet tops the parfait, and the whole thing is served with a Pineapple Chip and Tapioca Sauce made with grains of large-pearl tapioca.

MAKES 8 SERVINGS

COMPONENTS

COCONUT SORBET
PINEAPPLE GELÉE
SEARED PINEAPPLE
SPICE MIX
TAPIOCA SAUCE
TAPIOCA PARFAIT
PINEAPPLE CHIPS

SPECIAL EQUIPMENT | ice cream machine; mandoline; 8 by 4 by 3-inch loaf pan; ½-inch, plain pastry tip (Ateco #8); electric slicer

PERFECT MATCH | Rhum J.M. VSOP, Martinique

COCONUT SORBET

2½ cups (600 g/21 oz) coconut milk

1½ cups (350 g/12.34 oz) whole milk

1½ cups plus 2 Tbsp (330 g/11.6 oz) granulated sugar

1 cup (90 g/3.2 oz) unsweetened desiccated coconut

1.   In a medium saucepan, combine the coconut milk, whole milk, and sugar and bring to a gentle boil over medium heat, stirring to dissolve the sugar. Stir in the coconut. Transfer the sorbet base to a medium bowl and place the bowl into a bowl of ice water. Let stand, stirring occasionally, until completely cool. Cover the bowl and refrigerate the sorbet base for at least 4 hours, or overnight.

2.   Process the base in an ice cream machine according to the manufacturer's instructions. Transfer the sorbet to an airtight container and freeze until ready to serve.

PINEAPPLE GELÉE

6 sheets (12 g/0.42 oz) gelatin (silver grade)

2 cups (450 g/15.8 oz) pineapple purée

1.　Line an 8 by 4-inch loaf pan with plastic wrap. Fill a medium bowl halfway with cold water and add the gelatin sheets. Allow to soften for 10 minutes.

2.　In a small saucepan, heat half of the pineapple purée over medium heat until just hot. Remove the pan from the heat. Drain the gelatin, squeezing it to remove the excess water, and add it to the hot purée. Stir until the gelatin has dissolved. Add the remaining purée and stir until blended. Pour the mixture into the prepared loaf pan and freeze until firm, at least 1 hour.

SPICE MIX

1 Tbsp (3 g/0.1 oz) ground sumac

2 Tbsp (20 g/0.7 oz) sesame seeds

¼ cup (8 g/0.28 oz) dried thyme

¼ tsp (1 g/0.03 oz) dried oregano

¼ tsp (1 g/0.03 oz) dried marjoram

Grind the spices together in a spice grinder until finely ground.

SEARED PINEAPPLE

1 large pineapple

Spice Mix (above)

1 Tbsp (14 g/0.5 oz) unsalted butter

⅓ cup (85 g/3 oz) Simple Syrup (page 339)

1.　Cut the peel off the pineapple. Slice the pineapple lengthwise into ½-inch-thick slabs. Cut the slabs into 2¼-inch squares; you will need a total of 8. Sprinkle the squares on both sides with some of the Spice Mix.

2.　Place a sauté pan over high heat and add the butter, swirling the pan until the butter has melted. Add the pineapple squares and cook until their bottom sides are well colored. Turn the squares over and add the Simple Syrup. Continue to cook until the syrup has begun to caramelize and the pineapple is tender, about 3 minutes. Remove from the heat and cool.

TAPIOCA SAUCE

⅓ cup (60 g/2.1 oz) premium large-pearl tapioca, such as Bob's Red Mill brand (see Sources, page 349)

1 cup (250 g/8.8 oz) coconut milk

1 cup (250 g/8.8 oz) heavy cream

Seeds of ½ vanilla bean (save the pod for later use)

¼ cup plus 2 Tbsp (75 g/2.6 oz) granulated sugar

3 large (60 g/2.1 oz) egg yolks

1.　Pour the tapioca into a medium bowl and cover it with cold water. Cover the bowl and allow the tapioca to soak in the refrigerator for 6 hours, or overnight.

2.　In a medium saucepan, combine the coconut milk, cream, 3 tablespoons (37 g/1.3 oz) of the sugar, and the vanilla bean seeds. Bring to a boil over medium-high heat, stirring occasionally. Remove the pan from the heat.

3. Drain the tapioca and set aside. Place the egg yolks and remaining 3 tablespoons (37 g/1.3 oz) sugar in a medium bowl and whisk until pale. Whisk about ½ cup of the hot coconut milk mixture into the yolks, then return this mixture to the remaining coconut milk mixture in the saucepan. Add the tapioca and cook over medium-low heat, stirring constantly to prevent the tapioca from scorching, for about 20 minutes, or until the tapioca is translucent. Remove the pan from the heat. Set aside 1¼ cups (300 g/10.5 oz) of the Tapioca Sauce for the Tapioca Parfait; reserve the rest for garnish.

TAPIOCA PARFAIT

2 sheets (4 g/0.14 oz) gelatin (silver grade)

1¼ cups (300 g/10.5 oz) Tapioca Sauce (left)

1¼ cups (300 g/10.5 oz) heavy cream

1. Fill a medium bowl halfway with cold water and add the gelatin sheets. Allow to soften for 10 minutes.

2. Place the Tapioca Sauce in a small saucepan. Heat over medium-low heat until warm (if it's already warm, you can skip this step). Drain the gelatin, squeezing it to remove the excess water, and add it to the sauce. Stir until the gelatin has dissolved. Transfer the mixture to a medium bowl and cool completely.

3. Line a half-sheet pan with parchment paper. In the bowl of a stand mixer fitted with the whisk attachment, whip the cream to medium peaks. Gently fold the whipped cream into the tapioca mixture. Scrape the mixture into a pastry bag fitted with a ½-inch, plain tip. Pipe the parfait mixture onto the prepared sheet pan in long tube shapes, spacing them ½ inch apart. Place the pan in the freezer until the parfait tubes are firm, at least 2 hours.

4. Cut 5-inch-long logs from the tubes; you will need a total of 8. Freeze the logs, loosely covered, until ready to serve.

PINEAPPLE CHIPS (page 345)

Prepare the Pineapple Chips as directed and while they are still warm, curl them around a small dowel or pencil, forming a cigarette shape. Cool and store as directed.

ASSEMBLY

Passion fruit seeds

1. Using a mandoline or electric slicer, shave a very thin sheet from the frozen Pineapple Gelée (about a 4 by 8-inch rectangle) and place it on a sheet of plastic wrap. Starting with a long side, use the plastic to help roll the gelée around one of the frozen Tapioca Parfait logs (defrosting it slightly will help the gelée stick). The bottom of the gelée roll should overlap slightly and should form a tight roll. Cut away the excess gelée on the bottom and ends. Use the plastic to wrap the log tightly and freeze again. Repeat with the remaining logs, and freeze them for about 1 hour before serving.

2. Take a square of Seared Pineapple and place it in the center of a plate. Cut the frozen parfait logs by trimming the ends and cutting them crosswise in half. Each log should yield two 2¼-inch rolls. Place 2 logs on the pineapple square. Place a quenelle of Coconut Sorbet on the gelée and garnish with the Pineapple Chip. Decorate the plate with the reserved Tapioca Sauce and passion fruit seeds.

QUINCE COOKED in CARAMEL with CHOCOLATE-BANANA BEIGNET

⧆ ⧆ PHILIPPE BERTINEAU, my chef at Payard, loved quince, and he always complained that I never made any desserts with it. Quince is a pear-shaped, golden yellow fruit that is very dense and difficult to cook, which is probably why I use it so infrequently. But here I took the idea of a Tatin, without the puff pastry, and roasted wedges of quince in a buttery caramel, which gives them a sweet, almost floral flavor. I served the caramelized quince with a Chocolate Banana Beignet, perched on a baked Phyllo Round, and it's a wonderful combination. Philippe loved it, and so do I.

MAKES 8 SERVINGS

COMPONENTS

CARAMELIZED QUINCE

PHYLLO ROUNDS

CHOCOLATE BANANA BEIGNETS

    CHOCOLATE-BANANA GANACHE

    BEIGNET BATTER

SPECIAL EQUIPMENT | 9 by 13-inch rectangular cake pan; 3-inch round pastry cutter; deep, straight-sided saucepan or deep fryer

PERFECT MATCH | 2004 Duché de Longueville Cidre Gros Oeillet, Normandy, France

CARAMELIZED QUINCE

2½ cups (500 g/17.6 oz) granulated sugar

½ cup (120 g/4 oz) water

5 Tbsp (70 g/2.4 oz) unsalted butter, cut into cubes

8 quinces

1. Preheat the oven to 350°F (177°C). Coat a large roasting pan generously with nonstick cooking spray.

2. Place the sugar in a small, heavy-bottomed saucepan with the water and cook over medium heat, occasionally washing down the sides of the saucepan with a wet pastry brush to prevent crystals from forming, until the sugar caramelizes and turns a medium caramel color. Immediately remove the pan from the heat and stir in the butter—be very careful, the mixture will foam up and may splatter. Pour the caramel into the prepared pan and let it sit for a few minutes to harden.

3. Peel the quinces and slice each one into 10 equal wedges. Using a paring knife, cut away the core from each wedge. Lay the wedges on top of the caramel in the pan, overlapping if necessary, and bake for 55 minutes, tossing the quinces with the caramel every 15 minutes, and rotating the pan halfway through the roasting time. Set the pan on a wire rack and cool completely.

PHYLLO ROUNDS

4 (9 by 14-inch) sheets phyllo dough

16 Tbsp (226 g/8 oz) unsalted butter, melted

Confectioners' sugar, as needed

1. Position a rack in the center of the oven and preheat the oven to 350°F (177°C). Line a half-sheet pan with a silicone baking mat.

2. Place a sheet of the phyllo dough on a piece of parchment paper and brush it with the melted butter. Dust the sheet with confectioners' sugar. Repeat the layering process until you have used 4 phyllo sheets. Brush the top sheet with butter and dust with confectioners' sugar. Refrigerate the phyllo layers for 30 minutes, or until the butter has firmed up.

POACHED PEARS

6 ripe pears (Anjou, Bosc, or Bartlett)

2 cups (472 g/16.6 oz) water

2 cups (400 g/14.1 oz) granulated sugar

3 vanilla beans, split lengthwise and seeds scraped

Peel the pears, cut them in half lengthwise, and core them. Place the pears in a medium saucepan with the water, sugar, and vanilla bean pods and seeds. Bring the liquid to a boil over medium-high heat, then reduce to a simmer. Simmer the pears until they are tender, about 25 minutes. Transfer the pears and the poaching liquid to a medium bowl and set aside to cool.

WALNUT PASTRY CREAM

2½ cups (605 g/21.3 oz) whole milk, plus more as needed

1⅓ cups (150 g/5.3 oz) finely chopped toasted walnuts (see Toasted Nuts, page 346)

½ cup (100 g/3.5 oz) granulated sugar

⅓ cup (40 g/1.4 oz) cornstarch

5 large (93 g/3.3 oz) egg yolks

1 Tbsp (14 g/0.5 oz) unsalted butter

½ cup (120 g/4.2 oz) heavy cream

1.   In a medium saucepan, combine the milk and the walnuts and bring to a boil over medium heat. Remove from the heat, cover the pan, and allow to infuse for 10 minutes.

2.   Strain the milk into a glass measuring cup. You should have 2 cups; add more milk if you need to. Return the infused milk to the saucepan and bring to a boil. Remove the pan from the heat.

3.   In a medium bowl, combine the sugar and cornstarch. Whisk in the egg yolks, whisking until the mixture is pale. Whisk about one-quarter of the hot milk into the yolk mixture, then whisk the yolk mixture into the pan with the remaining milk. Cook over medium-high heat, whisking constantly, until the custard thickens and boils. Remove the pan from the heat and whisk in the butter until it is completely melted. Scrape the pastry cream through a fine-mesh sieve into a stainless steel bowl and cover the pastry cream with plastic wrap pressed directly on the surface to prevent a skin from forming. Set the bowl in an ice bath and stir frequently until cold.

4.   In the bowl of a stand mixer fitted with the whisk attachment, whip the heavy cream to medium peaks. Gently fold the whipped cream into the cold pastry cream. Cover the bowl and refrigerate the cream until ready to serve.

POIRE WILLIAM CRÈME ANGLAISE

Crème Anglaise (page 335)

2 Tbsp (30 g/1 oz) Poire William

Stir the Poire William into the Crème Anglaise. Transfer to an airtight container and refrigerate until ready to serve.

ASSEMBLY

Put the Walnut Pastry Cream in a pastry bag fitted with a medium, plain tip. Take one of the Poached Pear halves and pat it dry with a paper towel. Cut the pear half crosswise into ¼-inch-thick slices. Lay down a Phyllo Pear shape and pipe some of the pastry cream from the top to the bottom of the shape, piping a little more cream at the bottom; this will help it stand up once assembled. Place a poached pear slice on top. Top with another Phyllo Pear shape and repeat the layering, until you have used 4 Phyllo Pears. Pipe a dollop of the pastry cream onto a plate and lean the dessert against it, so that the pear shape is standing up. Place the other Poached Pear half on the plate and spoon some Poire William Crème Anglaise onto the plate.

PASTRIES, MERINGUES, and OTHER
BAKED DESSERTS

THE RECIPES IN THIS CHAPTER were inspired by desserts typically found in a French pâtisserie. I took the techniques and elements of these classics and transformed them into restaurant-style plated desserts. Many of the components that make up these desserts can be made in advance, a factor that is extremely important if you work in a small kitchen or with a limited staff. Many of the desserts are also fairly easy to assemble, which is also an important consideration when you are thinking about adding a dessert to your menu.

There are several napoleons in this chapter, some of which are made with classic layers of puff pastry, while others are constructed with thin layers of tuile, nougatine, phyllo dough, or chocolate. I always find it interesting to use unusual elements in a classic form, like the Peppered Nougatine Rectangles that make up my Red Currant Napoleon, or the squares of milk chocolate found in my Peanut Butter and Milk Chocolate Crispy Napoleon.

One of my favorite recipes here is the Cassis Japonais with Japonais Noodles and Cassis Port Sauce, which, with its crown of deep-fried pink bean thread noodles and garnish of ruby-colored Cassis Port Sauce, is as pleasing to the eye as it is to the palate. The scone, a bakery staple, takes on a more sophisticated guise in my Buttermilk Scones with Strawberry and Tomato Jam, an unusual combination of sweet and acidic flavors. My Blueberry Pavlova, which features perfect spheres of crispy baked meringue, is assembled à la minute, combining a colorful filling of Blueberry Sorbet and whipped cream.

BUTTERMILK SCONES with STRAWBERRY and TOMATO JAM

THIS IS A DESSERT THAT WE USED TO MAKE at Payard in the summertime, when strawberries were at their peak. The ripe, farm-fresh strawberries pair well with sweet tomatoes in a jam that tops a tender buttermilk scone. A tangy Buttermilk Ice Cream is a nice contrast to the sweet jam, and a bright mint syrup and Buttermilk Crème Anglaise turn something simple into something really exceptional. It's a really great dessert to make for parties, because once the *mise en place*—the ice cream, the scones, the jam—is done, there are only four steps to plating it. We used to make 500 or 600 of them at a time for large events, and they were always a big hit.

MAKES 8 SERVINGS

COMPONENTS

BUTTERMILK ICE CREAM
BUTTERMILK CRÈME ANGLAISE
STRAWBERRY AND TOMATO JAM
BUTTERMILK SCONES
MINT SYRUP

SPECIAL EQUIPMENT | ice cream machine; 2-inch round pastry cutter; squeeze bottle

PERFECT MATCH | Avignonesi Vin Santo di Montepulciano, Tuscany, Italy

BUTTERMILK ICE CREAM

1 cup (250 g/8.8 oz) heavy cream

1 vanilla bean, split lengthwise and seeds scraped

6 large (112 g/4 oz) egg yolks

½ cup plus 2 Tbsp (125 g/4.4 oz) granulated sugar

1 cup (242 g/8.8 oz) buttermilk

1.   In a medium saucepan, combine the cream and vanilla bean pod and seeds and bring to a gentle boil over medium heat.

2.   In a medium bowl, whisk together the egg yolks and sugar until pale. Whisk about half of the hot cream into the yolks, then return this mixture to the remaining cream mixture in the saucepan and stir in the buttermilk. Cook over medium heat, stirring constantly with a wooden spoon, until the mixture thickens enough to coat the back of the spoon and reaches 175°F (79°C) on an instant-read thermometer; do not let the mixture boil, or the egg yolks will curdle. Remove the pot from the heat and strain the ice cream base immediately into a bowl. Set the bowl in an ice bath and stir until completely cool.

3. Transfer the ice cream base to an airtight container and refrigerate for at least 4 hours, or overnight.

4. Process the base in an ice cream machine according to the manufacturer's instructions. (Be careful not to overchurn the ice cream or it will become grainy.) Transfer the ice cream to an airtight container and freeze until ready to serve.

BUTTERMILK CRÈME ANGLAISE

1 cup (232 g/8.18 oz) heavy cream

1 vanilla bean, split lengthwise and seeds scraped

6 large (110 g/3.8 oz) egg yolks

¼ cup plus 2 Tbsp (75 g/2.6 oz) granulated sugar

1 cup (242 g/8.5 oz) buttermilk

1. In a medium saucepan, combine the cream and vanilla bean pod and seeds and cook over medium-high heat until the mixture comes to a gentle boil. Remove the pan from the heat.

2. In a medium bowl, whisk together the egg yolks and sugar until pale. Whisk about half of the hot cream mixture into the yolks, then return this mixture to the saucepan with the remaining cream and stir in the buttermilk. Cook over medium heat, stirring constantly with a wooden spoon, until the mixture thickens enough to coat the back of the spoon and reaches 175°F (79°C) on an instant-read thermometer; do not let the mixture boil, or the egg yolks will curdle. Remove the pot from the heat and pass the mixture through a fine-mesh sieve into a bowl. Set the bowl in an ice bath and stir frequently until cold. Transfer to an airtight container and refrigerate until ready to serve, or for up to 3 days.

STRAWBERRY AND TOMATO JAM

Finely grated zest and juice of 2 lemons

Finely grated zest and juice of 1 orange

1 cup (200 g/7 oz) granulated sugar

3 Tbsp plus 2 tsp (50 g/1.76 oz) light brown sugar

⅓ cup (80 g/2.8 oz) water

2 Tbsp (30 g/1 oz) apple cider vinegar

4½ cups (250 g/8.8 oz) fresh strawberries, washed, hulled, and quartered

5 medium (600 g/1 lb 5.16 oz) ripe tomatoes, peeled, seeded, and diced

In a medium saucepan, combine the citrus zests and juices, sugars, water, and vinegar and bring to a boil over medium-high heat. Add the strawberries and tomatoes and cook over medium-low heat, stirring occasionally, until the mixture thickens to the consistency of melted jam, 25 to 30 minutes. Cool completely.

BUTTERMILK SCONES

1¾ cups plus 2 Tbsp (240 g/8.5 oz) all-purpose flour

¾ tsp (3 g/0.1 oz) salt

2½ Tbsp (30 g/1 oz) granulated sugar

¾ tsp (3 g/0.1 oz) baking powder

½ tsp plus ⅛ tsp (3 g/0.1 oz) baking soda

6 Tbsp plus 1 tsp (90 g/3.17 oz) unsalted butter, cold and cut into ½-in pieces

1 cup (242 g/8.5 oz) buttermilk

1 egg, whisked with a fork with a small amount of water, for egg wash

1. Preheat the oven to 375°F (191°C). Line a half-sheet pan with a silicone baking mat.

2. Combine the dry ingredients in a medium bowl. Add the butter pieces and, using 2 knives or a pastry blender, cut them into the flour mixture until the largest pieces are the size of peas and the rest resembles coarse meal. Add the buttermilk and stir gently with a rubber spatula just until the dough comes together.

3. Transfer the dough to a lightly floured work surface and gather it into a rough rectangle. Fold the dough in half and roll it out to a thickness of ¾ inch. Using a 2-inch round pastry cutter, cut out 8 rounds from the dough and arrange them on the prepared sheet pan. Brush the tops of the dough rounds with the egg wash and bake for 10 to 12 minutes, or until golden brown. Transfer the scones to a wire rack and cool.

MINT SYRUP

1 cup loosely packed (20 g/0.7 oz) fresh mint leaves

¼ cup plus ½ Tbsp (90 g/3.17 oz) light corn syrup

Fill a medium bowl halfway with ice water and set aside. Fill a small saucepan halfway with water and bring to a boil; blanch the mint leaves for 20 seconds. Remove the leaves with a skimmer and immediately plunge them into the ice water. Once the leaves are cold, pat them dry with paper towels. Coarsely chop the blanched leaves and place them in a blender with the corn syrup. Blend until smooth. Transfer the syrup to a squeeze bottle and refrigerate until ready to use.

ASSEMBLY

1 pint (226 g/8 oz) fresh strawberries, washed, hulled, and diced

Fried mint leaves (page 346)

Cut a Buttermilk Scone in half and place the bottom half in the center of a plate. Right before serving, mix the diced strawberries into the Strawberry and Tomato Jam and spoon some on top of the scone bottom. Scoop a quenelle of the Buttermilk Ice Cream on top of the jam and place the other scone half on top. Spoon some of the Buttermilk Crème Anglaise around the plate and dot some of the Mint Syrup on top. Garnish with a fried mint leaf.

ALMOND-PRUNE NAPOLEON with PRUNE-ARMAGNAC ICE CREAM

WHEN I WORKED AT DANIEL, we frequently had special wine dinners at which various wines were paired with each course. It was always a little tricky to come up with desserts that go well with wine, but the flavors of this napoleon match beautifully with a variety of wines—you can serve it with a Banyuls, or a Château d'Yquem, or even a port. The layers here are made of baked phyllo, which is even flakier than puff pastry, and they sandwich a Prune Pastry Cream filling topped with prunes that have been simmered in sangria. The base is a baked almond cream, and we serve a Prune-Armagnac Ice Cream alongside. For the sangria, it's not necessary to use expensive wine, because it's reduced so much and has so many flavors mixed with it. If possible, let the Sangria Prunes macerate in the refrigerator for two to three days before using. The recipe will yield more prunes than you need for this dessert, but they are wonderful served warm alongside vanilla ice cream.

MAKES 10 SERVINGS

COMPONENTS

PRUNE-ARMAGNAC ICE CREAM
PHYLLO RECTANGLES
ALMOND RECTANGLES
SANGRIA PRUNES
PRUNE PASTRY CREAM
STREUSEL

SPECIAL EQUIPMENT | ice cream machine; cheesecloth; kitchen twine; medium, plain pastry tip (Ateco #6)

PERFECT MATCH | 1980 Armagnac Baron de Lustrac

PRUNE-ARMAGNAC ICE CREAM

1 cup (250 g/8.8 oz) whole milk

1 cup (250 g/8.8 oz) heavy cream

6 large (112 g/4 oz) egg yolks

½ cup plus 2 Tbsp (125 g/4.4 oz) granulated sugar

¾ cup (166 g/5.8 oz) Armagnac or Cognac

1 cup (142 g/5 oz) pitted prunes

1.   In a medium saucepan, combine the milk and cream and bring to a gentle boil over medium heat.

2.   In a medium bowl, whisk together the egg yolks and sugar until pale. Whisk about half of the hot milk mixture into the yolks, then return this mixture to the remaining milk mixture in the saucepan and cook over medium heat, stirring constantly with a wooden spoon, until it thickens enough to coat the back of the spoon and reaches 175°F (79°C) on an

instant-read thermometer; do not let the mixture boil, or the egg yolks will curdle. Remove the pot from the heat and strain the ice cream base immediately into a bowl. Set the bowl in an ice bath and stir frequently until cold.

3.   Transfer the ice cream base to an airtight container and refrigerate for at least 4 hours, or overnight.

4.   In a medium saucepan, combine the Armagnac and prunes. Bring to a boil over medium heat, then reduce the heat to low,

partially cover, and simmer until the prunes are tender but not mushy, about 20 minutes. Add some water if the liquid has reduced too quickly and the prunes are not yet tender. Let stand until cool.

5.   Just before processing the ice cream, drain the prunes and reserve the liquid; add a little extra Armagnac if there is less than ¼ cup. Stir the reserved Armagnac into the chilled ice cream base. Cut the prunes into quarters.

CHESTNUT ICE CREAM NAPOLEON with WHIPPED CREAM and CHOCOLATE-GINGER SAUCE

I DEVELOPED THIS DESSERT when I was working at Le Bernardin. When I first made it, I used puff pastry for the layers, but I wanted sleeker look, so I started using baked phyllo dough instead, and it worked perfectly. I love the subtle, earthy flavor of chestnuts, especially in the luscious ice cream that makes up the filling. Garnishing the napoleon are candied chestnuts enrobed in a beautiful chocolate-colored caramel. To color the caramel, you use just enough cocoa powder to give a nice brown color—too much and the caramel will take too long to drip off the chestnuts and you won't get that elegant long tail.

MAKES 8 SERVINGS

COMPONENTS

WHIPPED CREAM
CHESTNUT ICE CREAM
CHOCOLATE-GINGER SAUCE
PHYLLO TRIANGLES
CANDIED CHESTNUT GARNISH

SPECIAL EQUIPMENT   medium, plain pastry tip (Ateco #6); immersion blender; ice cream machine; bamboo skewers

PERFECT MATCH   Nocello Walnut Liqueur, Emilia-Romagna, Italy

WHIPPED CREAM

1 cup plus 1 Tbsp (250 g/8.8 oz) heavy cream

2½ Tbsp (30 g/2 oz) granulated sugar

1 vanilla bean, split lengthwise and seeds scraped

1.   Place the cream, sugar, and vanilla bean pod and seeds in an airtight container and refrigerate overnight.

2.   Remove the vanilla bean from the cream mixture. In the bowl of a stand mixer fitted with the whisk attachment, whip the cream on medium speed until medium peaks form. Transfer the Whipped Cream to a pastry bag fitted with a medium, plain tip and refrigerate until ready to serve.

CHESTNUT ICE CREAM

1 cup (250 g/8.8 oz) whole milk

1 cup (250 g/8.8 oz) heavy cream

6 large (112 g/4 oz) egg yolks

½ cup plus 2 Tbsp (125 g/4.4 oz) granulated sugar

⅓ cup plus 1 Tbsp (100 g/3.5 oz) unsweetened chestnut paste

2 Tbsp (34 g/1.2 oz) Simple Syrup (page 339)

1.   In a medium saucepan, combine the milk and cream and bring to a gentle boil over medium heat.

2. In a medium bowl, whisk together the egg yolks and sugar until pale. Whisk about half of the hot milk mixture into the yolks, then return this mixture to the remaining milk mixture in the saucepan and cook over medium heat, stirring constantly with a wooden spoon until it thickens enough to coat the back of the spoon and reaches 175°F (79°C) on an instant-read thermometer; do not let the mixture boil, or the egg yolks will curdle. Remove the pot from the heat and pass the ice cream base immediately through a fine-mesh sieve into a bowl.

3. In a small bowl, whisk the chestnut paste with the Simple Syrup until smooth. Stir the paste into the hot ice cream base and, using an immersion blender, blend on low speed until smooth. Set the bowl in an ice bath and stir frequently until cold.

4. Transfer the ice cream base to an airtight container and refrigerate for at least 4 hours, or overnight.

5. Process the base in an ice cream machine according to the manufacturer's instructions. (Be careful not to overchurn the ice cream or it will become grainy.) Spread the soft ice cream into an even layer in a 10½ by 15½-inch jelly roll pan that has been lined with plastic wrap. Cover the ice cream with plastic wrap and freeze until firm, at least 3 hours.

6. Cut out 24 equilateral triangles with 2-inch sides from the ice cream rectangle. Place the triangles on a half-sheet pan, cover with plastic wrap, and freeze until ready to serve.

CHOCOLATE-GINGER SAUCE

7 oz (200 g) 72% bittersweet chocolate, finely chopped

8 Tbsp (113 g/4 oz) unsalted butter, cut into ½-inch cubes

1 cup (250 g/8.8 oz) whole milk

2 sticks cinnamon

¼ cup (30 g/1 oz) peeled and coarsely chopped fresh ginger

1. Place the chocolate and butter in a medium bowl and set aside.

2. In a small saucepan, combine the milk, cinnamon sticks, and ginger and bring to a boil over medium-high heat. Strain the hot milk over the chocolate, discard the cinnamon sticks and ginger, and stir gently until the chocolate has melted and the sauce is completely smooth.

PHYLLO TRIANGLES

4 (13 by 18-inch) sheets phyllo dough

17¾ Tbsp (250 g/8.8 oz) unsalted butter, melted

Confectioners' sugar, for dusting

1. Position two racks near the center of the oven and preheat the oven to 350°F (177°C). Line two half-sheet pans with silicone baking mats. Place a sheet of phyllo dough on a piece of parchment paper and brush it with some of the melted butter. Dust with confectioners' sugar. Repeat the layering process until you have used all 4 phyllo sheets. Brush the last sheet with butter and dust with confectioners' sugar. Refrigerate the phyllo layers for 30 minutes, or until the butter has firmed up.

2. Using a pastry wheel or sharp knife, cut out 32 equilateral triangles with 2½-inch sides. Arrange the triangles on the prepared sheet pans and place another silicone baking mat on top of them to keep them flat. Bake the triangles for 10 minutes, or until crisp. Cool the triangles on the pans set on wire racks.

CANDIED CHESTNUT GARNISH

32 candied chestnuts in syrup

1½ cups (500 g/17.6 oz) fondant (see Sources, page 349)

¾ cup (250 g/8.8 oz) glucose syrup

2 tsp (4 g/0.14 oz) unsweetened alkalized cocoa powder, sifted

1. Drain and dry the candied chestnuts well with paper towels. Stick 24 of the candied chestnuts on both ends of a bamboo skewer, arranging them so that the points of the chestnuts are facing downward. Place the skewers on a box that is between 4 and 6 inches wide and at least 6 inches high. Set the box on top of a silicone baking mat–lined half-sheet pan. The skewers should be at least 6 inches above the sheet pan with the chestnuts hanging over the edge at each end.

2. In a medium, heavy-bottomed saucepan, combine the fondant and glucose syrup and cook over medium-high heat until the mixture caramelizes and turns a light amber, about 8 minutes. Remove the pan from the heat and let the caramel cool until it thickens enough so that it drips slowly off a spoon, about 5 minutes.

3. Stir the cocoa powder into the caramel just until combined. Dip the chestnuts on the skewers in the sugar, one at a time, and place the skewers back on the box. Allow the sugar to run off of the chestnuts in a steady stream. As the sugar starts to cool and drops from the chestnuts, the sugar thread should bend. Do not move or touch the chestnuts until the sugar has set. Allow the Candied Chestnuts to cool completely.

4. Remove the chestnuts and store them in an airtight container until ready to serve.

5. Reheat the caramel and cool until thickened, as before. Spoon a little thickened caramel onto the remaining 8 candied chestnuts for garnish.

ASSEMBLY

Confectioners' sugar, for dusting

Place a Phyllo Triangle on a plate and top with a triangle of Chestnut Ice Cream. Pipe a dollop of Whipped Cream on top of the ice cream and top with another Phyllo Triangle, slightly askew. Repeat the layering and top with the fourth Phyllo Triangle, which has been lightly dusted with confectioners' sugar. Top with one of the Candied Chestnuts that has been topped with a spoonful of caramel. Arrange 3 of the Candied Chestnuts with the long caramel stems next to the dessert on the plate. Spoon some Chocolate-Ginger Sauce onto the plate.

FOUR-HOUR BAKED APPLE NAPOLEON with CARAMEL CHANTILLY and CARAMEL SAUCE

⧖⧖ DANIEL BOULUD WAS THE INSPIRATION for this fall dessert. He adores apples, so I designed a dessert that presents comfort food—baked apples—in an elegant way. The apples are baked slowly, for about 4 hours, at a very low temperature, which makes them juicy and so tender that they almost melt in your mouth. The apples become the filling for the napoleon, with spiced tuiles separating the layers. I serve a simple Caramel Chantilly on top, and a luscious Caramel Sauce that spills over onto the plate, allowing you to have some with every bite. I like to use Granny Smith apples here, but you can use any firm-textured apple, such as Fuji or Braeburn.

MAKES 8 SERVINGS

COMPONENTS

SPICED TUILES
CARAMEL CHANTILLY
FOUR-HOUR BAKED APPLES
CARAMEL STICKS
CARAMEL SAUCE

SPECIAL EQUIPMENT | 3½-inch round pastry cutter; 1-inch round pastry cutter; small 1½-inch ice cream scoop; medium, plain pastry tip (Ateco #6)

PERFECT MATCH | Brasserie Duyck Jenlain Ambrée Beer, France

SPICED TUILES

4 large (120 g/4.2 oz) egg whites

1 cup (200 g/7 oz) granulated sugar

¾ cup plus 1 Tbsp plus 1 tsp (100 g/3.5 oz) all-purpose flour

½ tsp (0.75 g/0.03 oz) ground cinnamon

¼ tsp (0.5 g/0.02 oz) ground anise

¾ tsp (0.75 g/0.03 oz) freshly grated nutmeg

8¾ Tbsp (125 g/4.4 oz) Clarified Butter (page 348)

1.   Half fill a small saucepan with water and bring to a simmer. In a medium stainless steel bowl, whisk together the egg whites and granulated sugar and place the bowl over the pot of simmering water. Continue to whisk gently until the mixture is just warm to the touch and the sugar has dissolved. Remove the bowl and whisk in the flour and spices until blended. Mix in the Clarified Butter. Transfer the batter to an airtight container and refrigerate for at least 2 hours, or up to 3 days, before using.

2.   Preheat the oven to 350°F (177°C). Line a half-sheet pan with a silicone baking mat.

Spread some of the tuile batter in a thin, even layer over the mat. Bake for 10 minutes, until partially baked. While the tuile sheet is still warm and pliable, using a 3¼-inch round pastry cutter, cut out as many rounds as possible from the sheet. Using a 1-inch round pastry cutter, cut out a hole from the center of 8 of the rounds. Return the tuiles to the oven and bake for another 5 minutes, or until golden brown. Repeat to make at least 40 tuile rounds, with 8 having center holes.

CARAMEL CHANTILLY

1 cup (200 g/7 oz) granulated sugar

Pinch of salt

2 Tbsp (30 g/1 oz) water

4 cups plus 5 Tbsp (1 kg/35.2 oz) heavy cream

8½ Tbsp (120 g/4.2 oz) unsalted butter

1. In a medium, heavy-bottomed saucepan, combine the sugar, salt, and water and cook over medium-high heat, occasionally washing down the sides of the pan with a wet pastry brush to prevent crystals from forming, and watching carefully, until the sugar caramelizes and turns a deep amber color, 3 to 5 minutes. Remove the pan from the heat and gradually add 2 cups plus 2½ tablespoons (500 g/17.6 oz) of the cream. Return the pan to the heat and stir until any hardened bits of caramel have dissolved, about 2 minutes. Add the butter and stir until melted. Cool the mixture, then transfer to an airtight container and refrigerate for at least 6 hours, or overnight. Reserve half of the chilled caramel to use with the apples.

2. In the bowl of a stand mixer fitted with the whisk attachment, whip the remaining 2 cups plus 2½ tablespoons (500 g/17.6 oz) cream to medium peaks. Fold the remaining caramel into the whipped cream. Using a 1½-inch ice cream scoop, scoop out 8 balls of the chantilly onto a plate. Loosely cover the plate and refrigerate the scoops until ready to serve. Transfer the remaining chantilly to a pastry bag fitted with a medium, plain tip and refrigerate until ready to serve.

FOUR-HOUR BAKED APPLES

6 Granny Smith apples, peeled, cored, and halved crosswise (so that each round has a hole in the center)

Caramel reserved from the Caramel Chantilly

1. Preheat the oven to 300°F (149°C).

2. Arrange the apple halves, cut side up, in a large baking pan and pour the reserved caramel on top. Bake the apples for 4 hours, turning them every 30 minutes, until they are caramelized and tender. If the caramel on the bottom of the pan starts to burn at any point, add 2 tablespoons of water to the pan as needed. Cool completely.

3. Cut each apple half in half crosswise to form 2 rounds from each half. Set aside at room temperature, loosely covered with aluminum foil, until ready to serve.

CARAMEL STICKS

Caramel Garnishes (page 336)

1.   Follow the instructions for the Caramel Garnishes through step 2. Dip a thick wooden spoon in the caramel and move the spoon back and forth over the silicone baking mat, drizzling the caramel in solid, even lines. Allow the caramel to harden.

2.   When the caramel lines have hardened, cut them to the desired size with a knife. Store the sticks in an airtight container at room temperature.

CARAMEL SAUCE (page 334)

ASSEMBLY

Pipe a small dollop of the Caramel Chantilly on a plate and top with a Spiced Tuile (without a center hole). Place a Four-Hour Baked Apple quarter on top of the tuile and fill the apple's center cavity with some piped Caramel Chantilly. Top with another tuile. Repeat the layering until you have used 4 tuiles and 3 apple quarters, ending with a tuile on top. Arrange 1 of the reserved Caramel Chantilly scoops on top of the fourth tuile. Arrange a tuile with a center hole on top of the scoop at an angle. Garnish with 2 Caramel Sticks coming from the top. Garnish the dessert and the plate with Caramel Sauce.

RED CURRANT NAPOLEON with PEPPERED NOUGATINE

RED CURRANTS ARE VERY ACIDIC, very tart, so they should always be combined with sweet elements. I decided to use them in a nontraditional napoleon, made with Peppered Nougatine Rectangles, which are very sweet, but with a slightly peppery endnote that complements the tart berries. I add some red currant purée and a little grenadine to the pastry cream to turn it a beautiful soft pink color, then layer it on the rectangles along with red currants, raspberries, and strawberries. The nougatine rectangles are very fragile, so the dessert needs to be assembled à la minute.

MAKES 8 SERVINGS

COMPONENTS

PEPPERED NOUGATINE RECTANGLES

RED CURRANT PASTRY CREAM

RED BERRIES IN VANILLA SYRUP

RED CURRANT SAUCE

SPECIAL EQUIPMENT | pepper mill; 1½ by 3½-inch rectangular tuile stencil; medium, plain pastry tip (Ateco #4)

PERFECT MATCH | Les Brasseurs de Gayant Tequieros, Douai, France

PEPPERED NOUGATINE RECTANGLES

½ cup plus 1¾ Tbsp (200 g/7 oz) glucose or light corn syrup

1 cup (300 g/10.6 oz) fondant (see Sources, page 349)

2 Tbsp (28 g/1 oz) unsalted butter

Pinch of salt

5 turns freshly ground pepper

1.   Line a half-sheet pan with a silicone baking mat. In a small saucepan, combine the glucose or light corn syrup and fondant and cook over medium-high heat until the mixture caramelizes and turns a light amber color. Remove the pan from the heat and stir in the butter, salt,

and pepper. Pour the mixture onto the baking mat and, using a small offset metal spatula, spread it out into a thin layer. Cool completely.

2.   Break the nougatine into chunks and pulse it in a food processor until it forms a powder.

3.   Preheat the oven to 350°F (177°C). Line a half-sheet pan with a silicone baking mat and place the rectangular stencil on the mat. Sprinkle a layer of the nougatine powder over the stencil so that it just covers it; you don't want to spread too thick a layer. Repeat to form as many rectangles as you can fit on the sheet pan. Bake for 3 to 5 minutes, watching the nougatine carefully. Once it melts and turns a caramel color, it is ready. (It's OK if the rectangle has some holes in it—the most important

thing is that it should be very thin.) Remove the rectangles from the oven and cool completely on a wire rack. Repeat until you have at least 32 rectangles.

RED CURRANT PASTRY CREAM

1½ cups (375 g/13.2 oz) whole milk

1¼ cups (375 g/13.2 oz) red currant purée

1 cup plus 2 Tbsp (225 g/8 oz) granulated sugar

½ cup (60 g/2.1 oz) cornstarch

7¼ large (135 g/4.7 oz) egg yolks

1 Tbsp (16 g/0.5 oz) grenadine syrup

1 Tbsp (21 g/0.5 oz) unsalted butter

¾ cup (174 g/0.7 oz) heavy cream

1.   In a medium saucepan, bring the milk and red currant purée to a boil over medium heat. Remove from the heat.

2.   In a medium bowl, combine the sugar and cornstarch. Whisk in the egg yolks, whisking until the mixture is pale. Whisk about

one-quarter of the milk into the yolk mixture, then whisk the yolk mixture into the pan with the remaining milk mixture and cook over medium-high heat, whisking constantly, until the custard thickens and boils. Remove the pan from the heat and whisk in the grenadine syrup and butter, and continue to whisk until the butter has completely melted. Scrape the pastry cream through a fine-mesh sieve into a stainless steel bowl and press a piece of plastic wrap directly on the surface of the pastry cream to prevent a skin from forming. Set the bowl in an ice bath and stir frequently until cold.

3.   In the bowl of a stand mixer fitted with the whisk attachment, whip the cream to medium peaks. Gently fold the whipped cream into the cold pastry cream. Cover the bowl and refrigerate until ready to serve.

RED BERRIES IN VANILLA SYRUP

> 1 cup (113 g/4 oz) sliced small fresh strawberries
>
> 1 cup (113 g/4 oz) fresh red currants
>
> 1 cup (113 g/4 oz) fresh raspberries, halved
>
> 1 cup (250 g/8.8 oz) Simple Syrup (page 339)
>
> 1 vanilla bean, split lengthwise and seeds scraped

1.   Place the berries in a medium bowl and set aside.

2.   In a small saucepan, combine the Simple Syrup and vanilla bean pod and seeds and bring to a boil over medium-high heat. Remove the pan from the heat and set aside to cool until just warm.

3.   Pour the warm syrup over the berries and gently toss to coat them with syrup. Discard the vanilla bean pod. Set aside to cool at room temperature.

RED CURRANT SAUCE

> 3 cups (340 g/12 oz) fresh red currants
>
> ½ cup (125 g/4.4 oz) water
>
> ¼ cup plus 1 Tbsp (62 g/2.2 oz) granulated sugar
>
> Juice of 1 lemon

1.   In a medium saucepan, combine all the ingredients and bring to a boil over medium-high heat. Reduce the heat to a simmer and cook until the currants are very soft, about 10 minutes.

2.   Transfer the mixture to a blender and process until smooth. Pour through a fine-mesh sieve and set aside to cool.

3.   Refrigerate in an airtight container until ready to serve.

ASSEMBLY

Place the Red Currant Pastry Cream in a pastry bag fitted with a medium, plain tip. Pipe a dab of the cream onto a plate and top with a Peppered Nougatine Rectangle; the cream will make it stick. Pipe dollops of cream around the edge of the rectangle. Arrange some of the Red Berries in Vanilla Syrup on top of the cream. Pipe more cream onto the berries and top with another nougatine rectangle. Repeat until you have used 4 nougatine rectangles and top with some of the berries. Decorate the plate with the Red Currant Sauce.

BLUEBERRY PAVLOVA with WARM BLUEBERRY COULIS

EACH SEPTEMBER AT PAYARD, my chef de cuisine, Philippe Bertineau, would go to the farmers' market and bring back beautiful fresh blueberries. This simple dessert, my take on a classic pavlova, is a great way to showcase the tangy flavor of these ripe summer berries. My pavlova is all about contrasting textures (crispy meringue with smooth sorbet and creamy whipped cream) and temperatures (frozen sorbet with warm blueberry coulis). It's important to bake the meringue shells very slowly at a low temperature, as directed, so that they don't expand too much—they should retain their spherical shape for the best presentation.

MAKES 6 SERVINGS

COMPONENTS

BLUEBERRY SORBET
CRISPY MERINGUE
BLUEBERRY SAUCE
WHIPPED CREAM

SPECIAL EQUIPMENT | ice cream machine; twelve 3-inch dome-shaped silicone molds; medium, plain pastry tip (Ateco #6)

PERFECT MATCH | 2007 Di Majo Norante Moscato del Molise Apianae, Italy

BLUEBERRY SORBET

1¾ cups (420 g/14.8 oz) water

1½ tsp (5 g/0.17 oz) sorbet stabilizer

1 cup (200 g/7 oz) granulated sugar

2½ Tbsp (50 g/1.7 oz) glucose syrup

1⅔ cups (500 g/17.6 oz) blueberry purée

1. In a small bowl, combine 2 tablespoons (28 g/1 oz) of the water with the sorbet stabilizer until smooth.

2. In a small saucepan, combine the remaining water with the sugar, sorbet stabilizer mixture, and glucose syrup and bring to a boil over medium-high heat, stirring to dissolve the sugar. Transfer the sorbet base to a medium bowl and stir in the blueberry

purée. Cover and chill for at least 4 hours, or overnight.

3. Process the base in an ice cream machine according to the manufacturer's instructions. Transfer the sorbet to an airtight container and freeze until ready to serve.

CRISPY MERINGUE

4 large (125 g/4.4 oz) egg whites

½ cup plus 2 Tbsp (125 g/4.4 oz) granulated sugar

1 cup plus 1½ Tbsp (125 g/4.4 oz) confectioners' sugar, sifted

½ cup (42 g/1.5 oz) sliced almonds

1. Preheat the oven to 175°F (79°C). Place twelve 3-inch silicone dome molds on a half-sheet pan

2. In the bowl of a stand mixer fitted with the whisk attachment, whip the egg whites on medium speed until soft peaks begin to form. Gradually add the granulated sugar and whip on high speed until the whites form stiff peaks. Gently fold in the confectioners' sugar by hand. Transfer the meringue to a pastry bag fitted with a medium, plain tip (Ateco #6). Place about ¾ tablespoon sliced almonds in the bottom of each mold. Pipe the meringue into each dome, filling them halfway (you won't use all the meringue). Use a spoon to spread the meringue up the sides of the molds, creating hollow half-spheres. Bake for 1½ to 2 hours, or until the meringue is dry and crisp. Cool the half-spheres completely in the molds.

3. Very carefully turn the molds inside-out and pop out the half-spheres.

BLUEBERRY SAUCE

8 cups (1 kg/2.2 lb) fresh blueberries

¼ cup (60 g/2.1 oz) crème de cassis

1. Place the blueberries in a large saucepan and cook over medium-low heat, stirring occasionally, until they release their liquid and are soft, about 10 minutes. Remove the pan from the heat and cool.

2. Purée the blueberries with their liquid and the crème de cassis in a blender. Strain through a fine-mesh sieve into an airtight container and refrigerate until ready to serve.

WHIPPED CREAM

2 cups (464 g/16.4 oz) heavy cream

¼ cup (50 g/1.7 oz) granulated sugar

¼ vanilla bean, split lengthwise and seeds scraped

In the bowl of a stand mixer fitted with the whisk attachment, whip the cream with the sugar and vanilla bean seeds to medium peaks. Cover the bowl and refrigerate until ready to serve.

ASSEMBLY

Confectioners' sugar, for dusting

Warm the Blueberry Sauce in the microwave for 1 minute on high power. Spoon some warm sauce into the center of a shallow bowl. Place some of the Whipped Cream into a pastry bag fitted with a medium, plain tip. Right before serving, place a small scoop of Blueberry Sorbet in a half-sphere of Crispy Meringue. Pipe some of the cream into the meringue sphere, on top of the sorbet. Pipe a little cream around the top edge of the sphere. Top the half-sphere with the cream around the edge with another half-sphere topped with almond slices, forming a full sphere. Place the sphere in the center of the bowl and serve immediately.

RHUBARB NAPOLEON filled with BRAISED RHUBARB

THE INSPIRATION FOR THIS RECIPE came from my friend Claude Troisgros, son of the great chef Pierre Troisgros. Claude has a restaurant called Olympe in Rio de Janeiro, where he serves a dessert that includes crispy wafers made from a thin, baked crêpe batter. These delicious little rounds are lacy and very crisp, and a fork goes through them very easily without making a big mess, so I decided to layer them in this fresh rhubarb napoleon, a great spring dessert. Because they're so light, Claude's wafers are a good alternative to more traditional puff pastry or phyllo. To make them successfully, however, you must use Teflon cake pans, or they will stick and be impossible to unmold. The filling is a Rhubarb Pastry Cream and chunks of Braised Rhubarb, and I spoon a little passion fruit pulp on top to break up the color and add a tropical note.

MAKES 8 SERVINGS

COMPONENTS

RHUBARB SAUCE
RHUBARB PASTRY CREAM
CRISPY WAFERS
BRAISED RHUBARB

SPECIAL EQUIPMENT
cheesecloth; kitchen twine; 4-inch-diameter by 1-inch-high round Teflon pans; medium, plain pastry tip (Ateco #6)

PERFECT MATCH   Nicolas Feuillatte Rosé Champagne, France

RHUBARB SAUCE

1 stalk fresh lemongrass, chopped

2 cups plus 2 Tbsp (500 g/17.6 oz) water

¼ cup plus 1 Tbsp (62 g/2.2 oz) granulated sugar

About 2 medium stalks (250 g/8.8 oz) rhubarb, coarsely chopped

Finely grated zest of 1 lemon

Finely grated zest of 1 orange

¼ cup (60 g/2.1 oz) grenadine syrup

1.   Place the lemongrass in the center of a 7-inch square of cheesecloth and gather the ends of the cheesecloth together to form a pouch. Tie a string around the neck of the pouch to secure it.

2.   Place the cheesecloth pouch and the remaining ingredients in a medium saucepan and bring to a boil over medium-high heat. Reduce the heat to a simmer and cook until the rhubarb is very soft, 7 to 10 minutes. Remove the pan from the heat. Remove the pouch of lemongrass with a slotted spoon and discard.

3.   Transfer the mixture to a blender and blend until smooth. Strain the sauce through a fine-mesh sieve into a bowl, cover, and set aside. Some of the sauce will be used in the Rhubarb Pastry Cream, and the rest will be used to garnish the plate.

RHUBARB PASTRY CREAM

1 cup (250 g/8.8 oz) Rhubarb Sauce (page 119)

1 cup (250 g/8.8 oz) whole milk

½ cup (100 g/3.5 oz) granulated sugar

⅓ cup (40 g/1.4 oz) cornstarch

5 large (90 g/3.17 oz) egg yolks

1 Tbsp (15 g/0.5 oz) unsalted butter

3 Tbsp plus 1 tsp (50 g/1.76 oz) grenadine syrup

1 cup plus 1 Tbsp (250 g/8.8 oz) heavy cream

1.   In a medium saucepan, combine the Rhubarb Sauce and milk and bring to a boil over medium heat. Remove from the heat.

2.   In a medium bowl, combine the sugar and cornstarch. Whisk in the egg yolks, whisking until the mixture is pale. Whisk about one-quarter of the milk mixture into the yolk mixture, then whisk the yolk mixture into the pan with the remaining milk mixture. Cook over medium-high heat, whisking constantly, until the custard thickens and boils.

3.   Remove the pan from the heat and whisk in the butter and grenadine syrup, whisking until the butter is completely melted. Scrape the pastry cream through a fine-mesh sieve into a stainless steel bowl and press a piece of plastic wrap directly on the surface of the pastry cream to prevent a skin from forming. Set the bowl in an ice bath and stir frequently until cold.

4.   In the bowl of a stand mixer fitted with the whisk attachment, whip the cream to medium peaks. Gently fold the whipped cream into the cold pastry cream. Cover the bowl and refrigerate until ready to serve.

CRISPY WAFERS

¾ cup plus 1 Tbsp (100 g/3.5 oz) all-purpose flour

7 Tbsp (100 g/3.5 oz) unsalted butter, melted and hot

¾ cup plus 1 Tbsp (165 g/5.8 oz) granulated sugar

7½ large (225 g/8 oz) egg whites

6 cups (1.4 kg/3.12 lb) warm water

1.   Place the flour in a large bowl and whisk in the hot melted butter until smooth. Whisk in the sugar. Whisk in the egg whites, one-third at a time, to prevent lumps from forming. Whisk in the water last. Cover the bowl and refrigerate the batter for 24 hours.

2.   Position two racks near the center of the oven and preheat the oven to 375°F (191°C). Place twelve 4-inch-diameter by 1-inch-high round Teflon pans on each of two half-sheet pans. Stir the chilled wafer batter, then immediately pour 2 tablespoons (30g/1 oz) of it into each pan. Bake the wafers for about 15 minutes, or until they are an even golden brown. While they are still hot, run a small metal spatula around the edge of the pans to remove the wafers, and place them on a half-sheet pan. Top the pan with another half-sheet pan to flatten the wafers as they cool. Repeat the baking and cooling process with the remaining batter, leaving 8 of the wafers unflattened.

Reserve the cooled wafers in an airtight container to prevent them from becoming soft. This recipe makes about 50 wafers; you will need 48 wafers for this dessert.

BRAISED RHUBARB

About 4 medium stalks (454 g/1 lb) rhubarb

4 cups (944 g/33.3 oz) water

2½ cups (500 g/17.6 oz) granulated sugar

1 stalk lemongrass, cut into 2-inch pieces

Finely grated zest of 1 lemon

Finely grated zest of 1 orange

½ cup (100 g/3.5 oz) grenadine syrup

1. Preheat the oven to 375°F (191°C). Trim off and discard the ends from the rhubarb and place the stalks in a roasting pan.

2. Combine the remaining ingredients in a medium saucepan and bring to a boil over high heat. Remove the pan from the heat and strain the liquid over the rhubarb in the pan, pouring in just enough liquid to cover the rhubarb. Braise the rhubarb in the oven for about 15 minutes, or until tender. Set aside to cool.

3. Cut the cooled rhubarb into 1-inch pieces.

ASSEMBLY

Pulp of 4 passion fruits, for garnish

Scrape the Rhubarb Pastry Cream into a pastry bag fitted with a medium, plain tip. Pipe a small dab of the pastry cream in the center of a shallow soup bowl and top with a Crispy Wafer. Pipe a layer of pastry cream onto the wafer, and top with a few slices of Braised Rhubarb. Repeat the layering until you have five layers. Top with one of the unflattened Crispy Wafers, and top it with a few slices of Braised Rhubarb and some passion fruit pulp. Spoon some of the Rhubarb Sauce around the plate.

WHITE CHOCOLATE ROSE WATER NAPOLEON with LYCHEE CRÈME GLACÉ

EVEN THOUGH I DON'T THINK ROSE WATER is a very popular flavor in America, this dessert was a big seller at Payard. There's nothing classic about this napoleon; instead of puff pastry, it's composed of layers of almond dacquoise, White Chocolate Rice Crispy rectangles, and a floral Rose Mousse. I serve this dessert with a lychee ice cream, which has a soft perfume that brings all the flavors together. Caramelized raspberries bring a dash of color and a bright acidity to this pretty dessert.

MAKES 8 SERVINGS

COMPONENTS

ROSE MOUSSE
ALMOND DACQUOISE
WHITE CHOCOLATE RICE CRISPY
LYCHEE CRÈME GLACÉ
CARAMELIZED RASPBERRIES
WHITE CHOCOLATE RECTANGLES

SPECIAL EQUIPMENT | 8-inch square baking pan; ice cream machine; three 3 by 12-inch acetate rectangles; medium, plain tip (Ateco #6)

PERFECT MATCH | Carole Bouquet Passito di Pantelleria Sangue D'Oro, Sicily

ROSE MOUSSE

1¼ cups (290 g/10.22 oz) heavy cream

1 lb 7 oz (650 g) white chocolate, chopped

5 large (93 g/3.2 oz) egg yolks

1 Tbsp plus 1 tsp (20 g/0.7 oz) rose water

2 Tbsp (30 g/1 oz) grenadine syrup

1. In a small saucepan, bring 1 cup (232 g/ 8.18 oz) of the cream to a boil over medium heat. Reduce the heat to low.

2. Place the white chocolate in the bowl of a stand mixer and set the bowl over a pot half filled with barely simmering water. Heat, stirring frequently, until the chocolate is melted and smooth. Transfer the bowl to the mixer stand and, using the whisk attachment, mix on medium-low speed while gradually adding the egg yolks. The mixture will appear curdled, as if it has seized. Add the hot cream little by little, allowing the heat of the cream to remelt the chocolate. Add the rose water and grenadine syrup and mix until blended. Cover the bowl and refrigerate the mousse base for at least 6 hours, or overnight.

3. Place the cooled mousse base on the mixer stand and, using the whisk attachment, beat the mixture on high speed until it is pale and very thick, 1 to 2 minutes.

4. Place the remaining ¼ cup (58 g/2 oz) heavy cream in a medium bowl and, using a hand whisk, whip it to soft peaks. Fold the whipped cream into the rose mousse mixture. Cover the bowl and refrigerate the mousse until ready to serve.

ALMOND DACQUOISE

1 cup (90 g/3.17 oz) almond flour

¾ cup (90 g/3.17 oz) confectioners' sugar

4 large (120 g/4.2 oz) egg whites

3 Tbsp plus 1 tsp (42 g/1.5 oz) granulated sugar

1. Preheat the oven to 400°F (204°C). Line an 8-inch square baking pan with parchment paper and spray the sides of the pan with non-stick baking spray (alternatively, you can use a quarter-sheet pan).

2. Sift the almond flour and confectioners' sugar into a medium bowl and whisk to combine. Set aside.

3. In the bowl of a stand mixer fitted with the whisk attachment, whip the egg whites on medium speed until they are opaque and form soft peaks. Gradually add the sugar, then increase the speed to high and whip until stiff peaks form. Gently fold in the almond flour mixture. Spread the batter into the prepared pan. Bake for 9 to 12 minutes, or until lightly browned and baked through. Set on a wire rack and cool completely.

4. Unmold and cut the dacquoise into 1¼ by 3½-inch rectangles; you will need a total of 8 rectangles. Set aside until ready to serve.

WHITE CHOCOLATE RICE CRISPY

4.4 oz (125 g) white chocolate, chopped

1 Tbsp (14 g/0.5 oz) peanut oil

2¼ cups (65 g/2.3 oz) crispy rice cereal, such as Rice Krispies

1. Place the chocolate and peanut oil in a medium stainless steel bowl and place the bowl over a pot half filled with barely simmering water. Heat, stirring frequently, until the chocolate has melted and the mixture is smooth. Remove the bowl and fold in the cereal.

2. Place a silicone baking mat on a sheet pan. Spread the cereal mixture onto the mat, spreading it evenly into an 8-inch square. Place another silicone baking mat on top and freeze until firm, at least 1 hour.

3. Cut the bar into 1¼ by 3½-inch rectangles; you will need a total of 8 rectangles. Set aside until ready to serve.

LYCHEE CRÈME GLACÉ

2 cups (484 g/17 oz) whole milk

½ cup (50 g/1.7 oz) powdered milk

2 Tbsp (28 g/1 oz) unsalted butter

½ cup plus 1 Tbsp (112 g/4 oz) granulated sugar

⅓ cup (50 g/1.76 oz) powdered glucose (see Sources, page 349)

1½ cups (350 g/12.3 oz) lychee purée (see Sources, page 349)

1. In a medium saucepan, combine all of the ingredients and place over medium-high heat, stirring occasionally, until the mixture reaches

180°F (82°C) on an instant-read thermometer. Transfer the ice cream base to a medium bowl. Set the bowl in an ice bath and stir frequently until cold.

2.   Cover the bowl with plastic wrap and refrigerate the ice cream base for at least 4 hours, or overnight.

3.   Process the base in an ice cream machine according to the manufacturer's instructions. Transfer the ice cream to an airtight container and freeze until ready to serve.

CARAMELIZED RASPBERRIES

¼ cup (90 g/3.17 oz) light corn syrup

1 vanilla bean, split lengthwise and seeds scraped

1 cup (250 g/8.8 oz) raspberry purée

1¼ cups (300 g/10.6 oz) fresh raspberries

Place the corn syrup and vanilla bean pod and seeds in a small saucepan and cook over medium-high heat, stirring constantly, until the corn syrup caramelizes and turns a medium amber color. Remove from the heat and stir in the purée. Add the fresh raspberries and cook over medium heat until the raspberries break down, about 6 minutes. Set aside to cool.

WHITE CHOCOLATE RECTANGLES

12 oz (340 g) white chocolate, chopped

1.   Temper the white chocolate according to the directions on page 347.

2.   Lay three 3 by 12-inch acetate rectangles on a work surface (preferably marble). Using a small, offset metal spatula, spread a thin layer of chocolate over each piece of acetate. Allow the chocolate to set for 2 to 3 minutes; it should be partially set, but not hard. Using a chef's knife, cut the chocolate into twenty-four 1¼ by 3-inch rectangles. (If you find that the chocolate is sticking to the knife, wait another minute or two until the chocolate has set a bit more.) Let the chocolate rectangles set completely at room temperature.

3.   When ready to assemble the dessert, peel the rectangles off the acetate sheet.

ASSEMBLY

Crystallized rose petals (see Sources, page 349)

1.   Scrape about one-quarter of the Rose Mousse into a pastry bag fitted with a medium, plain tip. Arrange an Almond Dacquoise rectangle on a dessert plate and pipe a line of the mousse down the dacquoise. Top with a White Chocolate Rectangle. Pipe another line of mousse on top of the white chocolate rectangle, then lay a white chocolate rice crispy rectangle on top. Top with another white chocolate rectangle. Dip a spoon in hot water and form a quenelle from the Rose Mousse; arrange it on top of the white chocolate, then top with another white chocolate rectangle.

2.   Spoon some of the Caramelized Raspberries onto the plate. Spoon a quenelle of Lychee Crème Glacé on top of the raspberries and garnish with a crystallized rose petal.

FEUILLE DE BRICK filled with SAUTÉED APPLES, PAIN D'ÉPICES, and CARAMEL SAUCE

FEUILLE DE BRICK IS AN ULTRATHIN, flaky dough that is similar to phyllo. It's commonly used in Tunisian pastries and savory dishes, and I like to use it when I want to add texture to a dessert. In this fall dessert, the baked feuille de brick serves as a cup for a filling of sautéed apples mixed with cubes of Pain d'Épices, the French version of gingerbread. I drizzle it with Caramel Sauce, but you could also serve it with a scoop of caramel or vanilla ice cream or some sweetened whipped cream.

MAKES 10 SERVINGS

COMPONENTS

PAIN D'ÉPICES
APPLE CUPS
CARAMEL SAUCE

SPECIAL EQUIPMENT
9 by 5-inch loaf pan; ten 4-ounce disposable aluminum cups or a muffin pan

PERFECT MATCH | LeMorton Reserve Calvados, Domfrontais, France

PAIN D'ÉPICES

2½ cups (300 g/10.6 oz) all-purpose flour

¼ cup plus ½ Tbsp (33 g/1.16 oz) cornstarch

2 tsp (10 g/0.35 oz) baking powder

1½ tsp (8.3 g/0.3 oz) baking soda

1 cup plus 1 Tbsp (250 g/8.8 oz) water

½ cup (167 g/5.8 oz) honey

¼ cup (83 g/3 oz) light corn syrup

¼ cup plus 2½ Tbsp (83 g/3 oz) granulated sugar

1 tsp (1 g/0.035 oz) whole fennel seeds

½ Tbsp (3.3 g/0.11 oz) ground star anise

¼ tsp plus ⅛ tsp (1.3 g/0.04 oz) Chinese five-spice powder

⅛ tsp (0.6 g/0.02 oz) salt

½ Tbsp (2.6 g/0.09 oz) ground cinnamon

Finely grated zest of 2 limes

2½ Tbsp (33 g/1.16 oz) Myers's dark rum

1. Preheat the oven to 325°F (163°C). Line a 9 by 5-inch loaf pan with parchment paper.

2. In a medium bowl, sift together the flour, cornstarch, baking powder, and baking soda and whisk to combine. Set aside.

3. In a medium saucepan, combine the remaining ingredients, except for the rum, and bring to a boil over medium-high heat. Remove the pan from the heat and allow to infuse for 10 minutes. Stir in the rum and cool completely.

4. Transfer the cooled liquid to the bowl of a stand mixer fitted with the paddle attachment. With the mixer on low speed, add the dry ingredients in three additions, mixing until the ingredients are blended and there are no lumps. Scrape the batter into the prepared pan and bake the cake for 40 to 50 minutes, until a knife inserted in the center of the cake comes out clean. Cool the cake in the pan, set on a wire rack.

APPLE CUPS

6 medium (1 kg/35.3 oz) Fuji or Macoun apples, peeled, cored, and cut into ¼-inch dice

3¾ cups (250 g/8.8 oz) cubed (¼-inch/6-mm) Pain d'Épices (page 127)

2 Tbsp (30 g/1 oz) Calvados

12¼ Tbsp (227 g/8 oz) unsalted butter

10 (12-inch-square) sheets feuille de brick

¼ cup (50 g/1.76 oz) granulated sugar

1. Preheat the oven to 375°F (191°C). Coat the interiors of ten 4-ounce disposable aluminum cups with nonstick cooking spray.

2. Heat a large sauté pan over medium-high heat until hot. Add 4¼ tablespoons (60 g/2.1 oz) of the butter and swirl it in the pan until melted. Add the diced apples and sauté until tender, about 3 minutes. Add the diced Pain d'Épices and cook until most of the juice in the pan has evaporated, but the apples still hold their shape, about 5 minutes. Remove the pan from the heat and stir in the Calvados. Set the mixture aside to cool.

3. In a small, microwavable cup, melt the remaining 8 tablespoons (113 g/4 oz) butter. Place a feuille de brick square on a work surface and brush it with some of the melted butter. Sprinkle the square with ½ tablespoon (6 g/0.21 oz) sugar. Press the center of the square into one of the prepared aluminum cups, letting the edges stick up to form an open pouch. Repeat with the remaining sheets and cups and fill each with the apple and Pain d'Épices mixture, packing it down slightly. Place the cups on a sheet pan and bake for 15 to 20 minutes, or until the feuille de brick is golden brown. Serve the cups warm.

CARAMEL SAUCE (page 334)

ASSEMBLY

Remove a warm Feuille de Brick and Apple Cup from the aluminum cup and place it on a plate. Garnish with a drizzle of the Caramel Sauce.

SOUFFLÉ OF PUFF PASTRY with ORANGE-SCENTED PASTRY CREAM, CANDIED PECANS, and CARAMEL BUTTER SAUCE

DANIEL BOULUD ALWAYS HAD A PREFERENCE for classic French desserts, so I developed this recipe for the lunch menu when I was pastry chef at Daniel. The dessert itself is very simple: We bake an undocked, thick round of puff pastry, letting it puff up high, and serve it hot, filled with Orange-Scented Pastry Cream and topped with a buttery caramel sauce and a few Candied Pecans. The puff pastry rounds should be baked à la minute, never ahead of time, though the dough can be rolled out and cut in advance, and stored, covered, in the refrigerator for up to a day. Sometimes the best desserts are the simplest.

MAKES 10 SERVINGS

COMPONENTS

ORANGE-SCENTED PASTRY CREAM

CARAMEL BUTTER SAUCE

CANDIED PECANS

PUFF PASTRY ROUNDS

SPECIAL EQUIPMENT | medium, plain tip (Ateco #6); 3-inch round pastry cutter

PERFECT MATCH | 2004 Duché de Longueville Cidre Gros Oeillet, Normandy, France

ORANGE-SCENTED PASTRY CREAM

½ cup (120 g/4.2 oz) heavy cream

Pastry Cream (page 341)

Finely grated zest of 1 orange

1.   In the bowl of a stand mixer fitted with the whisk attachment, whip the cream to soft peaks.

2.   Whisk the Pastry Cream until smooth. Gently fold in the orange zest and whipped cream. Transfer the cream to a pastry bag fitted with a medium, plain tip and refrigerate until ready to serve.

CARAMEL BUTTER SAUCE

1½ Tbsp (12 g/0.42 oz) cornstarch

2 cups plus 2 Tbsp (500 g/17.6 oz) water

1 cup (225 g/8 oz) firmly packed light brown sugar

1 vanilla bean, split lengthwise and seeds scraped

2 Tbsp (30 g/1 oz) unsalted butter

Pinch of salt

1 Tbsp (15 g/0.5 oz) Myers's dark rum

1.   In a small bowl, combine the cornstarch with 2 tablespoons (30 g/1 oz) of the water.

2. In a small saucepan, combine the brown sugar, vanilla bean pod and seeds, and remaining 2 cups (470 g/16.5 oz) water and bring to a boil over medium-high heat. Add the cornstarch mixture and cook, whisking, for another minute. Remove the pan from the heat and whisk in the butter, salt, and rum. Keep the sauce warm until serving, or refrigerate it, covered, and rewarm before serving.

CANDIED PECANS

1¼ cups (125 g/4.4 oz) pecan halves

¼ cup (60 g/2.1 oz) water

¼ cup (50 g/1.76 oz) granulated sugar

1. Preheat the oven to 350°F (177°C). Place the pecans in a medium bowl and set aside.

2. In a small saucepan, combine the water and sugar and bring to a boil over medium-high heat, stirring, just until the sugar has dissolved. Pour the syrup over the pecans and toss until combined. Spread the coated pecans on a half-sheet pan and bake for about 8 minutes, tossing once during baking, until browned and fragrant.

PUFF PASTRY ROUNDS

Puff Pastry (page 343)

Confectioners' sugar, for dusting

1. Preheat the oven to 400°F (204°C). Line a half-sheet pan with a silicone baking mat.

2. On a lightly floured work surface, roll the puff pastry out to a thickness of ½ inch. Using a 3-inch round pastry cutter, cut out 10 rounds from the dough. Arrange the rounds on the prepared sheet pan and top with another silicone baking mat and half-sheet pan; this will allow the rounds to rise evenly. Bake for 45 to 55 minutes, or until the rounds are browned and nicely puffed. Remove the top sheet pan and baking mat. Preheat the broiler and dust the rounds liberally with confectioners' sugar. Place the rounds under the broiler until they are caramelized. Assemble the desserts immediately.

ASSEMBLY

While the Puff Pastry Rounds are still hot from the oven, split them in half. Scoop out any undercooked dough from the center of each half and pipe a generous amount of cold Orange-Scented Pastry Cream on the bottom half of the puff. Replace the top of the puff. Place the dessert on a plate and spoon some Caramel Butter Sauce on top of the warm pastry. Garnish with some Candied Pecans.

PEANUT BUTTER and MILK CHOCOLATE CRISPY NAPOLEON

⧊⧊⧊ THIS CRISPY NAPOLEON features the great American combination of chocolate and peanut butter. It is made of alternating layers of hazelnut dacquoise, milk chocolate, and crunchy squares of milk chocolate blended with Rice Krispies, with a quenelle of creamy Milk Chocolate and Peanut Butter Chantilly on top. Shards of peanut brittle, scattered around the plate, contribute even more crunch. If you prefer, you can use white chocolate instead of the milk chocolate, but not dark chocolate, as it would overpower the peanut flavor.

MAKES 8 SERVINGS

COMPONENTS

MILK CHOCOLATE SQUARES

MILK CHOCOLATE AND PEANUT BUTTER CHANTILLY

HAZELNUT DACQUOISE

MILK CHOCOLATE RICE CRISPY

PEANUT BRITTLE

SPECIAL EQUIPMENT | one 19 by 24-inch acetate sheet; 8-inch square baking pan; medium, plain tip (Ateco #5)

PERFECT MATCH | 2010 Alphonse Mellot Sancerre Blanc Generation XIX, Loire, France

MILK CHOCOLATE SQUARES

1 lb (454 g) milk chocolate, tempered (see Tempered Chocolate, page 347)

1. Cut out three 2¼ by 24-inch strips from an acetate sheet. Spread the tempered chocolate onto the strips in a very thin, even layer. (You won't use all of the chocolate; spread the remaining chocolate onto a piece of parchment paper, allow it to set, and store it for later use.) Let the chocolate partially set, about 5 minutes.

2. Using a sharp knife, cut the chocolate into 2¼-inch squares; you will need a total of 24 squares. Let the chocolate set completely, about 1 hour.

MILK CHOCOLATE AND PEANUT BUTTER CHANTILLY

7 oz (200 g) milk chocolate, chopped

2 Tbsp (30 g/1 oz) peanut butter

¾ cup plus 2 Tbsp (200 g/7 oz) heavy cream

1. Put the chocolate and peanut butter in a medium, stainless steel bowl. Set the bowl over a pot filled one-third of the way with simmering water and heat, stirring frequently, until melted and smooth. Remove the bowl from the heat and set aside to cool.

2. In the bowl of a stand mixer fitted with the whisk attachment, whip the cream to medium peaks. Fold half of the whipped cream into the cooled chocolate and peanut

butter mixture to lighten it. Fold in the remaining whipped cream. Cover the bowl and refrigerate until ready to serve.

HAZELNUT DACQUOISE

1 cup (90 g/3.17 oz) hazelnut flour

¾ cup (90 g/3.17 oz) confectioners' sugar

4 large (120 g/4.2 oz) egg whites

3 Tbsp plus ¾ tsp (40 g/1.4 oz) granulated sugar

1. Preheat the oven to 400°F (204°C). Line an 8-inch square baking pan with a piece of parchment paper and spray the sides with nonstick cooking spray (alternatively, you can use a quarter-sheet pan).

2. In a medium bowl, sift together the hazelnut flour and confectioners' sugar and set aside.

3. In the bowl of a stand mixer fitted with the whisk attachment, whip the egg whites on medium speed until soft peaks begin to form. Gradually add the granulated sugar and whip on high speed until the whites are stiff and glossy. Gently fold in the hazelnut flour mixture. Spread the meringue into the prepared pan in an even layer and bake for 9 to 12 minutes, or until lightly browned and baked through. Cool the dacquoise in the pan, set on a wire rack.

4. Unmold the dacquoise and cut it into 2¼-inch squares; you will need 8 squares. Store in an airtight container until ready to serve.

MILK CHOCOLATE RICE CRISPY

1.76 oz (50 g) milk chocolate, chopped

1.4 oz (40 g) white chocolate, chopped

1 cup (250 g/8.8 oz) smooth peanut butter

2 tsp (10 g/0.35 oz) peanut oil

1¾ cups (50 g/1.76 oz) crispy rice cereal, such as Rice Krispies

2 Tbsp (15 g/0.5 oz) crushed toasted peanuts

1. Put the milk chocolate, white chocolate, peanut butter, and peanut oil in a medium, stainless steel bowl. Place the bowl over a pot filled one-third of the way with simmering water and heat, stirring occasionally, until the chocolate has melted and the mixture is smooth. Remove from the heat.

2. Line a 9-inch square baking pan with a piece of parchment paper, leaving an overhang of at least 2 inches on each side. Place the rice cereal and peanuts in a large bowl and gently fold in the melted chocolate mixture, tossing to coat the cereal. Spread the mixture into the prepared pan in an even layer. Freeze until firm, about 1 hour.

3. Using the parchment paper as handles, remove the square from the pan and invert it onto a cutting board. Peel off the parchment paper and cut the rectangle into 2¼-inch squares; you will need a total of 8 squares. Cover the squares loosely and refrigerate until ready to serve.

PEANUT BRITTLE

1 cup plus 3 Tbsp (237 g/8.37 oz) granulated sugar

½ cup plus 1¾ Tbsp (200 g/7 oz) light corn syrup

½ cup plus 1½ Tbsp (140 g/5 oz) water

3¾ cups (450 g/15.87 oz) unsalted peanuts

¼ tsp plus ⅛ tsp (2 g/0.07 oz) salt

¾ tsp (4 g/0.14 oz) unsalted butter

½ tsp (3 g/0.1 oz) baking soda

1. Line a half-sheet pan with a silicone baking mat.

2. In a medium saucepan, combine the sugar, corn syrup, and water and place over medium-high heat. Cook, occasionally washing down the sides of the saucepan with a wet pastry brush to prevent crystals from forming, until the sugar caramelizes and turns a light amber color, 3 to 5 minutes. Remove the pan from the heat and stir in the peanuts and salt. Add the butter and baking soda and stir just until the butter has melted. Spread the mixture onto the prepared sheet pan and allow it to cool slightly. Using two forks, lift and pull the peanut mixture into a layer that has the thickness of a single nut. Cool completely.

3. Break the brittle up into ragged shards.

ASSEMBLY

Put one-quarter of the Milk Chocolate Peanut Butter Chantilly in a pastry bag fitted with a medium, plain tip. Pipe a small dollop of mousse onto a Hazelnut Dacquoise square and press a Milk Chocolate Square on top. Top with a Milk Chocolate Rice Crispy square. Pipe another small dollop of mousse on top and press a Milk Chocolate Square on top. Place the dessert on a plate. Using a hot spoon, make a quenelle out of the remaining Milk Chocolate Peanut Butter Chantilly and place it on top of the chocolate square. Top with a final square of chocolate. Place some Peanut Brittle pieces around the plate.

CASSIS JAPONAIS with JAPONAIS NOODLES and CASSIS PORT SAUCE

※※※ I LOVE THE LOOK OF THIS DESSERT, with its deep-fried pink bean thread noodles piled high on top and ruby-colored Cassis Port Sauce around the plate. The heart of the dessert is a Cassis Chantilly, scooped into quenelles on top of a Chocolate Raspberry Ganache. The base is a dacquoise, or *meringue Japonaise*, a meringue that is combined with ground hazelnuts and baked until crisp. The crunchy elements, the noodles and the Japonais, contrast nicely with the smooth ganache and chantilly; while the flavors, cassis, raspberry, chocolate, and port, are a perfect balance of sweet and tart.

MAKES 8 SERVINGS

JAPONAIS DISKS

¼ cup plus 3 Tbsp (50 g/1.7 oz) confectioners' sugar

½ cup (40 g/1.4 oz) hazelnut flour (see Sources, page 349)

1 Tbsp plus 1 tsp (10 g/0.35 oz) all-purpose flour

3 large (90 g/3.17 oz) egg whites

½ cup (100 g/3.5 oz) granulated sugar

1. Position a rack in the center of the oven and preheat the oven to 300°F (149°C). Line a baking sheet with a silicone baking mat or parchment paper.

2. In a medium bowl, sift together the confectioners' sugar, hazelnut flour, and all-purpose flour.

3. In the bowl of a stand mixer fitted with the whisk attachment, whip the egg whites on low speed until foamy. Increase the speed to medium and whip until soft peaks just begin to form. Gradually add the granulated sugar, then increase the speed to high and whip until the meringue is glossy and stiff peaks form. Remove the bowl from the machine and gently fold the dry ingredients into the meringue. Scrape the mixture in a pastry bag fitted with a ¼-inch, plain tip. Pipe the meringue onto the prepared baking sheet, forming 2¾-inch disks. You will need at least 8 disks, but make a few extra, in case of breakage. Place the meringues in the oven and turn off the heat. Leave them in the oven for 2 hours, checking occasionally, until they are completely dry and crispy. Store the disks in an airtight container until ready to serve.

CUSTARDS, MOUSSES, and OTHER
CREAMY DESSERTS

MANY OF THE DESSERTS IN THIS CHAPTER are versions of cakes that I sold at Payard, refashioned as plated desserts. It includes recipes that feature mousses, creams, or custards as a main element. You never want to serve something like a mousse or custard on its own, because that would be very boring. The balance of a dessert is very important, and here the key is pairing the creamy element with a contrasting texture—you always need something crisp or crunchy, such as a layer of nuts or a tuile, to go with the mousse or custard. Every element in a dessert should be in the proper ratio. Take the Palet d'Or filled with Hazelnut Wafer and Manjari Mousse, for example: On the bottom you have a Succès, which is very dry, then a little bit of feuilletine for some extra crunch, then a very dense chocolate mousse. Every bite of this dessert is perfectly balanced, with something crunchy and smooth, with all the flavors working together beautifully.

Many of the components in these desserts can be made a week or so in advance, but most of the desserts must be assembled no more than a day in advance so that they don't absorb other flavors and their texture remains superior. And some, such as the Cranberry Gelée filled with Pear Bavarian, Nougatine, and Poached Pear, or the Deconstruction of Crema Catalan, must be composed at the last minute.

BEET and MINT CRÈME BRÛLÉE— A MARKET INSPIRATION

I DEVELOPED THIS DESSERT AT PAYARD for a chef's tasting menu that revolved around beets. Most people don't think of using beets in dessert, but beets, like tomatoes, are very versatile because they are sweet. Here I use beet juice, not the pulp, which I get by passing the beets through a juicer. Try to use small beets, as they are sweeter than the large ones and don't require peeling. If you can only find large ones, peel them before juicing.

MAKES 10 SERVINGS

SPECIAL EQUIPMENT   pepper mill; ten 4-ounce ramekins; blowtorch

PERFECT MATCH   2011 Jean-Luc Colombo Cape Bleue Rosé, Provence, France

---

8 large (149 g/5.24 oz) egg yolks

¾ cup plus 2½ Tbsp (180 g/6.3 oz) granulated sugar

3⅓ cups (773 g/27.26 oz) heavy cream

⅔ cup (166 g/5.8 oz) beet juice, preferably from small beets

12 fresh mint leaves

1 to 2 turns of freshly ground pepper

1. Preheat the oven to 250°F (121°C). Place 10 ramekins in a hotel or roasting pan.

2. In a medium bowl, whisk together the egg yolks and ⅜ cup (90 g/3.15 oz) of the sugar until well blended.

3. In a small saucepan, combine the cream, the remaining ⅜ cup (90g/3.15 oz) sugar, and the beet juice and bring to a boil over medium-high heat. Whisk about ½ cup (120 g/4.2 oz) of the hot cream mixture into the yolk mixture, then whisk this mixture into the remaining cream mixture in the saucepan. Add the mint leaves and ground pepper and let the mixture stand off the heat, covered, for 15 minutes to infuse.

4. Strain the mixture and divide it equally among the ramekins. Place the pan with the ramekins in the oven and pour enough hot water into the pan so that it comes ½ inch up the sides of the ramekins. Bake the custards for about 45 minutes, or until just set. Remove the ramekins from the water bath and set aside to cool.

5. Refrigerate the custards for at least 2 hours, or until chilled.

ASSEMBLY

1 cup packed (217 g/7.6 oz) light brown sugar, sifted

Sprinkle the top of each chilled custard evenly with about 2 tablespoons (28 g/1 oz) of the brown sugar. Using a propane or butane blowtorch, caramelize the tops of the custards. Serve immediately.

PUMPKIN CRÈME BRÛLÉE with VANILLA CHANTILLY, CRISPY MERINGUE, and CHESTNUT PURÉE

THIS DESSERT EVOLVED AS AN ADAPTATION of the classic Mont Blanc, which has a crunchy meringue base, whipped cream filling, and a spaghetti-like mound of sweetened chestnut purée on top. Since pumpkin has the same starchy texture as chestnut, I used it as the key ingredient in the dome-shaped crème brûlée filling, which I coated with a layer of Vanilla Chantilly. Like its classic cousin, my version also has a baked meringue base and an impressive mountain of chestnut purée on top.

MAKES 8 SERVINGS

COMPONENTS

PUMPKIN CRÈME BRÛLÉE
MERINGUE DISKS AND STICKS
CHESTNUT PURÉE
VANILLA CHANTILLY

SPECIAL EQUIPMENT | eight 3-inch silicone dome molds; medium, plain pastry tip (Ateco #5); potato ricer

PERFECT MATCH | 2004 Duché de Longueville, Cidre Gros Oeillet, Normandy, France

PUMPKIN CRÈME BRÛLÉE

½ cup (100 g/3.5 oz) granulated sugar

3 Tbsp (40 g/1.4 oz) light brown sugar

1½ tsp (3 g/0.1 oz) ground ginger

1 tsp (2 g/0.07 oz) ground cloves

4 large (200 g/7 oz) eggs

1⅔ cups (400 g/14 oz) pumpkin purée

¾ cup (180 g/6.3 oz) whole milk

½ cup (120 g/4.2 oz) evaporated milk

1. Preheat the oven to 250°F (121°C). Place eight 3-inch silicone dome molds in a hotel or roasting pan.

2. In a small bowl, combine both sugars with the ground ginger and cloves.

3. In the bowl of a stand mixer fitted with the paddle attachment, combine the eggs and pumpkin and beat on medium speed until smooth. Add the sugar mixture and mix until blended. Add the whole milk and evaporated milk and mix until combined. Pour the batter into the molds, dividing it evenly. Place the pan with the molds in the oven and pour enough hot water into the pan so that it comes halfway up the sides of the molds. Bake the custards for 35 to 45 minutes, or until just set. Remove the molds from the water bath and set aside on a wire rack to cool.

4.   Place the molds in the freezer for at least 2 hours, or until firm. Unmold and freeze, loosely covered, until ready to serve.

MERINGUE DISKS AND STICKS

3 large (90 g/3.17 oz) egg whites

⅓ cup plus 2 Tbsp (90 g/3.17 oz) granulated sugar

1.   Preheat the oven to 300°F (149°C). Line a half-sheet pan with a silicone baking mat. Fill a medium saucepan one-third of the way with water and bring to a simmer over medium heat.

2.   Place the egg whites and sugar in the bowl of a stand mixer and place the bowl on top of the pot of simmering water. Heat, whisking constantly, until the whites are warm to the touch and the sugar has dissolved. Transfer the bowl to the mixer stand and, using the whisk attachment, whip the whites on high speed until they are completely cool, about 5 minutes. Scrape the meringue into a pastry bag fitted with a medium, plain tip. Pipe eight 3-inch disks of meringue in spirals onto the prepared sheet pan, piping from the center out. Pipe at least eight 6-inch-long sticks of meringue on the sheet in between the disks. Place the sheet pan in the oven and turn the oven off. Let the meringues dry for 1 to 2 hours, until crisp. Cool completely and store in an airtight container until ready to serve.

VANILLA CHANTILLY

1 cup (232 g/8.18 oz) heavy cream

2 Tbsp (25 g/0.88 oz) granulated sugar

½ vanilla bean, split lengthwise and seeds scraped

In the bowl of a stand mixer fitted with the whisk attachment, whip the heavy cream, sugar, and vanilla bean seeds together on high speed until the cream forms soft peaks. Cover and refrigerate until ready to serve.

CHESTNUT PURÉE

2 cups (540 g/19 oz) sweetened chestnut paste

1 cup (142 g/5 oz) candied chestnuts

In the bowl of a stand mixer fitted with the paddle attachment, beat the chestnut paste and candied chestnuts together on medium speed until very smooth. Cover and refrigerate until ready to use.

ASSEMBLY

Candied chestnut pieces

Place a frozen Pumpkin Crème Brûlée dome onto a Meringue Disk and allow to thaw. Spread Vanilla Chantilly over the dome, covering it completely. Place some Chestnut Purée in a potato ricer and push it through over the dome, covering it with strings of purée. Garnish the dessert with Meringue Sticks and some candied chestnut pieces.

SHOT of BUTTERMILK PANNA COTTA with TARRAGON-SCENTED MANGO

Panna cotta, the traditional Italian "cooked milk" dessert, is actually made with cream, which makes it fairly rich. In this recipe I cut its richness by substituting low-fat buttermilk for some of the cream, and layering it with cubes of mango that have been sautéed with tarragon. Mango and tarragon go very, very well together—the mango has a bright sweetness, while the tarragon has the tongue-numbing flavor of anise. Served in a tall shot glass with an orange chip, this elegant dessert is great for summer parties.

MAKES 10 SERVINGS

COMPONENTS

CRYSTALLIZED TARRAGON LEAVES
ORANGE CHIPS
BUTTERMILK PANNA COTTA
SAUTÉED MANGO WITH TARRAGON

SPECIAL EQUIPMENT | ten 4-ounce shot glasses

PERFECT MATCH | Ca' del Bosco, Cuvée Annamaria Clementi, Lombardy, Italy

CRYSTALLIZED TARRAGON LEAVES

3 sprigs fresh tarragon

1 large (30 g/1.05 oz) egg white

½ cup (50 g/1.76 oz) granulated sugar

Pick 20 large leaves off the tarragon stems. Place the egg white in a small bowl and whisk it a little to loosen it. Place the sugar in another bowl. Using a small pastry brush, brush both sides of a tarragon leaf with egg white, then coat it with sugar and place it on a plate. Repeat with the remaining leaves and allow them to dry at room temperature for at least 8 hours, or overnight.

ORANGE CHIPS

2 medium oranges

2 cups (472 g/16.64 oz) water

1¼ cups (250 g/8.8 oz) granulated sugar

Confectioners' sugar, for dusting

1.   Preheat the oven to 200°F (93°C). Line 3 half-sheet pans with silicone baking mats.

2.   Cut the top and bottom portion of the peel off each of the oranges. Using an electric slicer, slice the oranges crosswise into very thin rounds (as thin as possible). Arrange the slices in stacks and place toothpicks through them. Place them in a shallow pan, keeping the stacks intact.

3.   In a large saucepan, combine the water and sugar and bring to a boil over high heat, stirring, just until the sugar has dissolved. Pour the hot syrup over the orange slices in the pan. Let them stand for 30 minutes.

4.   Dust the silicone mats generously with confectioners' sugar. Remove the oranges from the syrup with a slotted spoon and separate the slices. Arrange the orange slices on the prepared sheet pans; make sure they do not overlap, or they will stick together. Dust the oranges with more confectioners' sugar and let stand for 10 minutes.

5.   After the sugar has dissolved, dry the orange slices with paper towels. Place them back on the sheet pans and dust with more confectioners' sugar. Bake for 2 to 3 hours, or until they are dry. Cool completely; the chips will become crisp as they cool. Store the Orange Chips in an airtight container at room temperature.

BUTTERMILK PANNA COTTA

4 sheets (8 g/0.28 oz) gelatin (silver grade)

1¼ cups plus 2 Tbsp (320 g/11.3 oz) heavy cream

1½ cups (360 g/12.7 oz) buttermilk

½ cup plus 2 Tbsp (124 g/4.4 oz) granulated sugar

1 vanilla bean, split lengthwise and seeds scraped

1.   Half fill a medium bowl with cold water and add the gelatin sheets. Set aside to soften for 10 minutes.

2.   In a small saucepan, combine the cream, buttermilk, sugar, and vanilla bean pod and seeds and bring to a boil over medium-high heat, stirring to dissolve the sugar. Remove the pan from the heat. Drain the gelatin, squeezing it to remove the excess water, and add it to the hot cream mixture. Stir until the gelatin has dissolved. Strain the mixture through a fine-mesh sieve into a bowl and set aside, covered, at room temperature until ready to use.

SAUTÉED MANGO WITH TARRAGON

4 medium (1.5 kg/3.3 lb) ripe mangoes

2 Tbsp (28 g/1 oz) unsalted butter

2 Tbsp (14 g/0.8 oz) granulated sugar

Leaves from 2 sprigs fresh tarragon, finely chopped

1.   Peel the mangoes and cut them into ¼-inch dice.

2.   Melt the butter in a sauté pan over medium-high heat. Add the mango and sprinkle the sugar on top. Sauté the mango for 2 minutes. Remove from the heat and sprinkle with the tarragon.

ASSEMBLY

1.   Spoon enough of the Sautéed Mango with Tarragon to come one-quarter of the way up a 4-ounce shot glass. Pour some of the liquid Buttermilk Panna Cotta on top, so that it comes halfway to the top of the glass. Place in the freezer to set for about 30 minutes. Cover the remaining mango and refrigerate until ready to use again.

2. Spoon more of the mango to fill the glass three-quarters full. Finish by filling with panna cotta to just beneath the rim of the glass. Refrigerate until set, at least 3 hours.

3. Serve the dessert garnished with an Orange Chip, 2 Crystallized Tarragon Leaves, and a little more mango.

RECONSTRUCTION of CAFÉ LIÉGEOIS with CACAO NIB–ESPRESSO TUILE and MERINGUE STICKS

I DRINK A LOT OF ESPRESSO, so it's no surprise that one of my favorite desserts, Café Liégeois, is flavored with coffee. It's a cold dessert made with layers of coffee ice cream, lightly sweetened coffee, and chantilly cream, but, for me, there's something missing in the classic recipe—texture. My version, a reconstruction of the original, features the same espresso and whipped cream layers, but includes a crispy Cacao Nib–Espresso Tuile balanced on top of the glass. The ice cream is set on top of the tuile and, when the tuile is broken with a spoon, it falls into the glass and mixes with the espresso, cream, and bits of crunchy tuile, creating an unbelievable combination of texture and flavors. Cacao nibs and roasted coffee go very well together, especially in this delicious dessert.

MAKES 10 SERVINGS

COMPONENTS

VANILLA ICE CREAM

MERINGUE STICKS

WHIPPED CREAM

CACAO NIB–ESPRESSO TUILE

SPECIAL EQUIPMENT | ice cream machine; ¼-inch, plain pastry tip (Ateco #3); ½-inch, plain pastry tip (Ateco #6)

PERFECT MATCH | Di Majo Norante Moscato del Molise Apianae, Italy

VANILLA ICE CREAM
(page 340)

MERINGUE STICKS

3 large (90 g/3.17 oz) egg whites

⅓ cup plus 2 Tbsp (90 g/3.17 oz) granulated sugar

1. Preheat the oven to 300°F (149°C). Line a half-sheet pan with a silicone baking mat. Fill a medium saucepan one-third of the way with water and bring to a simmer over medium heat.

2. Place the egg whites and sugar in the bowl of a stand mixer and place the bowl on top of the pot of simmering water. Heat, whisking constantly, until the whites are warm to the touch and the sugar has dissolved. Transfer the bowl to the mixer stand and, using the whisk attachment, whip the whites on high speed until they are completely cool, about 5 minutes. Scrape the meringue into a pastry bag fitted with a ¼-inch, plain tip. Pipe as many 6-inch-long sticks of meringue as possible onto the sheet pan; you will need a total of 20 sticks. Place the sheet pan in the oven and turn the oven off. Let the meringue dry for 2 hours, or until crisp. Cool completely and store in an airtight container until ready to serve.

CRANBERRY GELÉE

2 sheets (4 g/0.14 oz) gelatin (silver grade)

3 cups (340 g/12 oz) fresh or frozen cranberries

¼ cup plus 1 Tbsp (62 g/2.2 oz) granulated sugar

Finely grated zest of 1 orange

1¼ cups (300 g/10.5 oz) water

1. Fill a medium bowl halfway with cold water and add the gelatin sheets. Allow to soften for 10 minutes.

2. In a medium saucepan, combine the cranberries, sugar, orange zest, and water and cook over medium-high heat, stirring occasionally, until the cranberries are soft and have given up some of their juice, about 10 minutes. Remove the pan from the heat.

3. Drain the gelatin and squeeze it to remove the excess water. Add the drained gelatin to the hot cranberry mixture and stir until dissolved. Allow to cool slightly.

4. Divide the Cranberry Gelée equally among eight 8-ounce wineglasses and chill until set, about 2 hours.

PEAR BAVARIAN

5 sheets (10 g/0.35 oz) gelatin (silver grade)

1 cup (250 g/8.8 oz) pear purée (page 153)

1 cup (232 g/8.18 oz) Crème Anglaise (page 335)

2 cups plus 2½ Tbsp (500 g/17.6 oz) heavy cream

1. Fill a medium bowl halfway with cold water and add the gelatin sheets. Allow to soften for 10 minutes.

2. Place half of the purée in a small saucepan over medium heat and heat until hot to the touch. Remove the pan from the heat. Drain the gelatin and squeeze it to remove the excess water. Add the drained gelatin to the hot purée, stirring until dissolved. Stir in the remaining pear purée and the Crème Anglaise; the mixture should be at room temperature. If it is not, cool to room temperature. Transfer the mixture to a medium bowl and stir in the reserved diced pear. In the bowl of a stand mixer fitted with the whisk attachment, whip the cream to soft peaks. Gently fold the whipped cream into the crème anglaise mixture. Transfer the Pear Bavarian to a pastry bag with no tip.

ASSEMBLY

Nougatine (page 345), finely chopped, for sprinkling on top

1. Pipe a layer of Pear Bavarian into each glass on top of the chilled Cranberry Gelée and refrigerate until set, about 2 hours.

2. When ready to serve, sprinkle the Pear Bavarian with some chopped Nougatine and garnish with a reserved Poached Pear top.

DECONSTRUCTION of CREMA CATALANA: BLOOD ORANGE GELÉE, FOAMED CRÈME BRÛLÉE, and CINNAMON ICE CREAM

  Crema catalana is similar to the French crème brûlée, but it's made with milk, not cream, which gives it a very different texture. It's traditionally served in Spain on March 19, St. Joseph's Day, which is the equivalent of Father's Day in the United States. Here is my deconstructed version, which is anything but classic. I bake the custard in a bain marie, then chill it and place it in an N_2O-charged whipped cream canister. When it's piped out, it becomes very light and foamy. I serve it with a beautiful Blood Orange Gelée and Cinnamon Ice Cream, elements that add bright and spicy notes to the subtle crema.

MAKES 10 SERVINGS

COMPONENTS

CINNAMON ICE CREAM
CREMA CATALANA
BLOOD ORANGE GELÉE
ORANGE-SCENTED STREUSEL

SPECIAL EQUIPMENT | ice cream machine; 9 by 13-inch baking pan; N_2O-charged whipped cream canister; 10 serving plates with 4 sections (alternatively, the dessert can be arranged in 4 small, shallow bowls)

PERFECT MATCH | Sanguinella cocktail: a mixture of Campari, Limoncello, and freshly squeezed lime and orange juice over ice

CINNAMON ICE CREAM

- 1 cup (250 g/8.8 oz) whole milk
- 1 cup (250 g/8.8 oz) heavy cream
- 2 sticks cinnamon
- 6 large (112 g/4 oz) egg yolks
- ½ cup plus 2 Tbsp (125 g/4.4 oz) granulated sugar
- 1½ tsp (3 g/0.1 oz) ground cinnamon

1. In a medium saucepan, combine the milk, cream, and cinnamon sticks and bring to a gentle boil over medium heat. Remove the pan from the heat, cover, and allow to infuse for 30 minutes.

2. Return the pan to medium heat and bring to a boil. In a medium bowl, whisk together the egg yolks and sugar until pale. Whisk about half of the hot milk mixture into the yolks, then return this mixture to the remaining milk mixture in the saucepan and cook over medium heat, stirring constantly with a wooden spoon, until it thickens enough to coat the back of the spoon and reaches 175°F (79°C) on an instant-read thermometer; do not let the mixture boil, or the egg yolks will curdle. Remove the pot from the heat and strain the ice cream base immediately into a bowl. Stir in the ground cinnamon. Set the bowl in an ice bath and stir frequently until cold.

RICE PUDDING with SZECHUAN PEPPERCORN ANGLAISE and CARAMEL BALSAMIC SAUCE

PASTRY CHEF FRANCK IGLESIAS, who was my nighttime sous-chef at Payard, came up with this dessert: a rice pudding parfait with mixed berries, a Szechuan Peppercorn Anglaise, and a caramel-flavored balsamic sauce.

According to Franck, his grandmother made the best rice pudding ever, which he ate warm as a kid—it was impossible for him to wait for it to cool. Franck used her handwritten recipe to create this version, a sophisticated reinterpretation of the original. Here Szechuan peppercorns lend a subtle floral accent, while the light acidity of balsamic vinegar balances the sweetness of the caramel. Meringue sticks add a bit of crunch to this elegant parfait, a tribute to Franck's "Mémé."

MAKES 8 SERVINGS

COMPONENTS

CARAMEL BALSAMIC SAUCE
SZECHUAN PEPPERCORN ANGLAISE
RICE PUDDING
MERINGUE STICKS
MIXED BERRIES

SPECIAL EQUIPMENT ¼-inch, plain pastry tip (Ateco #3); eight 8-ounce wineglasses

PERFECT MATCH Château-Chalon Vin Jaune du Jura, France

CARAMEL BALSAMIC SAUCE

1¼ cups (250 g/8.8 oz) granulated sugar

3 Tbsp (60 g/2.1 oz) glucose syrup

½ cup plus 2 Tbsp (150 g/5.3 oz) water

¼ cup (60 g/2.1 oz) balsamic vinegar (use an ordinary one, nothing too concentrated)

In a small, heavy-bottomed saucepan, combine the sugar, glucose, and ¼ cup plus 2 tablespoons (90 g/3.17 oz) of the water and cook over medium-high heat, occasionally washing down the sides of the saucepan with a wet pastry brush to prevent crystals from forming, and watching carefully, until the syrup caramelizes and turns a medium amber color, 3 to 5 minutes. Remove from the heat and carefully add the balsamic vinegar and the remaining ¼ cup (60 g/2.1 oz) water. Return the pan to medium heat and cook, stirring, just until any hardened bits of sugar have dissolved, about 2 minutes. Remove from the heat and strain through a fine-mesh sieve. Set aside to cool.

BANANA LEAF BOAT with LEMONGRASS CHIBOUST and CITRUS SAUCE

THIS WHIMSICAL DESSERT was inspired by a shipment of bright green banana leaves that arrived in the kitchen one day at Daniel. I wanted to make something exotic, something a little different, so I used the banana leaves to form little boats, which I filled with a Lemongrass Chiboust. I even made little oar-shaped tuiles for the boats. Unfortunately, I could never come up with a good way to secure the leaves—bamboo skewers kept breaking—so I ended up using staples, which you really can't use for a restaurant dessert. It was a learning experience, but I still love this dessert for its refreshing mix of tropical flavors and its fanciful presentation, both of which remind me of holidays in the sun. Banana leaves are available from several sources online, including www.gourmetsleuth.com.

MAKES 8 SERVINGS

COMPONENTS

PINEAPPLE CHIPS
OAR-SHAPED TUILES
LEMONGRASS CHIBOUST
CITRUS SAUCE

SPECIAL EQUIPMENT electric slicer; 6-inch-long oar-shaped tuile stencil; candy thermometer; medium, plain pastry tip (Ateco #6); blowtorch

PERFECT MATCH 2004 Duché de Longueville, Cidre Gros Oeillet, Normandy, France

PINEAPPLE CHIPS (page 345)

Prepare the Pineapple Chips as directed and while still warm, curl them around a rolling pin to give them a curved shape. Cool and store as directed.

OAR-SHAPED TUILES

Vanilla Tuile batter (page 338)

1. Preheat the oven to 350°F (177°C). Line a half-sheet pan with a silicone baking mat.

2. Place a 6-inch-long oar-shaped stencil on the baking mat and spread the batter over it in a thin layer. Repeat to make 4 more tuiles. Bake for about 8 minutes, or until golden brown around the edges. Cool the tuiles on the sheet pan, then transfer them to an airtight container. Repeat to make a total of 8 tuiles.

HAZELNUT PRALINE DOME with GANACHE CITRON and HONEYED PHYLLO LEAVES

THIS DESSERT IS RELATIVELY SIMPLE, but has an intriguing look. At its center is a dome made from layers of Praline Bavarian, Hazelnut Dacquoise, and a white chocolate–lemon ganache. I freeze the dome, then unmold it and push shards of honey-brushed phyllo into it, fanning them all around the dessert. Because the phyllo pieces are irregular, each dessert looks a little different every time. Continuing with the hazelnut theme, I garnish this with a few Caramelized Hazelnuts, which glisten like jewels on the plate.

MAKES 10 SERVINGS

COMPONENTS

HAZELNUT DACQUOISE
GANACHE CITRON
PRALINE BAVARIAN CREAM
PHYLLO LEAF SHARDS
CARAMELIZED HAZELNUTS

SPECIAL EQUIPMENT | 2½-inch round pastry cutter; 1-inch round pastry cutter; immersion blender; bamboo skewers; small boxes 3 inches square and 6 inches high; 2 medium, plain pastry tips (Ateco #6); ten 3-inch silicone dome molds

PERFECT MATCH | 2011 Domaine Paul Blanck Riesling, Alsace, France

HAZELNUT DACQUOISE

2 cups (175 g/6.17 oz) hazelnut flour

1½ cups (175 g/6.17 oz) confectioners' sugar

8 large (250 g/8.8 oz) egg whites

¼ cup plus 2 Tbsp (75 g/2.6 oz) granulated sugar

⅓ cup (50 g/1.76 oz) hazelnuts, coarsely chopped

1. Preheat the oven to 400°F (204°C). Line a half-sheet pan with a silicone baking mat.

2. In a medium bowl, sift together the hazelnut flour and confectioners' sugar and set aside.

3. In the bowl of a stand mixer fitted with the whisk attachment, whip the egg whites on medium speed until soft peaks begin to form. Gradually add the sugar, increase the speed to high, and whip until the meringue is stiff and glossy. Remove the bowl from the mixer stand and gently fold in the dry ingredients. Spread the mixture out in an even layer onto the prepared sheet pan. Sprinkle the hazelnuts on top and bake for 9 to 12 minutes, or until lightly browned and baked through. Set the sheet pan on a wire rack and cool completely.

4. Using the 2½-inch round pastry cutter, cut out 10 rounds from the dacquoise. Using the 1-inch round pastry cutter, cut out 10 or more rounds from the dacquoise and store all the rounds in an airtight container until ready to serve.

RICE CRISPIES with MILK CHOCOLATE and CRISPY CHOCOLATE PHYLLO

THIS DESSERT, which combines the flavors of milk chocolate, nuts, and caramel, was very popular at Payard, and it was also great for the kitchen from a production standpoint. Every element could be prepared ahead, and it was very easy to plate, so we could make it for parties of 600 or 700 with no problem. The Chocolate Phyllo is very elegant, and it's also very easy to make in large quantities, a bonus for the kitchen. I think diners loved this dessert not only for its rich flavors, but also for its contrasting textures: creamy Chocolate Chantilly combined with a crispy milk chocolate–hazelnut cereal base and cocoa phyllo garnish, and a luxurious caramel sauce. In the texture department, this dessert has it all!

MAKES 8 SERVINGS

COMPONENTS

RICE CRISPY DISKS
CHOCOLATE CHANTILLY
CHOCOLATE PHYLLO
CARAMELIZED NUTS
CARAMEL SAUCE

SPECIAL EQUIPMENT | 2¾-inch round pastry cutter; candy thermometer; squeeze bottle

PERFECT MATCH | 2004 Duché de Longueville, Cidre Gros Oeillet, Normandy, France

RICE CRISPY DISKS

4.2 oz (120 g) milk chocolate, melted

3.2 oz (90 g) white chocolate, melted

1½ cups (500 g/17.6 oz) praline paste

2 tsp (10 g/0.32 oz) peanut oil

4 cups (120 g/4.2 oz) crispy rice cereal, such as Rice Krispies

1. Line a half-sheet pan with parchment paper. In a large bowl, stir together the melted chocolates, praline paste, and peanut oil until blended and completely smooth. Add the cereal and gently fold into the chocolate mixture until evenly coated. Spread the mixture onto the prepared pan into an even 8 by 12-inch rectangle. Place the sheet pan into the freezer for 10 minutes, or until set.

2. Using a 2¾-inch round cutter, cut out 8 rounds from the cereal rectangle. Refrigerate the rounds until ready to serve; the mixture softens up at room temperature, which makes it easy to cut through with a fork.

CHOCOLATE CHANTILLY

1¼ cups (360 g/12.6 oz) heavy cream

6.3 oz (180 g) milk chocolate, melted

In the bowl of a stand mixer, whip the cream on high speed to soft peaks. Fold half of the whipped cream into the melted chocolate. Fold in the remaining cream. Cover the bowl and refrigerate until ready to serve.

CHOCOLATE PHYLLO

7 Tbsp (100 g/3.5 oz) Clarified Butter (page 348)

¼ cup plus 1 Tbsp (30 g/1 oz) unsweetened alkalized cocoa powder

8 (9 by 14-inch) sheets phyllo dough

1.   Preheat the oven to 375°F (191°C). Line a half-sheet pan with parchment paper and brush the paper with melted butter.

2.   In a small saucepan, melt the Clarified Butter over medium heat and whisk in the cocoa powder.

3.   Place a sheet of phyllo dough on the parchment paper–lined pan and brush it with some of the butter mixture. Place another sheet of phyllo on top. Repeat the layering until you have used 4 phyllo sheets. Brush the last sheet with the butter mixture and refrigerate the phyllo layers for 30 minutes, or until the butter has firmed up.

4.   Transfer the layers to a cutting board and, using a sharp chef's knife, cut the phyllo stack into 5 by 2¼-inch rectangles. Cut each rectangle in half diagonally, forming long triangles; you will need 16 triangles. Arrange the triangles on the lined sheet pan and cover with another silicone baking mat to keep them flat during baking. Bake for 10 minutes, or until the phyllo triangles are crisp. Place the sheet pan on a wire rack and cool completely.

CARAMELIZED NUTS

½ cup (60 g/2.1 oz) walnuts

½ cup (60 g/2.1 oz) peanuts

½ cup (60 g/2.1 oz) hazelnuts

½ cup (60 g/2.1 oz) almonds

½ cup (60 g/2.1 oz) pistachios

½ cup (60 g/2.1 oz) pine nuts

1¼ cups (250 g/8.8 oz) granulated sugar

¼ cup (60 g/2.1 oz) water

1.   Position two racks near the center of the oven and preheat the oven to 350°F (177°C). On a half-sheet pan, combine the walnuts, peanuts, hazelnuts, and almonds. On another half-sheet pan, combine the pistachios with the pine nuts. Bake the nuts for about 5 minutes, or until lightly toasted (see Toasted Nuts, page 346). Set aside to cool.

2.   Line a half-sheet pan with a piece of parchment paper. In a medium, heavy-bottomed saucepan, combine the sugar and water and cook over medium-high heat until the sugar registers 242°F (117°C) on a candy thermometer (soft ball stage). Add the toasted nuts and stir to coat them with the sugar syrup. Continue to stir the nuts over the heat until the sugar begins to crystallize and the nuts have turned golden brown. Using a wooden spoon, spread the nuts out onto the prepared sheet pan and let them cool completely.

3.   Once the nuts are cool, use your hands to break apart the clusters.

CARAMEL SAUCE (page 334)

ASSEMBLY

Cocoa powder, for dusting

Place a Rice Crispy Disk in the center of a plate. Dip a spoon in a container of hot water, dry it, and form a quenelle of Chocolate Chantilly. Place it on one half of the disk. Pile a mound of Caramelized Nuts in a mound next to the chantilly, filling up the rest of the space on the disk. Place another quenelle of Chocolate Chantilly next to the first quenelle. Dust the Phyllo Triangles with cocoa powder and lean two of the triangles against the chantilly. The triangles should cross at one point, forming an X shape. Pour the Caramel Sauce into a squeeze bottle and make three 1-inch dots of sauce on the plate; pull the tip of the squeeze bottle through them to connect them. Pipe a few smaller dots of sauce around the plate and garnish with a few more Caramelized Nuts.

LEMONGRASS CHIBOUST with POMEGRANATE PINEAPPLE

THIS REFRESHING DESSERT features an array of exotic flavors: pineapple, pomegranate, pink peppercorn, and lemongrass. The flavors blend together perfectly, with a citrusy Lemongrass Chiboust offering an interesting contrast to chunks of sweet and slightly spicy sautéed pineapple. The chiboust is sprinkled with sugar and caramelized with a blowtorch right before serving, giving it a slightly crunchy texture and complex sweetness. A Pineapple Chip makes a pretty and flavorful garnish.

MAKES 10 SERVINGS

COMPONENTS

LEMONGRASS CHIBOUST
SABLÉ ROUNDS
POMEGRANATE PINEAPPLE
PINEAPPLE CHIPS

SPECIAL EQUIPMENT | candy thermometer; medium, plain pastry tip (Ateco #6); ten 3-inch silicone dome molds; 3-inch round pastry cutter; pepper mill; electric slicer; blowtorch

PERFECT MATCH | Carole Bouquet Sangue D'Oro Passito di Pantelleria, Sicily

LEMONGRASS CHIBOUST

1½ cups (375 g/13.2 oz) whole milk

1 stalk fresh lemongrass, cut into 1-inch pieces

¾ cup plus 3 Tbsp (192 g/6.7 oz) granulated sugar

¼ cup plus ½ Tbsp (37 g/1.3 oz) cornstarch

4½ large (84 g/3 oz) egg yolks

4½ large (135 g/4.76 oz) egg whites

1. In a small saucepan, combine the milk and lemongrass pieces and bring to a boil over medium-high heat. Remove the pan from the heat, cover, and allow to infuse for 20 minutes.

2. In a medium bowl, combine 1½ tablespoons (19 g/0.66 oz) of the sugar with the cornstarch. Whisk in the egg yolks until smooth and set aside.

3. Strain the milk, discarding the lemongrass, and return it to the saucepan. Bring the infused milk to a boil over medium-high heat. Whisk about ½ cup of the hot milk into the yolk mixture, then whisk this mixture into the remaining milk in the saucepan. Cook over medium heat, whisking constantly, until the mixture begins to bubble and thicken. Remove from the heat.

4. In a small saucepan, combine the remaining ¾ cup plus 1½ tablespoons (170 g/6 oz) granulated sugar with 2 tablespoons (29 g/1 oz) water and cook over medium-high heat, occasionally washing down the sides of the pan with a wet pastry brush to prevent crystals from forming, and watching carefully, until the syrup registers 248°F (120°C) on a candy thermometer, 3 to 5 minutes. While the

sugar syrup is cooking, place the egg whites in the bowl of a stand mixer fitted with the whisk attachment and begin whipping them on medium speed. When the syrup is ready, gradually pour it in a steady stream into the whipping egg whites. Increase the speed to high and whip the whites until they are stiff. Do not overwhip; the whites should still be warm to the touch.

5.   Transfer the pastry cream to a large bowl and whisk in half of the meringue. Gently fold in the remaining meringue. Scrape the mixture into a pastry bag fitted with a medium, plain tip and pipe the mixture into ten 3-inch silicone dome molds, filling them. Place the molds in the freezer for at least 3 hours, or until the chiboust is firm.

6.   Unmold the domes, place each on a 3-inch square of parchment paper, and refrigerate until ready to use.

SABLÉ ROUNDS

Sablé Breton Dough (page 333)

1.   Position a rack in the center of the oven and preheat the oven to 375°F (191°C). Line a half-sheet pan with a silicone baking mat.

2.   Place the dough disk on a work surface and roll the dough out to a thickness of ½ inch. Using a 3-inch round cutter, cut out 10 rounds from the dough and prick them well with a fork. Place the rounds on the prepared sheet pan and bake for about 15 minutes, or until golden brown. Cool the rounds on the sheet pan, set on a wire rack.

POMEGRANATE PINEAPPLE

½ medium pineapple, peeled and cored

2 Tbsp (28 g/1 oz) unsalted butter

½ cup (86 g/3 oz) pomegranate seeds

3 to 5 turns freshly ground pink peppercorns

1.   Cut the pineapple into ¼-inch cubes.

2.   Melt the butter over high heat in a large sauté pan and add the cubed pineapple and the freshly ground pink peppercorns. Sauté for 2 minutes until tender. Remove the pan from the heat and stir in the pomegranate seeds. Strain the mixture, storing the pineapple and pomegranate in a covered container in the refrigerator, and reserving the liquid in a separate container to garnish the dessert.

PINEAPPLE CHIPS (page 345)

Prepare the Pineapple Chips as directed and, while they are still warm, curl them around a rolling pin. Cool completely. Store in an airtight container.

ASSEMBLY

6 Tbsp (75 g/2.6 oz) granulated sugar

12 vanilla beans

1.   Preheat the oven to 375°F (191°C). Spoon about ⅓ cup Pomegranate Pineapple on a Sablé Round and place it in the center of a plate. Place the Lemongrass Chiboust domes on a half-sheet pan and sprinkle each with ½ tablespoon (6.5 g/0.23 oz) sugar. Pass a blowtorch over each dessert until they are browned. Place the desserts in the oven for 3 minutes to warm them.

2.   Arrange a warm chiboust on top of the Pomegranate Pineapple. Make a small hole in the center top of the dome and insert a vanilla bean. Thread the vanilla through a pineapple chip and slide the chip down to the top of the dome as a garnish. Drizzle the reserved liquid from the Pomegranate Pineapple around the plate.

STEAMED MERINGUE and RHUBARB CREAM with BERRIES in VANILLA BEAN SYRUP

⬚⬚ THIS IS ANOTHER DESSERT I CREATED at Daniel to entice the "ladies who lunch" into ordering dessert. The ladies always wanted something very light, and this dessert, a steamed meringue, is just that. The meringue must be steamed very gently, preferably in a professional steamer. I serve it with a light rhubarb cream (don't tell the ladies, but it has a little heavy cream in it) and fresh berries in a vanilla syrup. A baked phyllo crescent adds a crisp element to this dieter's-dream dessert.

MAKES 12 SERVINGS

COMPONENTS

RHUBARB SAUCE
RHUBARB PASTRY CREAM
STEAMED MERINGUE
PHYLLO CRESCENTS
BERRIES IN VANILLA SYRUP

SPECIAL EQUIPMENT
cheesecloth; kitchen twine; stacked bamboo or other large steamer (you can also use a perforated hotel pan, stacked on top of a regular hotel pan); 3-inch-diameter by 2¼-inch-high ring molds; 4-inch round pastry cutter; 1-inch-diameter pastry cutter; large, round tip (Ateco #8); blowtorch

PERFECT MATCH | Wel Scotch Beer, Brasseries Kronenbourg, Strasbourg, France

RHUBARB SAUCE

1 stalk lemongrass, chopped

2 cups plus 2 Tbsp (500 g/17.6 oz) water

¼ cup plus 1 Tbsp (62 g/2.2 oz) granulated sugar

About 2 medium stalks (250 g/8.8 oz) rhubarb, coarsely chopped

Finely grated zest of 1 lemon

Finely grated zest of 1 orange

¼ cup (60 g/2.1 oz) grenadine syrup

Place the chopped lemongrass in the center of a 7-inch square of cheesecloth and gather the ends of the cheesecloth together to form a pouch. Tie a string around the neck of the pouch to secure it. Place the cheesecloth pouch and the remaining ingredients in a medium saucepan and bring to a boil over medium-high heat. Reduce the heat to a simmer and cook until the rhubarb is very soft, 7 to 10 minutes. Remove the pan from the heat and remove the pouch of lemongrass with a slotted spoon; discard. Transfer the mixture to a blender and blend until smooth. Strain the sauce through a fine-mesh sieve, cover, and set aside.

RHUBARB PASTRY CREAM

1 cup (250 g/8.8 oz) Rhubarb Sauce
(page 183)

1 cup (250 g/8.8 oz) whole milk

½ cup (100 g/3.5 oz) granulated sugar

⅓ cup (40 g/1.4 oz) cornstarch

5 large (90 g/3.17 oz) egg yolks

1 Tbsp (15 g/0.5 oz) unsalted butter

3 Tbsp plus 1 tsp (50 g/1.76 oz) grenadine
syrup

1 cup plus 1 Tbsp (250 g/8.8 oz) heavy cream

1.   In a medium saucepan, combine the
Rhubarb Sauce and milk and bring to a boil
over medium heat. Remove from the heat.

2.   In a medium bowl, combine the sugar
and cornstarch. Whisk in the egg yolks, and
continue whisking until the mixture is pale.
Whisk about one-quarter of the milk mixture
into the yolk mixture, then whisk the yolk
mixture into the pan with the remaining milk
mixture. Cook over medium-high heat, whisking constantly, until the custard thickens and
boils. Remove the pan from the heat and whisk
in the butter and grenadine syrup. Continue
whisking until the butter has completely
melted. Scrape the pastry cream through a
fine-mesh sieve into a stainless steel bowl and
press a piece of plastic wrap directly on the
surface of the pastry cream to prevent a skin
from forming. Set the bowl in an ice bath and
stir frequently until cold.

3.   In the bowl of a stand mixer fitted with
the whisk attachment, whip the cream to
medium peaks. Gently fold the whipped
cream into the cold pastry cream. Cover the
bowl and refrigerate until ready to serve.

STEAMED MERINGUE

10 large (300 g/10.5 oz) egg whites

½ tsp (2.5 g/0.08 oz) freshly squeezed lemon
juice

¾ cup plus 1⅓ Tbsp (167 g/5.8 oz) granulated
sugar

1.   In the bowl of a stand mixer fitted with
the whisk attachment, begin whipping the egg
whites and lemon juice on low speed. Add
¼ cup (50 g/1.76 oz) of the sugar and increase
the speed to medium. Gradually add half of
the remaining sugar, then increase the speed
to medium-high. Gradually add the remaining sugar and whip on high speed until the
meringue forms firm peaks. Transfer the
meringue immediately to a piping bag fitted
with a large, round tip.

2.   Fill a large pot halfway with water. Bring
the water to a boil over high heat, then reduce
it to a simmer. Arrange the dessert rings in
the steamer and pipe the meringue into the
rings, filling them to the top. Make sure to use
one smooth motion, starting from the bottom
center and moving to the top of the ring. This
will make the meringue appear very smooth
on the outside and the top. Place the steamer
over the pot of simmering water and steam
for 5 minutes, or until the meringues are firm.
Remove the pot from the heat and place the
steamer insert directly into the refrigerator to
chill for at least 1 hour. The meringues will fall
slightly in the rings.

PHYLLO CRESCENTS

4 (13 by 18-inch) sheets phyllo dough

16 Tbsp (226 g/8 oz) unsalted butter, melted

Confectioners' sugar, as needed

1.   Position a rack in the center of the oven and preheat the oven to 350°F (177°C). Line a half-sheet pan with a silicone baking mat and set aside.

2.   Place a sheet of the phyllo dough on a piece of parchment paper and brush the sheet with melted butter. Dust the sheet with confectioners' sugar and top with another phyllo sheet. Repeat the layering process until you have used 4 phyllo sheets. Brush the top sheet with butter and dust with confectioners' sugar. Refrigerate the phyllo layers for 30 minutes, or until the butter has firmed up.

3.   Transfer the layers to a cutting board and, using a 4-inch round cutter, cut out a round from the stack. Move the cutter about ½ inch toward the center of the circle and cut to make a crescent shape. Place the crescent on the prepared sheet pan and repeat to make a total of 12 crescents. Cover the crescents with another silicone baking mat to keep them flat during baking. Bake for 10 minutes, or until the phyllo crescents are crisp. Place the sheet pan on a wire rack and cool completely.

BERRIES IN VANILLA SYRUP

1 cup (250 g/8.8 oz) Simple Syrup (page 339)

2 vanilla beans, split lengthwise and seeds scraped

1 cup (113 g/4 oz) fresh strawberries, washed, hulled, and sliced

1 cup (113 g/4 oz) fresh raspberries

1 cup (113 g/4 oz) fresh blueberries

1 cup (113 g/4 oz) fresh red currants

1.   In a small saucepan, combine the Simple Syrup with the vanilla bean pods and seeds and bring to a boil. Remove the pan from the heat, remove the vanilla bean pods, and cool the syrup until just warm.

2.   Place the berries in a medium bowl and toss them with the warm syrup. Set aside to cool.

ASSEMBLY

Vanilla bean slivers, for garnish

1.   Place one of the ring molds of Steamed Meringue in the center of a plate. Place a 1-inch-diameter pastry cutter into the center of the meringue and push it into the meringue, marking a circle. Lift out the pastry cutter and, using a small, offset spatula or paring knife, remove the circle of meringue from the center, going all the way to the bottom of the dessert. Lift off the outside ring mold.

2.   Using the blowtorch, caramelize the outside of the meringue evenly. Pipe some Rhubarb Pastry Cream into the center of the meringue, filling the hole. Garnish the top with a Phyllo Crescent, some Berries in Vanilla Syrup, and a sliver of vanilla bean. Spoon some additional berries and syrup around the plate.

BIG PALET D'OR filled with HAZELNUT WAFER and MANJARI MOUSSE

THE INSPIRATION FOR THIS BEAUTIFUL DESSERT came from Daniel Boulud. Daniel always wanted me to make desserts that were very French, so I decided to make a cake that looked like a classic *palet d'or,* a flat truffle coated with a thin layer of dark chocolate and topped with a fleck of gold leaf. The cake is all about contrasting textures—crispy meringue and milk chocolate–hazelnut wafer layered with a creamy dark chocolate mousse. The chocolate mousse has very little air in it—it's almost like a parfait—and has an intense chocolate flavor so that every bite you take is chocolate. It's not too heavy, though, because it's perfectly balanced. And it looks like a million dollars with its ultra-shiny chocolate finish and gold leaf accent.

MAKES 6 SERVINGS

COMPONENTS

SUCCÈS BISCUITS
HAZELNUT WAFERS
CHOCOLATE MOUSSE
CHOCOLATE GLAZE
CHOCOLATE DECORATIONS

SPECIAL EQUIPMENT | small, plain pastry tip (Ateco #2); 2¾-inch-diameter round pastry cutter; medium, plain pastry tip (Ateco #6); six 3-inch-diameter by 1-inch-high dessert rings; six 6-inch by 1-inch acetate strips; pastry comb; 3-inch rolling pin

PERFECT MATCH | Page 24 Triple Beer, Brasserie Saint-Germain, Aix-Noulette, France

SUCCÈS BISCUITS

⅔ cup (51 g/1.8 oz) hazelnut flour (see Sources, page 349)

1 Tbsp (8 g/0.28 oz) all-purpose flour

3 large (90 g/3.17 oz) egg whites

¾ tsp (3 g/0.1 oz) freshly squeezed lemon juice

⅔ cup (133 g/4.7 oz) granulated sugar

1. Position two racks near the center of the oven and preheat the oven to 300°F (149°C). Line two half-sheet pans with silicone baking mats.

2. In a medium bowl, sift together the hazelnut flour and all-purpose flour through a medium-mesh sieve and set aside.

3. Place the egg whites in the bowl of a stand mixer fitted with the whisk attachment and begin to whip them on low speed. When the whites are foamy, add the lemon juice, increase the speed to medium-high, and beat until soft peaks begin to form. Gradually add the sugar and continue to whip until the meringue is glossy and forms stiff peaks.

4.　Gently fold the dry ingredients into the meringue. Scrape the mixture into a pastry bag fitted with a ¼-inch, plain tip. Pipe the meringue onto the sheet pans, forming 2¼-inch disks, spaced about ½ inch apart. (You only need 6 disks for this recipe, but pipe out as many as you can, as they make excellent snacks.) Place the sheet pan in the oven and turn off the heat. Leave the meringues in the oven for 2 hours, checking on them occasionally, until they are completely dry and crisp. Cool, then store in an airtight container until ready to use.

HAZELNUT WAFERS

2 oz (60 g) milk chocolate, chopped

1¾ Tbsp (24 g/0.84 oz) unsalted butter

1 cup (300 g/10.6 oz) praline paste

1⅓ cups (90 g/3.17 oz) feuilletine or crisped rice cereal

½ cup (60 g/2.1 oz) skinless hazelnuts, toasted and finely chopped

1.　Line a half-sheet pan with a silicone baking mat.

2. In a small, microwave-safe bowl, combine the milk chocolate and butter and microwave on medium (50 percent) power, stirring every 20 seconds, for about 2 minutes, or until completely melted and smooth.

3. In another small bowl, mix the praline paste with a rubber spatula until it is smooth. Stir the praline paste into the chocolate mixture until combined. Fold in the feuilletine and hazelnuts. Spread the mixture onto a prepared sheet pan in a ⅛-inch-thick layer. Refrigerate for 30 minutes, or until firm.

4. Using a 2¾-inch round pastry cutter, cut out 6 rounds (the scraps are excellent snacks). Refrigerate until ready to serve; they will soften at room temperature.

CHOCOLATE MOUSSE

1 cup (232 g/8.2 oz) heavy cream

3 large (56 g/2 oz) egg yolks

¼ cup (75 g/2.6 oz) Simple Syrup (page 339)

1 Tbsp plus 2 tsp (25 g/0.88 oz) water

5½ oz (156 g) 72% bittersweet chocolate, chopped

1. In the bowl of a stand mixer fitted with the whisk attachment, beat the heavy cream on high speed until soft peaks just begin to form. Do not overwhip. Cover the bowl and refrigerate the cream until ready to use.

2. In the bowl of a stand mixer, whisk together the egg yolks, Simple Syrup, and water by hand. Place the bowl over a saucepan half full of barely simmering water and heat, whisking constantly, until light and thick, about 5 minutes. Continue to heat, whisking occasionally, until the mixture registers 180°F

(82°C) on an instant-read thermometer. Place the bowl in the mixer stand and, using the whisk attachment, beat on high speed until completely cool, about 5 minutes. Set aside.

3. While the yolk mixture is beating, place the chocolate in a medium, stainless steel bowl and set the bowl over the saucepan of simmering water; the water should not touch the bottom of the bowl. Heat until melted, stirring occasionally. Remove the bowl from the heat and set the melted chocolate aside to cool.

4. Whisk about one-quarter of the yolk mixture into the melted chocolate. Gently fold in the remaining yolk mixture. Fold about one-third of the whipped cream into the mixture, then gently fold in the remaining cream. Assemble the desserts as soon as the mousse is made.

ASSEMBLE THE DESSERTS

1. Scrape the Chocolate Mousse into a pastry bag fitted with a medium, plain tip. Take one of the dessert rings and place it on a baking sheet. The sheet must be able to fit in your freezer; if it doesn't, use a cardboard square or a plate. Pipe some mousse around the edge of the ring; this will ensure that the dessert has smooth sides, and the Succès Biscuit Round will not be poking through. Place a succès round in the center of the ring and push it to the bottom. Pipe a dollop of mousse in the center of the succès and place a Hazelnut Wafer on top. Press to compact the mousse. Fill the ring with mousse. Using a small, offset spatula, level the top and repeat with the remaining rings and ingredients to make 6 desserts. Place the rings in the freezer for at least 2 hours, or until the mousse is firm.

2. Once the desserts are set, remove the rings by placing the desserts on top of an inverted cup and then warming the sides with a propane blowtorch or hot, damp kitchen towel. Push down on the rings to remove them. Arrange the unmolded desserts on a wire rack and lay a single sheet of plastic wrap on top of the desserts; this will prevent condensation from forming. Allow the desserts to defrost at room temperature for about an hour.

CHOCOLATE GLAZE

9 oz (255 g) 61% bittersweet chocolate, finely chopped

1 Tbsp (20 g/0.7 oz) light corn syrup

1 cup (242 g/8.5 oz) heavy cream

1. Place the chocolate and corn syrup in a medium bowl and set aside.

2. In a small saucepan, bring the cream to a gentle boil. Pour the hot cream over the chocolate. Let stand for a minute to melt the chocolate, then stir with a spatula until smooth. Strain through a fine-mesh sieve into another bowl, cover the surface of the glaze with a piece of plastic wrap, and set aside at room temperature.

CHOCOLATE DECORATIONS

8 oz (227 g) bittersweet chocolate, tempered (see Tempered Chocolate, page 347)

Place an acetate strip on a work surface and pour some of the tempered chocolate onto one end of the strip. Run a pastry comb through the chocolate, drawing lines all the way to the end of the acetate strip. Draw a line of chocolate across each end of the strip to join the lines. Allow the chocolate to set for a few minutes at room temperature; the time will depend on the temperature of your kitchen. When the chocolate begins to set, lay the acetate strip on top of a rolling pin with the acetate side against the pin. Repeat to make a total of 6 garnishes. Allow the chocolate to set fully at room temperature, about 1 hour. Carefully remove the strips from the rolling pin and peel the chocolate decoration off the acetate.

FINAL ASSEMBLY

Sliced almonds, lightly toasted

Gold leaf

Remove the plastic wrap from the desserts. Place the bowl of Chocolate Glaze over a pot of hot water and warm it to 90°F (32°C). Pour the glaze over each dessert, and using an offset spatula, smooth it over the top and remove the excess before it sets. Carefully place each dessert on a plate and line the sides with the best of the sliced almonds. Place a Chocolate Decoration on the top of the mousse, and lay a piece of gold leaf on the chocolate.

CARRÉ PAYARD with CARAMEL ANGLAISE, FLEUR DE SEL, and CARAMEL ICE CREAM

At Payard I discovered that people love the idea of a cube-shaped dessert, so I created this one using plastic cubes I found down in Manhattan's Chinatown. The interiors of the cubes are painted with tempered chocolate, then filled with an intense chocolate mousse that has a secret salted caramel center. When you break the cube with your fork, the salted caramel pours out and mixes with the mousse, and it's really a fabulous combination of flavors. Not surprisingly, this was one of my most popular desserts at Payard.

MAKES 8 SERVINGS

COMPONENTS

CHOCOLATE SACHER CAKE
CHOCOLATE SABLÉ BRETON
CHOCOLATE CUBES
   CHOCOLATE MOUSSE
   SALTED CARAMEL CENTERS
CARAMEL CRÈME ANGLAISE
CARAMEL ICE CREAM
STREUSEL

SPECIAL EQUIPMENT | eight 3-inch plastic cubes (available from office supply stores); ice cream machine

PERFECT MATCH | Carole Bouquet Sangue D'Oro Passito di Pantelleria, Sicily

CHOCOLATE SACHER CAKE

¾ cup (70 g/2.5 oz) almond flour

⅓ cup plus 1 Tbsp (78 g/2.7 oz) granulated sugar

4 large (200 g/7 oz) egg yolks

5 large (150 g/5.3 oz) egg whites

3 Tbsp (25 g/0.88 oz) unsweetened alkalized cocoa powder, sifted

1. Preheat a convection oven to 425°F (218°C). Line a half-sheet pan with a silicone baking mat.

2. In the bowl of a stand mixer fitted with the whisk attachment, combine the almond flour, ⅓ cup (65 g/2.3 oz) of the sugar, the egg yolks, and 2½ (75 g/2.6 oz) of the egg whites and whip on medium-high speed until the mixture doubles in volume and becomes a pale yellow color, about 10 minutes. Gently fold the cocoa powder into the yolk mixture just until blended; do not overmix, or the batter will deflate.

3. In another, clean mixer bowl, using a clean whisk attachment, immediately whip the remaining 2½ (75 g/2.6 oz) egg whites on medium-high speed until soft peaks begin to form. Gradually add the remaining 1 tablespoon (13 g/0.45 oz) granulated sugar and beat on high speed until the whites form stiff peaks.

Fold the whites into the cocoa mixture. Spread the batter onto the prepared sheet pan (it will be a thin layer) and bake for 7 to 9 minutes, or until a toothpick inserted into the center of the cake comes out clean. Cool the cake in the pan, set on a wire rack, for 10 minutes.

4.   Unmold the cake and cool completely.

5.   Cut out eight 2¾-inch squares from the cake and place them in an airtight container until ready to serve.

CHOCOLATE SABLÉ BRETON

3 large (56 g/2 oz) hard-boiled egg yolks

12½ Tbsp (177 g/6.2 oz) unsalted butter

Pinch of salt

⅔ cup (75 g/2.6 oz) confectioners' sugar

1⅓ cups (170 g/6 oz) all-purpose flour

⅓ cup (30 g/1 oz) almond flour

3 Tbsp plus 1 tsp (30 g/1 oz) unsweetened alkalized cocoa powder

1.   Pass the cooked yolks through a fine-mesh sieve onto a piece of wax or parchment paper.

2.   In the bowl of a stand mixer fitted with the paddle attachment, beat the butter, salt, and confectioners' sugar on medium speed until well blended and smooth. Add the flour, egg yolks, almond flour, and cocoa powder and mix on low speed until the mixture comes together and forms a dough. Remove from the bowl, form the dough into a disk, wrap it in plastic wrap, and refrigerate for at least 1 hour.

3.   Preheat the oven to 375°F (191°C). Line a half-sheet pan with a silicone baking mat.

4.   Place the dough on a lightly floured work surface and roll it out to a thickness of ¼ inch. Cut out eight 3-inch squares from the dough and arrange them on the prepared sheet pan. Bake for about 10 minutes, or until the dough is baked through and no longer shiny. Cool completely.

CHOCOLATE CUBES

24 oz (680 g) bittersweet chocolate, chopped

Melt and temper the chocolate according to the directions on page 347. Pour some of the chocolate into a 3-inch plastic cube, filling it. Turn the cube over, pouring the chocolate back into the bowl and leaving a thin film of chocolate coating the interior of the cube. Repeat with the remaining chocolate and cubes. Set the chocolate cubes aside to set.

CHOCOLATE MOUSSE

5.3 oz (150 g) 72% bittersweet chocolate, chopped

1 large (50 g/1.76 oz) whole egg

1 large (19 g/0.65 oz) egg yolk

¼ cup plus 1 Tbsp (62 g/2.2 oz) granulated sugar

2 Tbsp (30 g/1 oz) water

1 cup plus 1 Tbsp (250 g/8.8 oz) heavy cream

1. Place the chocolate in a medium stainless steel bowl and set the bowl over a saucepan filled one-third of the way with barely simmering water. Heat, stirring frequently, until the chocolate is melted and smooth. Remove from the heat and set aside to cool.

2. In the bowl of a stand mixer fitted with the whisk attachment, beat the egg and egg yolk together on medium speed. Meanwhile, in a small saucepan, combine the sugar and water and cook over medium-high heat, occasionally washing down the sides of the pan with a wet pastry brush to prevent crystals from forming, until the syrup comes to a full boil. Allow to boil for 1 minute, then remove the pan from the heat and slowly pour the hot syrup into the beating egg and yolk. Increase the speed to high and beat the mixture until it is doubled in volume and completely cool, about 6 minutes.

3. In the bowl of a stand mixer fitted with the whisk attachment, whip the cream to soft peaks. Fold the melted chocolate into the egg mixture. Ideally, the chocolate should be at 104°F (40°C) when it's folded in; if it's too cool, rewarm it gently over the hot water. Gently fold in the whipped cream. Cover and refrigerate until ready to serve.

SALTED CARAMEL CENTERS

½ cup (125 g/4.4 oz) heavy cream

½ cup plus 2 Tbsp (125 g/4.4 oz) granulated sugar

2 Tbsp (30 g/1 oz) water

1½ tsp (12 g/0.4 oz) glucose syrup

9 Tbsp (125 g/4.4 oz) unsalted butter

Pinch of salt

1. In a small saucepan, heat the cream over medium heat until hot. Reduce the heat to low to keep it warm.

2. In a small, heavy-bottomed saucepan, combine the granulated sugar with the water and glucose and cook over medium-high heat, occasionally washing down the sides of the pan with a wet pastry brush to prevent crystals from forming, and watching carefully, until the sugar caramelizes and turns a dark amber color, 3 to 5 minutes. Remove the pan from the heat and gradually stir in the warm cream. Return the pan to the heat and stir until any hardened bits of caramel have dissolved, about 2 minutes. Add the butter and salt and stir until the butter has melted. Remove the pan from the heat and let the caramel cool to room temperature.

CARAMEL CRÈME ANGLAISE

2 cups plus 1 Tbsp (500 g/17.6 oz) whole milk

1 cup plus 2 Tbsp (225 g/8 oz) granulated sugar

Pinch of fleur de sel

7 large (125 g/4.4 oz) egg yolks

1. In a small saucepan, heat the milk over medium heat until hot. Reduce the heat to low and keep it warm.

2. In a small, heavy-bottomed saucepan, combine ½ cup plus 2 tablespoons (125 g/4.4 oz) of the granulated sugar with the salt and cook over medium-high heat, occasionally washing down the sides of the pan with a wet pastry brush to prevent crystals from forming, and watching carefully, until the sugar caramelizes and turns a medium amber color, 3 to 5 minutes. Remove the pan from the heat and gradually stir in the warm milk. Return the pan to the heat and stir until any hardened bits of caramel have dissolved, about 2 minutes. Remove the pan from the heat.

3. In a medium bowl, whisk together the egg yolks and the remaining ½ cup (100 g/3.5 oz) sugar until pale. Whisk about ½ cup of the hot caramel mixture into the yolks, then return this mixture to the remaining hot caramel mixture in the saucepan. Cook over medium heat, stirring constantly, until the mixture thickens enough to coat the back of a spoon and reaches 175°F (79°C) on an instant-read thermometer; do not let the mixture boil, or the egg yolks will curdle. Remove the pot from the heat and pass the mixture through a fine-mesh sieve into a bowl. Set the bowl in an ice bath and stir frequently until cold. Cover and refrigerate until ready to use.

CARAMEL ICE CREAM

(page 31)

STREUSEL, BAKED (page 342)

ASSEMBLY

Fleur de sel

Chocolate cigarettes

Gold leaf

1. Fill the Chocolate Cubes halfway with Chocolate Mousse. Press the square of Chocolate Sacher Cake into the mousse, allowing the mousse to push up the sides. Place about 1 tablespoon of the cooled Salted Caramel Center into the cavity created by the mousse. Pipe more of the chocolate mousse on top of the caramel layer, filling each cube. Level the top of the mousse with a spatula. Set the cubes on a sheet pan and place in the freezer until firm, at least 3 hours.

2. Unmold each chocolate cube from the plastic and place it onto the baked square of Chocolate Sablé Breton. Use a small bit of the Salted Caramel Center to anchor the dessert to the plate. Place a small piece of gold leaf on top of the cube. Sprinkle some baked Streusel on the other side of the plate and place a quenelle of Caramel Ice Cream on top of it. Garnish the ice cream with a sprinkling of fleur de sel and a chocolate cigarette. Spoon some Caramel Crème Anglaise onto one of the corners of the cube and allow it to drip down the side onto the plate.

DUO OF COFFEE and CHOCOLATE with a MASCARPONE-ESPRESSO SHOT

When you give flavor ideas to a chef, each chef will come back with something a little different. This dessert duo is my interpretation of tiramisú, presented in a very different way. The glass holds a Mascarpone Mousse paired with more assertive elements: a dark chocolate mousse and a very strong espresso granité. I don't use ladyfingers—instead, I serve a little napoleon on the side, made with chocolate phyllo triangles and alternating layers of Chocolate Mousse and Coffee Pastry Cream.

MAKE 8 SERVINGS

COMPONENTS

COFFEE GRANITÉ

MASCARPONE MOUSSE

COFFEE PASTRY CREAM

CHOCOLATE PHYLLO TRIANGLES

CHOCOLATE SAUCE

CHOCOLATE MOUSSE

SPECIAL EQUIPMENT | eight 8-ounce shot glasses; coffee filter; 2 medium, plain pastry tips (Ateco #6).

PERFECT MATCH | Faretti Biscotti Famosi Liqueur, Italy

COFFEE GRANITÉ

2 cups plus 2 Tbsp (500 g/17.6 oz) water

1 cup (60 g/2.1 oz) ground espresso beans

¼ cup plus 2 Tbsp (75 g/2.6 oz) granulated sugar

1 Tbsp (15 g/0.5 oz) coffee extract

1. In a small saucepan, bring the water to a boil. Remove from the heat and add the ground espresso. Cover the pan and allow to infuse for 10 minutes.

2. Strain the mixture through a coffee filter into a bowl. Stir in the sugar and coffee extract, stirring to dissolve the sugar. Pour into a 9 by 5-inch loaf pan or shallow container and freeze for at least 2 hours, or until firm.

3. When ready to serve, use a fork to scrape the coffee block to form the granité.

MASCARPONE MOUSSE

½ cup plus 2½ Tbsp (130 g/4.6 oz) granulated sugar

4 large (74 g/2.6 oz) egg yolks

4 large (120 g/4.2 oz) egg whites

2 cups (500 g/17.6 oz) mascarpone cheese

1. In the bowl of a stand mixer, whisk together ¼ cup plus 2 tablespoons (75 g/2.6 oz) of the granulated sugar with the egg yolks by hand. Place the bowl over a pot filled one-third of the way with simmering water and heat, whisking constantly, until the yolk mixture has thickened and is hot to the touch. Place the bowl on the mixer stand and, using the whisk attachment, whip the mixture on high speed until completely cool. Set aside.

2. In another clean bowl of a stand mixer, using a clean whisk attachment, whip the whites on medium speed until soft peaks begin to form. Gradually add the remaining ¼ cup plus ½ tablespoon (55 g/1.9 oz) sugar and whip on high speed until the whites are glossy and form stiff peaks.

3. Place the mascarpone in a large bowl and whisk it by hand until soft and smooth. Gently fold in the yolk mixture. Fold in the whipped egg whites, cover the bowl, and refrigerate until ready to serve.

COFFEE PASTRY CREAM

2 cups (484 g/17 oz) whole milk

½ cup plus 1 Tbsp (24 g/0.8 oz) instant coffee powder

½ cup (100 g/3.5 oz) granulated sugar

⅓ cup (40 g/1.4 oz) cornstarch

5 large (93 g/3.3 oz) egg yolks

1 Tbsp (14 g/0.5 oz) unsalted butter

¾ cup (180 g/6.3 oz) heavy cream

1. In a medium saucepan, bring the milk to a boil over medium heat. Stir in the coffee powder until it has dissolved. Remove from the heat.

2. In a medium bowl, combine the sugar and cornstarch. Whisk in the egg yolks, whisking until the mixture is pale. Whisk about one-quarter of the hot milk into the yolk mixture, then whisk this mixture into the pan with the remaining milk. Cook over medium-high heat, whisking constantly, until the custard thickens and boils. Remove the pan from the heat, whisk in the butter, and continue to whisk until the butter has melted completely. Scrape the pastry cream through a fine-mesh sieve into a stainless steel bowl and press a piece of plastic wrap directly on the surface of the pastry cream to prevent a skin from forming. Set the bowl in an ice bath and stir frequently until cold.

3. In the bowl of a stand mixer fitted with the whisk attachment, whip the cream to soft peaks. Gently fold the whipped cream into the cold pastry cream. Cover and refrigerate until ready to serve.

CHOCOLATE PHYLLO TRIANGLES

> 7 Tbsp (100 g/3.5 oz) Clarified Butter (page 348)
>
> ¼ cup (32 g/1.1 oz) unsweetened alkalized cocoa powder
>
> 8 (9 by 14-inch) sheets phyllo dough

1. Preheat the oven to 375°F (191°C). Line two half-sheet pans with parchment paper and brush the paper with melted butter.

2. In a small saucepan, melt the Clarified Butter over medium heat and whisk in the cocoa powder.

3. Place a sheet of phyllo dough on the parchment paper and brush the sheet with some of the butter mixture. Place another sheet of phyllo on top. Repeat the layering until you have used 4

phyllo sheets. Brush the last sheet with the butter mixture and, using the remaining phyllo sheets and cocoa-butter mixture, repeat the process on the other sheet pan. Refrigerate the phyllo layers for 30 minutes, or until the butter has firmed up.

4. Using a ruler as a guide, cut the phyllo layers into 3½-inch squares. Cut the squares in half diagonally, forming a total of 24 triangles. Place the triangles on a silicone baking mat–lined half-sheet pan and place another silicone baking mat on top to keep them flat. Bake for 10 minutes, or until crisp. Remove the top mat and cool the triangles on the sheet pan, set on a wire rack.

CHOCOLATE SAUCE (page 334)

CHOCOLATE MOUSSE (page 337)

ASSEMBLY

> Cocoa powder, for sprinkling

1. Scrape the Chocolate Mousse into a pastry bag fitted with a medium, plain tip. Scrape the Coffee Pastry Cream into another pastry bag fitted with a medium, plain tip. Pipe some mousse onto one of the Chocolate Phyllo Triangles. Place another triangle on top of the mousse and pipe a layer of Coffee Pastry Cream on top. Pipe on more mousse, and top with a final Chocolate Phyllo Triangle. Place the napoleon on a plate on its side, with the points facing up.

2. Fill a shot glass one-third of the way with Chocolate Mousse. Fill another third of the glass with Coffee Granité. Spoon the Mascarpone Mousse on top, filling the glass to the top. Sprinkle with cocoa powder, place the glass on the plate, and spoon some Chocolate Sauce onto the plate.

PYRAMID OF GIANDUJA with HIBISCUS BERRY GELÉE and HIBISCUS SAUCE

THIS CHOCOLATE-HAZELNUT PYRA-MID was one of my most popular dinner desserts at Payard. It is composed of a Gianduja Mousse with a Hibiscus Berry Gelée center and crisp Hazelnut Dacquoise base. After unmolding, the pyramids—and the plates they're sitting on—are sprayed with a mixture of melted chocolate and cocoa butter and garnished with overlapping chocolate triangles. A big fleck of gold leaf crowns the point on each triangle, making it look like a million dollars! After you spray the plates, they must be picked up from the bottom for serving, or the finish will be marred.

MAKES 8 SERVINGS

COMPONENTS

HIBISCUS BERRY GELÉE
HAZELNUT DACQUOISE
GIANDUJA MOUSSE
HIBISCUS SAUCE
CHOCOLATE TRIANGLES
CHOCOLATE SPRAY

SPECIAL EQUIPMENT | medium, plain pastry tip (Ateco #6); eight 3-inch silicone pyramid dessert molds; 8-inch square baking pan; 19 by 24-inch sheet of acetate; chocolate or paint sprayer

PERFECT MATCH | Il Gusto della Costa Limoncello Liqueur, Campania, Italy

HIBISCUS BERRY GELÉE

1 cup plus 1 Tbsp (250 g/8.8 oz) water

3 Tbsp (40 g/1.4 oz) granulated sugar

1 Tbsp plus 1 tsp (12 g/0.42 oz) dried hibiscus tea

4 sheets (8 g/0.3 oz) gelatin (silver grade)

¾ cup (250 g/8.8 oz) neutral glaze

1 cup (125 g/4.4 oz) fresh wild strawberries

1 cup (125 g/4.4 oz) fresh raspberries

1 cup (125 g/4.4 oz) fresh blackberries

1. In a small saucepan, combine the water and sugar and bring to a boil over medium-high heat. Remove the pan from the heat and add the hibiscus tea. Cover the pan and allow to infuse for 10 minutes.

2. Fill a medium bowl with cold water and add the gelatin sheets. Allow to soften for 10 minutes.

3. Strain the tea, and discard the hibiscus blossoms. Drain the gelatin, squeezing it to remove the excess liquid, and stir it into the tea along with the neutral glaze until the gelatin has dissolved (reheat over low heat, if necessary, to dissolve the gelatin).

4. Line an 8-inch square baking pan with plastic wrap and pour the hibiscus tea liquid into the pan. Arrange the berries evenly in the pan and freeze until set, at least 2 hours.

5. Unmold the gelée and cut it into 1½-inch squares. Refrigerate, covered, until ready to use.

HAZELNUT DACQUOISE

2 cups (180 g/6.3 oz) hazelnut flour

1½ cups (180 g/6.3 oz) confectioners' sugar

8 large (240 g/8.4 oz) egg whites

¼ cup plus 2 Tbsp (80 g/2.8 oz) granulated sugar

1.   Preheat a convection oven to 400°F (204°C). Line a half-sheet pan with a silicone baking mat.

2.   In a medium bowl, sift together the hazelnut flour and confectioners' sugar. Gently whisk to combine and set aside.

3.   In the bowl of a stand mixer fitted with the whisk attachment, whip the egg whites on medium-high speed to soft peaks. Gradually add the granulated sugar and whip on high speed until firm peaks form. Gently fold in the hazelnut flour mixture and spread the meringue on the prepared sheet pan. Bake for 9 to 12 minutes, or until lightly browned. Cool the dacquoise in the pan, set on a wire rack.

4.   Cut the dacquoise into eight 3-inch triangles that fit the base of the pyramid molds.

GIANDUJA MOUSSE

3¼ large (60 g/2.1 oz) egg yolks

2 Tbsp (30 g/1 oz) water

¼ cup plus 1 Tbsp (72 g/2.5 oz) Simple Syrup (page 339)

6.3 oz (180 g) gianduja chocolate, melted

1 cup plus 2½ Tbsp (270 g/9.5 oz) heavy cream

1.   In the bowl of a stand mixer fitted with the whisk attachment, begin whipping the yolks and water on high speed.

2.   Meanwhile, in a small saucepan, bring the Simple Syrup to a boil over medium-high heat. Reduce the mixer speed to medium and slowly add the hot syrup to the whipping egg yolks. Increase the speed to high and whip until the yolks are completely cool, about 5 minutes.

3.   Fold the melted gianduja into the whipped egg yolks.

4.   In the bowl of a stand mixer fitted with the whisk attachment, whip the heavy cream to soft peaks. Gently fold the whipped cream into the chocolate mixture until blended. Transfer the mousse to a pastry bag fitted with a medium, plain tip and refrigerate until ready to serve.

HIBISCUS SAUCE

1 cup (250 g/8.8 oz) red currant purée

½ cup (115g/4 oz) water

¼ cup plus 1 Tbsp (62 g/2.2 oz) granulated sugar

1 Tbsp (10 g/0.35 oz) dried hibiscus tea

1.   In a small saucepan, combine all of the ingredients and bring to a boil over medium-high heat. Remove the pan from the heat, cover, and allow to infuse for 5 minutes.

2.   Strain the sauce through a fine-mesh sieve. Discard the hibiscus blossoms. Cool completely, then refrigerate, covered, until ready to serve.

BEGIN ASSEMBLY

1. Pipe the Gianduja Mousse into eight 3-inch silicone pyramid dessert molds, filling them halfway. Using a spoon, spread the mousse up the sides of the mold. Press a square of Hibiscus Berry Gelée in the center. Fill the mold almost to the top with mousse. Press a Hazelnut Dacquoise square into the mousse until it is level with the base of the mold. Take a spatula and smooth the mousse over the dacquoise. Repeat to make a total of 8 desserts. Place the molds on a sheet pan and freeze until set, at least 3 hours.

2. Unmold the pyramids and freeze until ready to serve.

CHOCOLATE TRIANGLES

1 lb (454 g) bittersweet chocolate, tempered (see Tempered Chocolate, page 347)

1. Spread enough of the tempered chocolate onto a 19 by 24-inch sheet of acetate to make a thin, even layer. Let the chocolate set partially, about 10 minutes.

2. When the chocolate begins to set, cut out triangles that measure 3 inches at the base and have 5-inch sides. You will need 16 triangles total, or 2 for each dessert. Let the chocolate set completely.

CHOCOLATE SPRAY

7 oz (200 g) milk chocolate

7 oz (200 g) cocoa butter

Place the chocolate and cocoa butter in a medium, stainless steel bowl and set the bowl over a saucepan filled one-third of the way with barely simmering water. Heat, stirring frequently, until the chocolate has melted and the mixture is smooth. Strain through a fine-mesh sieve into another bowl. Place the bowl over the pan of hot water to keep it warm.

FINAL ASSEMBLY

Gold leaf

1. Place each pyramid on a plate. Place the warm chocolate into the sprayer. Evenly spray each pyramid, and the plate, with the chocolate mixture. Allow the desserts to defrost at room temperature for about 30 minutes.

2. Place the 2 Chocolate Triangles leaning on opposite sides of the pyramid. Use the Hibiscus Sauce to help stick the chocolate to the sides. Place some gold leaf on the tips of the triangles. Decorate the plate with dots of sauce.

CHOCOLATE DOME with VANILLA CRÈME BRÛLÉE and HAZELNUT DACQUOISE

BACK IN THE LATE 1990s, crème brûlée was at the peak of its popularity, and it was that classic that inspired this elegant dessert from my days at Daniel. Inside the understated chocolate dome are layers of Vanilla Crème Brûlée, crunchy Hazelnut Dacquoise, and Chocolate Mousse. The dessert is frozen, unmolded, and sprayed with a mixture of chocolate and cocoa butter, giving it a velvety finish. It's served with a Chocolate Sauce and Crème Anglaise, and garnished with a piped chocolate design and a chocolate cigarette. The cigarette can be purchased online at a variety of sources nowadays. The beauty of this dessert is that all its components can be made in advance and easily plated à la minute. In fact, I remember doing a party where I made 650 of these and decorated them all by myself!

MAKES 10 SERVINGS

COMPONENTS

VANILLA CRÈME BRÛLÉE

HAZELNUT DACQUOISE

CHOCOLATE MOUSSE

CHOCOLATE SAUCE

CHOCOLATE SPRAY

CRÈME ANGLAISE

CHOCOLATE GARNISH

SPECIAL EQUIPMENT | 9 by 13-inch baking pan; 2-inch and 2¾-inch round pastry cutters; medium, plain pastry tip (Ateco #6); ten 2¾-inch-diameter silicone dome molds (3.5-ounce capacity); chocolate or paint sprayer; parchment paper cone

PERFECT MATCH | 1994 Château Tirecul-la-Gravière Monbazillac Cuvée Madame, France

VANILLA CRÈME BRÛLÉE

2 cups plus 2½ Tbsp (500 g/17.6 oz) heavy cream

2 vanilla beans, split lengthwise and seeds scraped

7 large (125 g/4.4 oz) egg yolks

¾ cup plus 1 Tbsp (170 g/6 oz) granulated sugar

1. In a medium saucepan, bring the heavy cream and vanilla bean pods and seeds to a boil over medium-high heat.

2. Meanwhile, in the bowl of a stand mixer fitted with the whisk attachment, whip the egg yolks and sugar on high speed until pale and thickened, about 3 minutes. When the cream comes to a boil, add about one-quarter of it to the yolk mixture with the mixer on low speed. Add this mixture to the remaining cream in the pan and whisk until smooth. Transfer the

mixture to a medium bowl and place the bowl into an ice bath. Let stand, stirring occasionally, until slightly chilled. Cover the bowl and refrigerate overnight.

3. Preheat the oven (not an oven with a fan) to 250°F (121°C). Line the bottom and sides of a 9 by 13-inch baking pan with aluminum foil. Strain the chilled crème mixture through a fine-mesh sieve into the prepared pan. Place the pan into a roasting or hotel pan and pour enough water into the pan so that it comes halfway up the sides of the baking pan. Bake for 40 to 50 minutes, or until the custard is just set. Cool on a wire rack.

4. Freeze the crème until firm, at least 2 hours.

5. Remove the frozen crème from the pan and, using a 2-inch round pastry cutter, cut out 10 rounds from the crème. Place the rounds in an airtight container and freeze until ready to serve.

HAZELNUT DACQUOISE

2½ cups (175 g/6.17 oz) hazelnut flour

1½ cups (175 g/6.17 oz) confectioners' sugar

8⅓ large (250 g/8.8 oz) egg whites

¼ tsp (0.13 oz/3.7 g) freshly squeezed lemon juice

¼ cup plus 2 Tbsp (75 g/2.6 oz) granulated sugar

½ cup (50 g/1.76 oz) finely chopped hazelnuts

1. Preheat the oven to 400°F (204°C). Line a half-sheet pan with a silicone baking mat.

2. In a medium bowl, sift together the hazelnut flour and confectioners' sugar and gently whisk to combine. Set aside.

3. In the bowl of a stand mixer fitted with the whisk attachment, whip the egg whites on medium-low speed until frothy. Add the lemon juice, increase the speed to medium, and whip until soft peaks begin to form. Gradually add the sugar and whip on high speed until stiff peaks form. Remove the bowl from the mixer stand and gently fold in the dry ingredients. Spread the mixture onto the prepared sheet in an even layer. Sprinkle with the finely chopped hazelnuts. Bake for about 9 to 12 minutes, or until lightly browned and baked through. Cool the dacquoise in the sheet pan, set on a wire rack.

4. Using pastry cutters, cut out ten 2-inch rounds and ten 2¾-inch rounds from the dacquoise. Store the rounds in an airtight container until ready to serve.

CHOCOLATE MOUSSE (page 337)

CHOCOLATE SAUCE (page 334)

DOME ASSEMBLY

1.   Place the Chocolate Mousse in a pastry bag fitted with a medium, plain tip and pipe enough mousse into each mold to fill them halfway. Using a spoon, spread the mousse up the sides of each mold. Place a 2-inch Hazelnut Dacquoise disk in the center, then top with a disk of Vanilla Crème Brûlée. Pipe more mousse into each mold, almost filling them to the top. Press a 2¾-inch dacquoise disk on top. Freeze the desserts for at least 2 hours, or until firm.

2.   Unmold each dessert and return them to the freezer until ready to serve.

CHOCOLATE SPRAY

> 7 oz (200 g) milk chocolate, chopped
>
> 7 oz (200 g) cocoa butter, chopped

1.   Place the chocolate and cocoa butter in a medium, stainless steel bowl and set the bowl over a saucepan filled one-third of the way with barely simmering water. Heat, stirring frequently, until the chocolate has melted and the mixture is smooth. Strain through a fine-mesh sieve into another bowl. Place the bowl over the pan of hot water to keep it warm.

2.   Arrange the desserts on a wire rack that is set on top of a half-sheet pan. Place the warm chocolate into the sprayer. Evenly spray each dome with the chocolate mixture. Place each dome on a dessert plate and allow to defrost for 30 minutes at room temperature.

CRÈME ANGLAISE (page 335)

CHOCOLATE GARNISH

> 1 lb (454 g) bittersweet chocolate, tempered (see Tempered Chocolate, page 347)

1.   Line a half-sheet pan with a piece of parchment paper. Pour some tempered chocolate into a small parchment paper cone. Pipe the chocolate into 4 connected teardrop shapes in graduated sizes (refer to the photo on page 202), all coming together to a point at the base. Repeat to make a total of 10 chocolate garnishes. Pipe the same design on the plates next to the desserts. Allow the chocolate to set at room temperature, about 20 minutes.

2.   Carefully release the garnishes from the paper and set them aside until ready to serve.

FINAL ASSEMBLY

> 10 dark chocolate cigarettes

Make a small slit in the center of the top of each dome and insert a Chocolate Garnish into it. Lay a chocolate cigarette against each dome, threading it through one of the loops in the chocolate garnish. Place the Crème Anglaise in a squeeze bottle and fill the chocolate teardrops on the plate with some of the sauce. Garnish the plate with a few drops of Chocolate Sauce.

MILK CHOCOLATE CUBE filled with EARL GREY TEA MOUSSE and GRAPEFRUIT and ORANGE GELÉE

EARL GREY TEA, full of citrusy bergamot flavor, goes very well with chocolate because it can really stand up to its intensity. Here, a Chocolate Earl Grey Mousse is piped into a cube-shaped mold, and a cube of syrup-soaked Chocolate Génoise is tucked into its center. The mousse cube is frozen, then unmolded and sprayed with a thin coating of chocolate and cocoa butter. I serve it with a Grapefruit and Orange Gelée, which cuts through the richness of the chocolate and highlights the bergamot flavor. This is a great dessert to serve in a restaurant, because everything is prepared in advance, making it very easy to plate.

MAKES 10 SERVINGS

COMPONENTS

MERINGUE STICKS

CHOCOLATE GÉNOISE

CHOCOLATE EARL GREY TEA MOUSSE

EARL GREY TEA SYRUP

GRAPEFRUIT AND ORANGE GELÉE

CHOCOLATE SPRAY

SPECIAL EQUIPMENT | candy thermometer; small, plain pastry tip (Ateco #3); 9 by 5-inch loaf pan; medium, plain pastry tip (Ateco #6); ten 2¼-inch cube-shaped dessert molds (plastic or silicone); chocolate or paint sprayer

PERFECT MATCH | Carole Bouquet Sangue d'Oro Passito di Pantelleria, Sicily

MERINGUE STICKS

3 large (90 g/3.17 oz) egg whites

¼ cup plus 3 Tbsp (90 g/3.17 oz) granulated sugar

1.   Preheat the oven to 300°F (149°C). Line a half-sheet pan with a silicone baking mat.

2.   In the bowl of a stand mixer, whisk together the egg whites and sugar by hand a few times. Place the bowl in a saucepan half full of simmering water and continue to whisk the whites until the sugar has dissolved and the mixture is warm. Place the bowl on the mixer stand fitted with the whisk attachment and whip on high speed until the meringue is completely cool, about 5 minutes. Scrape the meringue into a pastry bag fitted with a small, plain tip. Pipe at least twenty 6-inch-long stick shapes onto the prepared sheet pan. Place them in the oven and turn off the heat. Leave the meringue sticks in the oven for 1 to 2 hours, checking occasionally, until they are completely dry and crispy. Store in an air-tight container until ready to serve.

CHOCOLATE GÉNOISE

1¼ cups (140 g/5 oz) cake flour

1½ Tbsp (10 g/0.35 oz) unsweetened alkalized cocoa powder

¼ tsp (1 g/0.03 oz) baking soda

5 large (250 g/8.8 oz) eggs

¾ cup (150 g/5.3 oz) granulated sugar

3½ Tbsp (50 g/1.76 oz) unsalted butter, melted

¾ tsp (4 g/0.14 oz) vanilla extract

1.   Preheat the oven to 400°F (204°C). Coat the sides of a half-sheet pan with nonstick cooking spray and line the bottom with a silicone baking mat.

2. In a bowl, sift together the cake flour, cocoa powder, and baking soda and whisk gently to combine.

3. In the bowl of a stand mixer fitted with the whisk attachment, beat the eggs on medium speed until blended, about 1 minute. Gradually add the sugar and beat on high speed until thick and fluffy, about 3 minutes. Fold in the sifted dry ingredients, then fold in the melted butter and vanilla extract. Immediately spread the batter onto the prepared sheet pan and bake for 12 to 15 minutes, or until the cake springs back when lightly touched. Cool the cake in the pan, set on a wire rack, for 10 minutes.

4. Unmold the cake and cool completely.

5. Trim the edges off the cake and cut out twenty 1½-inch squares from the cake.

CHOCOLATE EARL GREY TEA MOUSSE

3.5 oz (100 g) milk chocolate, finely chopped

3.5 oz (100 g) 61% bittersweet chocolate, finely chopped

2½ cups (580 g/20.45 oz) heavy cream

1½ Tbsp (15 g/0.5 oz) Earl Grey tea leaves

4½ large (83 g/3 oz) egg yolks

⅔ cup (133 g/4.7 oz) granulated sugar

3 Tbsp (44 g/1.5 oz) water

1. Place the chocolates in a medium bowl and set aside.

2. In a small saucepan, bring 1 cup (232 g/8.18 oz) of the cream to a gentle boil over medium-high heat. Stir in the tea leaves, remove the pan from the heat, cover, and allow to infuse for 8 minutes.

3. Strain the hot cream-tea mixture over the chocolate and let stand for 1 minute to melt the chocolate. Whisk until smooth.

4. In the bowl of a stand mixer fitted with the whisk attachment, begin beating the egg yolks on low speed.

5. While the yolks are beating, in a small saucepan, combine the sugar with the water and cook over high heat, occasionally brushing down the sides of the pan with a wet pastry brush to prevent crystals from forming, and watching carefully, until the syrup registers 248°F (117°C) on a candy thermometer. Slowly pour the hot syrup over the beating yolks. Increase the speed to medium-high and beat until cool.

6. In the bowl of a stand mixer fitted with the whisk attachment, whip the remaining 1½ cups (348 g/12.27 oz) of the cream at high speed until medium peaks form.

7. Gently fold the beaten yolks into the chocolate mixture. Fold in the whipped cream. Cover the bowl and refrigerate until ready to serve.

EARL GREY TEA SYRUP

¾ cup (175 g/6.17 oz) water

¾ cup plus 1½ Tbsp (170 g/6 oz) granulated sugar

1½ Tbsp (15 g/0.5 oz) Earl Grey tea leaves

1. In a small saucepan, combine the water and sugar and bring to a boil over medium-high heat. Stir in the tea, remove from the heat, cover, and allow to infuse for 5 minutes.

2. Strain the syrup and discard the tea leaves. Refrigerate, covered, until ready to serve.

GRAPEFRUIT AND ORANGE GELÉE

5 sheets (10 g/0.35 oz) gelatin (silver grade)

2 cups (484 g/17 oz) freshly squeezed orange juice

2 cups (484 g/17 oz) freshly squeezed grapefruit juice

⅓ cup (67 g/2.3 oz) granulated sugar

1¼ Tbsp (10 g/0.35 oz) cornstarch

1.   Line a 9 by 5-inch loaf pan with plastic wrap.

2.   Fill a medium bowl halfway with cold water and add the gelatin sheets. Allow to soften for 10 minutes.

3.   In a medium saucepan, combine the juices and sugar and bring to a boil. Continue to boil until the juices are reduced by half, about 30 minutes. In a small bowl, stir the cornstarch with a small amount of water to make a smooth mixture. Add to the reduced juice and bring to a boil. Continue to boil, stirring, for 1 minute. Strain the mixture through a fine-mesh sieve into a bowl. Drain the gelatin, squeezing it to remove the excess water, and add it to the hot juice mixture, stirring until the gelatin has dissolved. Pour the juice into the prepared pan and freeze for at least 1 hour, until firm.

4.   Unmold the block of gelée and, using a sharp knife, cut it into 1½-inch squares. Refrigerate, covered, or until ready to serve.

CHOCOLATE SPRAY

7 oz (200 g) milk chocolate, chopped

7 oz (200 g) cocoa butter, chopped

Place the milk chocolate and cocoa butter in a medium, stainless steel bowl and set the bowl over a saucepan filled one-third of the way with barely simmering water. Heat, stirring frequently, until melted. Strain through a fine-mesh sieve into another bowl. Place the bowl over a pan of hot water to keep it warm.

ASSEMBLY

Orange and grapefruit suprêmes (page 348)

1.   Scrape the Chocolate Earl Grey Mousse into a pastry bag fitted with a medium, plain tip and pipe the mousse halfway up the sides of eight 2¼-inch cube molds. Using a spoon, spread the mousse up the sides of each mold, forming a well in the center. Place a Chocolate Génoise square into each mold and brush it liberally with the Earl Grey Tea Syrup. Place a cube of Grapefruit and Orange Gelée on top of the cake and cover it with more mousse, almost filling each mold. Place another cake square on top, pressing it down slightly, and brush it with more syrup. Freeze until firm, at least 2 hours.

2.   Dip the bottom and sides of each mold into hot water and push the desserts out. Freeze the unmolded desserts for at least 1 hour, or until firm.

3.   Place the Chocolate Spray into the sprayer and coat the sides and top of each dessert cube. Place each cube on a dessert plate and allow to defrost for 30 minutes. Garnish each plate with 2 Meringue Sticks and some citrus suprêmes.

TARTS

SWEET TARTS CAN TAKE MANY FORMS, as you'll see in this chapter, which has a mix of classic tarts and newer variations. Though we often think of the classic pâte sucrée shell for tart bases, tarts can be made with a variety of different doughs. In my Banana Tart with White Chocolate Mousse and Passion Fruit Sauce, for example, I layer phyllo dough sheets with butter and finely chopped cashews in a tart ring for the shell. Puff pastry is the dough of choice in my Lucas Carton Fig Tart and my Apple Croustade, while the Carrot Cake Tart stretches the definition of tart: It's a dome of carrot cake inverted onto a round of Sablé Breton and then covered with meringue. Tarts can be made molded in tart rings or pans, or can be free-form. As for fillings, the possibilities are endless. Here you'll find everything from fruit to chocolate to red wine tarts. The tart really has no limits in how you present or interpret it.

APPLE CROUSTADE

THIS TART WAS INSPIRED BY THE CLASSIC *CROUSTADE AUX POMMES* from the southwest of France. In a traditional croustade recipe, you must use duck fat in the dough, which may not appeal to everyone's taste. I put my own twist on this dessert by topping it with strips of flaky phyllo dough, a crispy contrast to the tender apple filling. I also add a little Armagnac to the sautéed apples, which gives them a nice warm flavor. My favorite apple to use here is La Reine de Reinette, which we get from Canada, but I also recommend McCoy and Fuji apples.

MAKES 6 SERVINGS

> COMPONENTS
>
> **ALMOND CREAM**
> **PUFF PASTRY ROUNDS**
> **APPLE FILLING**
> **PHYLLO STRIPS**
>
> PERFECT MATCH | Étienne Dupont Organic Cidre Bouché Brut de Normandie, France

ALMOND CREAM (page 341)

Prepare the Almond Cream, cover, and refrigerate until ready to serve. (You'll only need a small amount, but you can freeze the extra, well-wrapped, for up to 3 months.)

PUFF PASTRY ROUNDS

1 lb (454 g) Puff Pastry (page 343)

Almond Cream (above)

1.   Preheat the oven to 375°F (191°C). Line a half-sheet pan with a silicone baking mat.

2.   On a lightly floured work surface, roll the Puff Pastry out to a rough circle with a thickness of about ⅛ inch. Dock the dough well with a pastry docker or the tines of a fork. Transfer the dough to a half-sheet pan and freeze for at least 20 minutes before cutting.

3.   Using a small plate or plastic lid as a guide, cut out six 5-inch rounds from the dough with a paring knife. Arrange the rounds on the prepared sheet pan and spread a thin layer of Almond Cream onto each round, leaving a 1-inch border around the edge.

4.   Bake the rounds until the pastry just begins to lightly brown and the Almond Cream is partially baked, about 10 minutes. Remove the pan from the oven and set it on a wire rack while you prepare the filling and topping.

APPLE FILLING

7 Tbsp (100 g/3.5 oz) unsalted butter

¼ cup (100 g/3.5 oz) granulated sugar

3 apples (La Reine de Reinette, McCoy, or Fuji), peeled, cored, and diced

⅓ cup (30 g/1 oz) pine nuts, toasted

2 Tbsp (28 g/1 oz) Armagnac

Melt the butter in a sauté pan over medium heat. Add the sugar and cook, stirring occasionally, until the sugar dissolves. Add the diced apples and cook, stirring occasionally, until the apples are tender, about 4 minutes. Stir in the toasted pine nuts and the Armagnac and cook for another minute. Remove from the heat and set aside.

PHYLLO STRIPS

12 (9 by 14-inch) sheets phyllo dough

12 Tbsp (146 g/5.16 oz) Clarified Butter (page 348)

Place a sheet of the phyllo dough on a cutting board and brush it with some of the Clarified Butter. Top with another phyllo sheet and brush with more butter. Cut the phyllo lengthwise into 2-inch-wide strips. Place the strips on a piece of parchment or wax paper, and top with another piece of paper. Repeat with the remaining phyllo sheets, to form strips from a total of 6 layered phyllo sheet pairs, stacking them on top of each other between sheets of paper. Place the stack in the refrigerator for 10 minutes to firm up the butter slightly and make the strips easier to handle.

ASSEMBLY

1.   Preheat the oven to 350°F (177°C). Pile a rounded mound of Apple Filling onto each parbaked Puff Pastry Round, leaving a ½-inch border around the edge. Take a chilled Phyllo Strip and, starting from the outside edge, place it on the filling, spiraling the strip toward the center, pinching and ruffling the strip as you go and working your way in rows toward the center. Use as many phyllo strips as necessary, overlapping the strips slightly. Repeat with the remaining Puff Pastry Rounds and Phyllo Strips.

2.   Bake the croustades for 8 to 10 minutes, or until the phyllo is golden brown. Serve immediately.

WARM LEMON TART with FRESH RASPBERRIES, LEMON-BASIL SHERBET, and BASIL OIL

THIS IS A VARIATION on one of the most popular recipes in my first book, *Simply Sensational Desserts* (Broadway Books, 1999). It's a perfect lemon tart that also happens to be incredibly easy to prepare. Of course you can serve it on its own, but here I dress it up with fresh raspberries, basil oil, Lemon-Basil Sherbet, and a lacy Lemon Tuile. The tart shells, sherbet, and tuiles can all be made the day before serving.

MAKES 8 SERVINGS

COMPONENTS

TART SHELLS
LEMON CREAM
LEMON-BASIL SHERBET
BASIL OIL
LEMON TUILES

SPECIAL EQUIPMENT | 4-inch pastry cutter; ten 3-inch tart rings; ice cream machine; squeeze bottle

PERFECT MATCH | Il Gusto della Costa Limoncello, Campania, Italy

TART SHELLS

Basic Sweet Tart Dough (page 332)

1. Preheat the oven to 375°F (191°C).

2. Place the dough on a lightly floured work surface and roll it out to a thickness of 1/10 inch. Using a 4-inch pastry cutter, cut out 8 rounds from the dough and press them into 3-inch-diameter by ¾-inch-high tart rings. Roll a rolling pin over the top of the rings and remove the excess dough. Prick the bottoms of the tart shells and arrange them on a sheet pan. Bake for 10 to 12 minutes, or until they are just beginning to turn golden brown. Cool on a wire rack and remove the rings.

LEMON CREAM

Finely grated zest and juice of 3 lemons

3 large (150 g/5.3 oz) eggs

⅔ cup (132 g/4.6 oz) granulated sugar

3 Tbsp (42 g/1.5 oz) unsalted butter, cubed

Fill a small pot with water and bring the water to a boil over high heat. Reduce the heat to medium-low so that the water is just at a simmer. Combine the lemon zest, lemon juice, eggs, and sugar in a heatproof medium bowl and place the bowl directly over the simmering water. Cook the mixture, whisking constantly, until it thickens, about 4 minutes. Remove from the heat, add the cubed butter, and whisk until the butter is completely emulsified. Pass the filling through a fine-mesh sieve into a bowl and set aside to cool.

LEMON-BASIL SHERBET

1 cup (250 g/8.8 oz) freshly squeezed lemon juice

1 cup (242 g/8.5 oz) whole milk

1 cup (236 g/8.3 oz) water

2 cups (400 g/14.1 oz) granulated sugar

1 tsp (3 g/0.1 oz) sorbet stabilizer

2 sprigs fresh basil

Zest of 3 lemons

1.   Combine all of the ingredients except for the lemon zest in a medium saucepan and bring to a boil over medium-high heat. Remove from the heat and remove and discard the basil sprigs. Add the lemon zest and transfer the mixture to a stainless steel bowl. Place the bowl in an ice bath and allow to stand, stirring occasionally, until cool. Cover the bowl and refrigerate the sherbet base for at least 4 hours, or overnight.

2.   Process the base in an ice cream machine according to the manufacturer's instructions. Scrape the sherbet into an airtight container and freeze for at least 3 hours before serving.

BASIL OIL

1 cup packed (60 g/2.1 oz) fresh basil leaves

¾ cup (175 g/6.17 oz) extra-virgin olive oil

Remove the stems from the basil. Fill a saucepan halfway with water and bring it to a boil over high heat. Add the basil leaves and cook just until the water returns to a boil. Drain the leaves and immediately plunge them into ice water. Pat the leaves dry with paper towels and place them in a blender with the olive oil. Process until smooth. Transfer the Basil Oil to a squeeze bottle.

LEMON TUILES

Orange Tuile batter (page 339)

1.   Prepare the Orange Tuile batter, replacing the orange juice with lemon juice.

2.   Preheat the oven to 350°F (177°C). Line a half-sheet pan with a silicone baking mat and, using a small, offset metal spatula, spread a thin, even layer of the tuile batter over the mat. Bake for about 8 minutes, or until just beginning to turn golden in spots. Cool completely.

3.   Break the cooled tuile rectangle into shards to garnish the dessert.

ASSEMBLY

4 cups (452 g/1 lb) fresh raspberries

Fried basil leaves (page 346)

1.   Position a rack in the center of the oven. Preheat the oven to 375°F (191°C).

2.   Place the tart shells on a sheet pan and divide the Lemon Cream equally among them. Bake the tarts for 5 to 7 minutes, or until the custard just begins to set.

3.   Arrange a warm tart in the center of a plate and arrange fresh raspberries around its top edge. Form a quenelle from the Lemon-Basil Sherbet and place it on the tart. Garnish the sherbet with a fried basil leaf. Drizzle some Basil Oil on the plate and garnish the tart with two shards of Lemon Tuile.

LUCAS CARTON FIG TART with CARAMELIZED FIGS

THIS WAS A SIGNATURE DESSERT AT LUCAS CARTON IN PARIS when I worked there, and it was a favorite of Chef Alain Senderens. It's a simple dessert, an open-faced tart that showcases the spicy, musky flavor of the Black Mission fig. I have to admit that I would bitch and moan every time I had to make this dessert, because it has to be "brûléed" à la minute, and you have to do it just right, or you'll end up burning the puff pastry base. The best technique is to sprinkle sugar on one area of the tart with one hand and immediately caramelize it with a blowtorch that you hold in your other hand. If you sprinkle the whole tart with sugar first, the sugar sinks into the figs and becomes difficult to caramelize.

MAKES 8 SERVINGS

COMPONENTS

PUFF PASTRY ROUNDS
SPICED FIG PULP

SPECIAL EQUIPMENT | 3-inch round pastry cutter; blowtorch

PERFECT MATCH | 2008 Zind-Humbrecht Riesling Brand Grand Cru, Alsace, France

PUFF PASTRY ROUNDS

1 lb (454 g) Puff Pastry (page 343)

Confectioners' sugar, for dusting

1.   Preheat the oven to 375°F (191°C).

2.   On a lightly floured work surface, roll the puff pastry out to a thickness of ⅛ inch. Using a 3-inch round pastry cutter, cut out 8 rounds from the dough and prick them well with the tines of a fork. Place the rounds on a half-sheet pan and place a piece of parchment paper, then another half-sheet pan, on top. Bake for 20 to 25 minutes, or until lightly browned. Remove the pan from the oven and preheat the broiler. Take off the top sheet pan and parchment paper. Dust the rounds with confectioners' sugar and broil until the sugar caramelizes, about 3 to 5 minutes. Cool the rounds on the sheet pan, set on a wire rack.

SPICED FIG PULP

20 (800 g/28.2 oz) ripe Black Mission figs

Pinch of Chinese five-spice powder

Pinch of ground cinnamon

Cut each fig in half and, using a small spoon, scoop the pulp into a bowl. Mash the pulp up a bit with a fork and stir in the spices.

ASSEMBLY

12 Black Mission figs

½ cup firmly packed (100 g/3.5 oz) light brown sugar

Spoon a rounded ¼ cup (90 g/3.17 oz) of the Spiced Fig Pulp onto a Puff Pastry Round and smooth it into a mound with a small, offset metal spatula. Repeat with the remaining Puff Pastry Rounds and fig pulp. Thinly slice the figs and lay the slices over each dome, overlapping the slices slightly and making sure that the puff pastry bases are covered, or they may burn. Holding some of the sugar in the fingers of your left hand and a blowtorch in your right hand, sprinkle some sugar onto the figs and immediately caramelize it with the torch. Continue working your way around the tart until all of the figs are caramelized. Serve immediately.

BANANA TART with WHITE CHOCOLATE CREAM and PASSION FRUIT SAUCE

THIS WAS A SIGNATURE DESSERT at Le Bernardin that I developed when I first came to New York in 1990. This simple tart has a dramatic presentation, featuring an elegant cylindrical tuile garnish on top. The tart itself has a phyllo crust baked with salted cashews, and a filling of warm sautéed bananas flavored with Myers's dark rum. A subtle White Chocolate Cream tops the bananas, and a Passion Fruit Sauce lends some acidity to counter the dessert's sweetness.

MAKES 8 SERVINGS

COMPONENTS

WHITE CHOCOLATE CREAM
PHYLLO TARTS
BANANA FILLING
PASSION FRUIT SAUCE
TUILE GARNISH

SPECIAL EQUIPMENT | 4-inch round pastry cutter; 5-inch round pastry cutter; eight 4-inch tart rings; eight 4-ounce ramekins; pastry comb with ¼-Inch square teeth; slender rolling pin; squeeze bottle

PERFECT MATCH | 1979 Rhum Trois Rivières, Martinique

WHITE CHOCOLATE CREAM

21 oz (600 g) white chocolate, chopped

2 cups (464 g/16.36 oz) heavy cream

1. Line a half-sheet pan with parchment paper.

2. Place the white chocolate in a medium stainless steel bowl and place the bowl over a pot filled one-third of the way with barely simmering water. Heat the chocolate, stirring occasionally, until melted and smooth. Set the chocolate aside to cool.

3. In the bowl of a stand mixer fitted with the whisk attachment, whip the cream to soft peaks. Stir about one-quarter of the whipped cream into the melted chocolate to lighten it, then gently fold in the remaining cream. Spread out the cream onto the prepared pan in an even layer and place the pan in the freezer for at least 2 hours, or until the cream is firm.

4. Remove the pan from the freezer and, using a 4-inch round pastry cutter, cut out 8 rounds from the cream. Place the rounds on a sheet pan, lightly cover them, and freeze until ready to serve.

PHYLLO TARTS

7 Tbsp (100 g/3.5 oz) Clarified Butter (see page 348), melted

4 (13 by 18-inch) sheets phyllo dough

¾ cup (100 g/3.5 oz) finely chopped salted cashews

1.   Position a rack in the center of the oven. Preheat the oven to 375°F (190°C). Line a half-sheet pan with parchment paper and brush the paper with Clarified Butter. Place a sheet of the phyllo dough on the parchment paper, brush with more clarified butter, sprinkle with some of the cashews, and cover with a second sheet of phyllo dough. Cover the dough with plastic wrap and flatten the phyllo by running the back of a heavy pot over it. Remove the plastic wrap and brush with more clarified butter. Cover with a third phyllo sheet, brush with clarified butter, add the fourth phyllo sheet, cover with plastic wrap, and flatten again with the pot.

2.   Using a 5-inch round pastry cutter, cut out 8 rounds from the phyllo layers. Place each round inside a 4-inch tart ring, pressing the dough against the sides. Chill in the refrigerator for 10 minutes.

3.   Place the chilled phyllo rings on a sheet pan. Place a 4-ounce ramekin in each phyllo shell to weigh it down, and bake for 5 minutes. Remove the ramekins and bake for another 2 to 3 minutes, or until the shells are golden. Cool completely.

BANANA FILLING

3½ Tbsp (50 g/1.76 oz) unsalted butter

6 medium (480 g/17 oz) bananas, sliced into ½-inch pieces

1 Tbsp (12 g/0.42 oz) granulated sugar

¼ cup (55 g/2 oz) Myers's dark rum

Melt the butter in a sauté pan over medium-high heat. Add the bananas and sauté while gradually adding the sugar. Cook until the sugar has dissolved. Pour in the rum and very carefully use a flame igniter to flambé the rum. Allow to cook until the alcohol is cooked off and the flame dies out.

PASSION FRUIT SAUCE

4 large (74 g/2.6 oz) egg yolks

¼ cup plus 2 Tbsp (75 g/2.6 oz) granulated sugar

1 Tbsp (8 g/0.28 oz) pastry cream powder (see Sources, page 349) or cornstarch

1 cup (250 g/8.8 oz) passion fruit purée

1 cup (250 g/8.8 oz) half-and-half

1.   Beat the egg yolks, sugar, and pastry cream powder or cornstarch in a large bowl with a wire whisk until blended and smooth.

2.   In a medium saucepan, bring the passion fruit purée and half-and-half to a boil and remove from the heat. Whisking rapidly, add about ½ cup (120 ml/4 fl oz) of the hot half-and-half mixture to the egg yolks. Pour this mixture back into the remaining half-and-half mixture and stir, scraping the bottom and sides of the saucepan constantly with a wooden spoon or silicone spatula to prevent lumps from forming. Continue stirring for several minutes, cooking gently over medium-low

heat until the sauce thickens slightly and coats the back of a spoon, about 3 minutes. Strain through a fine-mesh sieve into a bowl and set the bowl in an ice bath to cool. Keep refrigerated until ready to serve.

TUILE GARNISH

Vanilla Tuile batter (see page 338)

1. Position a rack in the center of the oven and preheat the oven to 375°F (191°C). Line a half-sheet pan with a silicone baking mat.

2. Spread some of the batter lengthwise onto the baking mat, forming a thin, 5 by 16-inch rectangle. Drag a pastry comb (with ¼-inch square teeth) lengthwise through the batter, making long, clean, unattached lines—make sure to leave one end of the lines connected to hold the garnish together. Bake the batter for 7 to 8 minutes, or until the tuile has colored slightly. Run a spatula under the entire length of the tuile to release it from the sheet. While still warm, wrap it around a slender rolling pin, until you have a spiral, tube-shaped tuile. Let it set and store it in an airtight container. Repeat to make a total of 8 tuile garnishes.

ASSEMBLY

Pulp of 4 passion fruits, for garnish

Place the Phyllo Tart on a plate. Arrange a layer of the Banana Filling on the bottom of the tart. Cover with a round of White Chocolate Cream. Decorate with the Tuile Garnish, placing the connected end at the bottom, toward the dessert. Place the Passion Fruit Sauce in a squeeze bottle and squeeze out teardrops of sauce on the plate all around the bottom edge of the tart. Garnish the plate with drops of passion fruit pulp.

CARROT CAKE TART with CREAM CHEESE ICE CREAM, HONEY-CARROT EMULSION, ORANGE BLOSSOM MERINGUE, and FRIED CARROTS

⁂ THIS DESSERT HAS ALL THE ELEMENTS of a classic carrot cake, but in quasi-tart form. First the carrot cake is baked in a dome shape, then it is unmolded onto a sablé round and frosted dramatically with an Orange Blossom Meringue that is lightly browned with a torch. The classic cream cheese frosting for carrot cake becomes an ice cream, which is served alongside the tart with a colorful stack of deep-fried julienne of carrots and a drizzle of carrot jus.

MAKES 8 SERVINGS

COMPONENTS

CARROT CAKES
SABLÉ ROUNDS
HONEY-CARROT EMULSION
FRIED CARROT GARNISH
CARROT JUS
CREAM CHEESE ICE CREAM
ORANGE BLOSSOM MERINGUE

SPECIAL EQUIPMENT | eight 3-inch silicone dome molds; 2¾-inch round pastry cutter; ice cream machine; blowtorch; candy thermometer

PERFECT MATCH | La Spinetta (Rivetti) Moscato d'Asti Vigneto Biancospino, Italy

---

CARROT CAKES

¾ cup (90 g/3.17 oz) cake flour

½ tsp (2 g/0.07 oz) baking powder

¼ tsp plus ⅛ tsp (2 g/0.07 oz) baking soda

2 tsp (3 g/0.1 oz) ground cinnamon

Pinch of freshly grated nutmeg

Pinch of salt

Pinch of freshly ground white pepper

2 large (100 g/3.5 oz) eggs

½ cup firmly packed (100 g/3.5 oz) light brown sugar

⅓ cup (75 g/2.6 oz) vegetable oil

2 Tbsp (28 g/1 oz) unsalted butter, melted

¼ cup (35 g/1.2 oz) golden raisins, plumped in hot water for 1 hour and drained

⅓ cup (28 g/1 oz) walnuts, toasted and chopped (see Toasted Nuts, page 346)

¾ cup (70 g/2.5 oz) peeled and grated carrots

1. Position a rack in the center of the oven. Preheat the oven to 350°F (177°C).

2. In a medium bowl, sift together the cake flour, baking powder, baking soda, cinnamon, nutmeg, salt, and pepper and gently whisk to combine.

3. In the bowl of a stand mixer fitted with the whisk attachment, beat the eggs and sugar together on high speed for 5 to 8 minutes, until light and thick. Reduce the speed to low and slowly drizzle in the vegetable oil and melted butter. Remove the bowl from the mixer stand and gently fold in the sifted dry ingredients by hand. Fold in the raisins, walnuts, and carrots. Divide the batter equally among eight 3-inch silicone dome molds and bake for 15 to 18 minutes, or until a tester inserted into the center of a cake comes out clean. Let the cakes cool in the molds for 10 minutes.

4. Unmold the cakes and cool completely on a wire rack.

SABLÉ ROUNDS

Sablé Breton Dough (page 333)

1. Position a rack in the center of the oven. Preheat the oven to 375°F (191°C). Line a half-sheet pan with a silicone baking mat.

2. Place the dough disk on a work surface and roll the dough out to a thickness of ¼ inch. Using a 2¾-inch round cutter, cut out 8 rounds from the dough and prick them well with the tines of a fork. Place the rounds on the prepared sheet pan and bake for 7 to 9 minutes, or until golden brown. Cool the rounds on the sheet pan, set on a wire rack.

HONEY-CARROT EMULSION

2 medium carrots, peeled and cut into 1-inch chunks

2 Tbsp (42 g/1.5 oz) honey

Fill a small saucepan halfway with water and bring the water to a boil. Add the carrot pieces and cook until soft, about 15 minutes. Drain the carrots and place them in the bowl of a food processor with the honey. Process until smooth. Transfer the emulsion to a small bowl, cover, and set aside at room temperature.

FRIED CARROT GARNISH

2 medium (170 g/6 oz) carrots, peeled

Vegetable oil, for deep frying

1. Using a mandoline set to the thinnest setting, slice the carrots lengthwise into thin strips (0.03 in/0.75 mm thick). Make a stack of several strips and, using a chef's knife, cut the stack lengthwise into very thin julienne.

2. Pour vegetable oil in a deep fryer or deep, straight-sided saucepan to a depth of 3 inches. Heat the oil to 370°F (188°C). Line a sheet pan with paper towels.

3. Working in batches, fry the carrot strips for 2 to 3 minutes, or until they just begin to brown lightly in spots. Using a slotted spoon or spider, transfer the fried carrots to the paper towels to drain and cool.

CARROT JUS

1 cup (250 g/8.8 oz) fresh carrot juice

1 cup (242 g/8.5 oz) freshly squeezed orange juice

1 Tbsp (8 g/0.28 oz) cornstarch

1 Tbsp plus 1 tsp (20 g/0.7 oz) water

1. In a small saucepan, bring the carrot and orange juices to a boil.

2. In a small bowl, combine the cornstarch and water until smooth. Whisk the cornstarch mixture into the juices and continue to boil, whisking constantly, for 1 minute. Remove the pot from the heat and set aside to cool.

CREAM CHEESE ICE CREAM

1 cup plus 3 Tbsp (250 g/8.8 oz) cream cheese, softened

1 cup (250 g/8.8 oz) whole milk

1 Tbsp (15 g/0.5 oz) freshly squeezed lemon juice

⅔ cup (133 g/4.7 oz) granulated sugar

Pinch of salt

½ cup (125 g/4.4 g) heavy cream, chilled

1. In a blender, combine the cream cheese, milk, lemon juice, sugar, and salt and blend until smooth. Transfer the mixture to a bowl and stir in the cream.

2. Process the ice cream base in an ice cream machine according to the manufacturer's instructions. Transfer to an airtight container and freeze for at least 3 hours, or until ready to use.

ORANGE BLOSSOM MERINGUE

1 cup (200 g/7 oz) granulated sugar

⅔ cup (157 g/5.5 oz) water

4 large (120 g/4.2 oz) egg whites

1 tsp (4 g/0.14 oz) orange blossom water

1. When you are ready to serve the desserts, prepare the meringue. In a small saucepan over medium heat, bring the sugar and water to a boil. Continue boiling until the syrup reaches 238°F (114°C) on a candy thermometer (soft-ball stage).

2. Meanwhile, place the egg whites in the bowl of a stand mixer fitted with the whisk attachment and whip on medium speed until opaque and soft peaks form; do not overbeat. With the mixer running on low speed, add the syrup to the whites in a steady stream. Increase the speed to high and beat until cool, about 5 minutes. Add the orange blossom water and mix until blended.

ASSEMBLY

Place a Sablé Round on a plate and spoon some Honey-Carrot Emulsion on top. Place a dome of Carrot Cake on the emulsion. Using a small, offset metal spatula, cover the dome and sablé round with the Orange Blossom Meringue, forming a peak on top so that it is kiss-shaped. Using a blowtorch, carefully brown the meringue. Spoon some emulsion on the plate and arrange a quenelle of the Cream Cheese Ice Cream on top, garnished with some of the Fried Carrot Garnish. Garnish the plate with Carrot Jus.

FROMAGE BLANC SOUFFLÉ TART with BLUEBERRY MARMALADE and FROMAGE BLANC SORBET with CUMIN

FROMAGE BLANC, OR "WHITE CHEESE," also known as *fromage frais*, or "fresh cheese," is a soft, creamy cheese with a mild flavor. It is very common in France, and is now becoming popular in the United States. Brightened with a little added lime zest, fromage blanc makes a wonderful filling for this souffléed tart. The filling puffs up dramatically when baked, and the tarts must then be served immediately, so timing is key here. Also make sure that your tart shells are completely baked before filling them because the baking time is relatively short. I serve these tarts with a quenelle of Fromage Blanc Sorbet with Cumin on top of a homemade Blueberry Marmalade flavored with blueberry liqueur.

MAKES 12 SERVINGS

COMPONENTS

FROMAGE BLANC SOUFFLÉ TART
  TART SHELL
  FROMAGE BLANC SOUFFLÉ
  TART FILLING
BLUEBERRY MARMALADE
FROMAGE BLANC SORBET WITH CUMIN

SPECIAL EQUIPMENT | 4-inch round pastry cutter; twelve 3-inch bottomless tart rings; ice cream machine; medium, plain tip (Atecco #6)

PERFECT MATCH | Di Majo Norante Apianae Moscato del Molise, Italy

TART SHELLS

Basic Sweet Tart Dough (page 332)

1. Preheat the oven to 375°F (191°C). Line a half-sheet pan with a silicone baking mat.

2. Place the dough on a lightly floured work surface and roll it out to a thickness of ⅛ inch. Using a 4-inch round pastry cutter, cut out 12 rounds from the dough. Drape each round over a 3-inch tart ring and gently pat it into the ring so that it is flush against the sides and "bottom" of the ring. Run a rolling pin over the tops of the rings and remove the excess dough. Prick the bottom of the shell well with the tines of a fork. Place each lined tart ring on the prepared sheet pan and bake for 12 to 15 minutes, or until golden brown around the edges and baked through. Cool the tart shells completely and remove the rings.

BLUEBERRY MARMALADE

3½ cups (450 g/15.8 oz) fresh blueberries

⅓ cup (86 g/3 oz) crème de mûre or crème de cassis liqueur

⅓ cup (66 g/2.3 oz) granulated sugar

Finely grated zest of 1 lime

In a small saucepan over medium heat, combine the blueberries, liqueur, and sugar. Cook, stirring, for about 5 minutes, until all of the sugar has dissolved and the blueberries have popped. Remove from the heat, add the lime zest, and set aside to cool.

FROMAGE BLANC SORBET WITH CUMIN

1¼ cups (300 g/10.5 oz) water

1 cup (200 g/7 oz) granulated sugar

2 tsp (4 g/0.14 oz) crushed cumin seeds

Finely grated zest of 1 lime

2 cups (500 g/17.6 oz) fromage blanc (see Sources, page 349)

1 cup (242 g/8.5 oz) sour cream

1 cup (242 g/8.5 oz) plain yogurt

1. In a small saucepan, combine the water, sugar, and cumin seeds. Bring to a boil over high heat, stirring occasionally to dissolve the sugar. Remove from the heat and let stand, covered, for 15 minutes to allow the flavors to infuse. Strain the syrup, then add the lime zest.

2. In a large bowl, using an immersion blender, combine the fromage blanc, sour cream, and yogurt. Add the sugar syrup and blend well. Cover the bowl and refrigerate the sorbet base for at least 4 hours.

3. Process the base in an ice cream machine according to the manufacturer's instructions. Transfer the sorbet to an airtight container and freeze for at least 2 hours, or until ready to serve.

FROMAGE BLANC SOUFFLÉ TART FILLING

½ cup (125 g/4.4 oz) fromage blanc

2 large (37 g/1.3 oz) egg yolks

2 Tbsp (16 g/0.56 oz) cornstarch

Finely grated zest of 1 lime

2 large (60 g/2.1 oz) egg whites

2½ Tbsp (33 g/1.16 oz) granulated sugar

1. Prepare the filling within an hour of the final baking. In a bowl, combine the fromage blanc, egg yolks, cornstarch, and lime zest.

2. In the bowl of a stand mixer fitted with the whisk attachment, whip the whites on high speed until they just turn opaque. Gradually add half of the sugar and continue to whip until they begin to stiffen. Add the remaining sugar and whip until stiff peaks form.

3. Using a rubber spatula, gently fold the whites into the fromage blanc mixture. Transfer the mixture to a pastry bag fitted with a medium, plain tip and pipe it into the prebaked tart shells, filling them. Refrigerate the filled tarts for 10 minutes.

ASSEMBLY

3 Tbsp cumin seeds, lightly toasted

Preheat the oven to 350°F (177°C). Bake the Fromage Blanc Soufflé Tarts for 10 to 12 minutes, or until the filling is puffed and cracked in spots. Spoon a pool of Blueberry Marmalade onto a dessert plate and place a quenelle of Fromage Blanc Sorbet with Cumin on top. Sprinkle some cumin seeds on top of the sorbet, place a hot tart next to the sauce, and serve immediately.

MASCARPONE TART with ROASTED FIGS and MASCARPONE ICE CREAM

The sweet, musky flavor of Black Mission figs, which become available in late June, is an ideal match for tangy mascarpone cheese. This beautiful tart features a mascarpone-fig filling, topped with glazed Roasted Figs and a garnet-colored Red Wine Sauce. I serve it with a Mascarpone Ice Cream, and it's the perfect combination of flavors. Figs don't ripen after they are picked, so make sure they are ripe when you buy them—they should be tender to the touch and have a sweet, earthy fragrance.

MAKES 8 SERVINGS

COMPONENTS

MASCARPONE ICE CREAM
TART SHELLS
MASCARPONE FIG CREAM
RED WINE SAUCE
ROASTED FIGS

SPECIAL EQUIPMENT | ice cream machine; 4-inch pastry cutter; eight 3-inch-diameter by ¾-inch-high tart rings; pepper mill

PERFECT MATCH | 2001 Hastae Grappa di Barbera d'Asti Quorum, Italy

MASCARPONE ICE CREAM

1 cup (250 g/8.8 oz) whole milk

⅔ cup (154 g/5.4 oz) heavy cream

1 vanilla bean, split lengthwise and seeds scraped

6 large (112 g/4 oz) egg yolks

½ cup plus 2 Tbsp (125 g/4.4 oz) granulated sugar

⅓ cup plus 1 Tbsp (100 g/3.5 oz) mascarpone cheese

1. In a medium saucepan, combine the milk, cream, and vanilla bean pod and seeds and bring to a gentle boil over medium heat.

2. In a medium bowl, whisk together the egg yolks and sugar until pale. Whisk about half of the hot milk mixture into the yolks, then return the entire mixture to the saucepan with the remaining milk mixture and cook over medium heat, stirring constantly with a wooden spoon until it thickens enough to coat the back of the spoon and reaches 175°F (79°C) on an instant-read thermometer; do not let the mixture boil, or the egg yolks will curdle. Remove the pot from the heat and pass the mixture immediately through a fine-mesh sieve into a bowl. Whisk in the mascarpone cheese until smooth. Set the bowl in an ice bath and stir frequently until cold.

3. Transfer the ice cream base to an airtight container and refrigerate for at least 4 hours, or overnight.

4. Process the base in an ice cream machine according to the manufacturer's instructions. (Be careful not to overchurn the ice cream or it will become grainy.) Transfer the ice cream to an airtight container and freeze until ready to serve.

TART SHELLS

Basic Sweet Tart Dough (page 332)

1. Preheat the oven to 375°F (191°C).

2. Place the dough on a lightly floured work surface and roll it out to a thickness of ⅒ inch. Using a 4-inch pastry cutter, cut out 8 rounds from the dough and press them into 3-inch-diameter by ¾-inch-high tart rings. Roll a rolling pin over the top of the rings and remove the excess dough. Prick the bottoms of the tart shells with the tines of a fork and arrange them on a sheet pan. Bake for 8 to 10 minutes, or until they are just beginning to turn golden brown in spots. Cool on a wire rack.

MASCARPONE FIG CREAM

4 ripe Black Mission figs

1¼ cups (300 g/10.5 oz) mascarpone cheese

3⅓ large (62 g/2.1 oz) egg yolks

¾ cup (150 g/5.3 oz) granulated sugar

4 large (120 g/4.2 oz) egg whites

232

1. Cut the figs in half and scoop out the pulp with a spoon. Pass the pulp through a fine-mesh sieve into a small bowl. Add the mascarpone cheese and mix until smooth. Set aside.

2. In the bowl of a stand mixer fitted with the whisk attachment, whip the egg yolks with ½ cup (100 g/3.5 oz) of the sugar on high speed until thick and doubled in volume, about 8 minutes. Fold in the mascarpone-fig mixture.

3. In a clean mixer bowl, using a clean whisk attachment, whip the egg whites on medium-high speed until soft peaks begin to form. Gradually add the remaining ¼ cup (50 g/1.7 oz) sugar and whip on high speed until stiff peaks form. Fold the meringue into the egg yolk mixture. Cover the bowl and refrigerate until ready to use.

RED WINE SAUCE

> 1 sheet (2 g/0.07 oz) gelatin (silver grade)
>
> 2 cups (500 g/17.6 oz) red wine
>
> ½ cup (100 g/3.5 oz) granulated sugar
>
> Finely grated zest of ½ lime
>
> Finely grated zest of ½ orange
>
> 1 whole clove
>
> 2 whole black peppercorns

1. Fill a medium bowl halfway with cold water and add the gelatin sheet. Allow to soften for 10 minutes.

2. In a small saucepan, combine the remaining ingredients and bring to a boil over medium-high heat, stirring, just until the sugar has dissolved. Continue to boil the red wine mixture until it has reduced by half, about 6 minutes. Strain the mixture into a bowl. Drain the gelatin, squeezing it to remove the excess water, and stir it into the red wine mixture until dissolved. The sauce should be served warm.

ROASTED FIGS

> 3 Tbsp (42 g/1.5 oz) unsalted butter
>
> ½ cup (100 g/3.5 oz) granulated sugar
>
> 1 tsp (1.5 g/0.05 oz) ground cinnamon
>
> 24 ripe Black Mission figs

Preheat the oven to 400°F (204°C). Preheat an ovenproof sauté pan over medium-high heat for 1 minute. Add the butter and swirl the pan until it is almost melted. Add the sugar and cinnamon and stir to combine. Add the figs and cook, tossing them gently to coat them with the sugar mixture, for about 1 minute. Transfer the pan to the oven and roast the figs for 5 minutes, or until they are tender.

ASSEMBLY

> 3 to 5 turns freshly ground black pepper
>
> 2 ripe Black Mission figs, sliced

Fill each Tart Shell three-quarters full with Mascarpone Fig Cream and place on a plate. Arrange 3 Roasted Figs, stem side up, on top of the cream on each tart. Glaze the figs with some of the warm Red Wine Sauce and top with a few turns of freshly ground black pepper. Drizzle some sauce on the plate. Place a fig slice on the plate and top with a quenelle of Mascarpone Ice Cream.

MEDITERRANEAN FENNEL TART filled with ANISE CREAM and CANDIED FENNEL

░░ ░░ THERE'S A CERTAIN LEMON TART popular in the South of France that's made with poached fennel, and I love it. When I opened Payard, I decided to make a version of this classic tart, and here's my interpretation. The base is a round of caramelized puff pastry, and on it is a layer of Anise Pastry Cream, with paper-thin slices of Poached Fennel topping the cream. A quenelle of Meyer Lemon Sherbet and a crisp Fennel Chip transform this simple tart, with its unusual combination of flavors, into something really memorable.

MAKES 10 SERVINGS

COMPONENTS

MEYER LEMON SHERBET

ANISE CREAM

PUFF PASTRY ROUNDS

POACHED FENNEL

FENNEL CHIPS

SPECIAL EQUIPMENT | ice cream machine; 3½-inch round pastry cutter; mandoline; medium, plain pastry tip (Ateco #6)

PERFECT MATCH | Vin d'Orange, Provence, France

MEYER LEMON SHERBET

2 cups (400 g/14.1 oz) granulated sugar

1 tsp (5 g/0.17 oz) sorbet stabilizer

Finely grated zest of 3 Meyer lemons

1 cup (236 g/8.3 oz) freshly squeezed Meyer lemon juice

1 cup (242 g/8.5 oz) whole milk

1 cup (236 g/8.3 oz) water

1.   In a small bowl, combine ½ cup (3.5 oz/ 100 g) of the sugar with the sorbet stabilizer and set aside. In a medium saucepan, combine the remaining ½ cup sugar with the lemon zest, lemon juice, milk, and water. Place the pan over medium-high heat and gradually whisk in the sugar mixture. Bring to a boil, whisking occasionally, until the sugar has dissolved. Remove from the heat and transfer the sherbet base to a medium bowl. Set the bowl in an ice bath and stir frequently until cold.

2.   Transfer the base to an airtight container and refrigerate for at least 4 hours, or overnight.

3.   Process the base in an ice cream machine according to the manufacturer's instructions. Transfer the sherbet to an airtight container and freeze until ready to serve.

CARAMELIZED PINEAPPLE-PECAN TART with BROWN BUTTER ICE CREAM

THIS IS A FALL DESSERT I DEVELOPED AT PAYARD, and it combines caramelized pineapple with a pecan tart. I cook the pineapple in caramel and unfiltered apple juice from the farmers' market, giving it a candied, toasty flavor that is a great match for the sweet, roasted nut flavor of the pecan tart. When it's done, the pineapple should be tender, but should offer a slight resistance when pierced with a fork. This tart must be served warm, with a quenelle of Brown Butter Ice Cream melting seductively on top.

MAKES 8 SERVINGS

COMPONENTS

BROWN BUTTER ICE CREAM

CARAMELIZED PINEAPPLE PECAN TART

   PECAN MIX

   CANDIED PECANS

   TART SHELLS

PINEAPPLE CHIPS

CARAMELIZED PINEAPPLE AND SAUCE

SPECIAL EQUIPMENT | ice cream machine; eight 3-inch tart pans; electric slicer; 3½-inch round pastry cutter; 1½-inch round pastry cutter

PERFECT MATCH | Matusalem Gran Reserva 18-Year-Old Rum, Dominican Republic

BROWN BUTTER ICE CREAM

⅓ cup plus 2 Tbsp firmly packed (100 g/3.5 oz) light brown sugar

½ cup (100 g/3.5 oz) granulated sugar

½ tsp (1 g/0.03 oz) sorbet stabilizer

½ tsp (1 g/0.03 oz) glycerol monostearate (available from l'Épicerie, see Sources, page 350)

10 large (192 g/6.7 oz) egg yolks

2 cups (480 g/17 oz) whole milk

½ vanilla bean, split lengthwise and seeds scraped

1⅜ cups (270 g/9.5 oz) Beurre Noisette (page 348)

1. In a medium bowl, combine the brown sugar, sugar, sorbet stabilizer, and glycerol monostearate. Add the egg yolks and whisk until well blended.

2. In a medium saucepan, bring the milk and vanilla bean pod and seeds to a boil over medium heat. Whisk about half of the hot milk mixture into the yolk mixture, then return the entire mixture to the saucepan and cook over medium heat, stirring constantly with a wooden spoon until it thickens enough to coat the back of the spoon and reaches 175°F (79°C) on an instant-read thermometer; do not let the mixture boil, or the egg yolks

will curdle. Remove the pot from the heat and pass the mixture immediately through a fine-mesh sieve into a bowl.

3.   In a medium bowl, mix the Beurre Noisette with an immersion blender until smooth. While blending, gradually add the hot milk mixture and blend until emulsified and smooth.

4.   Fill a large bowl with ice water and place the bowl containing the ice cream base into the bowl of ice water. Let stand, stirring occasionally, until cool. Cover the bowl and refrigerate for 24 hours.

5.   Process the base in an ice cream machine according to the manufacturer's instructions. Transfer the ice cream to an airtight container and freeze until ready to serve.

PECAN MIX

1½ Tbsp (12 g/0.44 oz) all-purpose flour

2 extra-large (110 g/3.8 oz) eggs

½ cup (170 g/6 oz) light corn syrup

⅓ cup firmly packed (75 g/2.6 oz) light brown sugar

Pinch of salt

6⅓ Tbsp (90 g/3.17 oz) unsalted butter, melted

In the bowl of a stand mixer fitted with the whisk attachment, combine the flour, eggs, corn syrup, brown sugar, and salt and whip on medium speed for 10 minutes, or until the mixture has doubled in volume. Stir in the melted butter. Cover the bowl and refrigerate for at least 8 hours, or overnight.

CANDIED PECANS

½ cup (120 g/4.2 oz) water

½ cup plus 1⅛ Tbsp (120 g/4.2 oz) granulated sugar

2 cups (200 g/7 oz) pecan halves

1.   Preheat the oven to 350°F (177°C). Line a half-sheet pan with parchment paper.

2.   In a small saucepan, combine the water and sugar and bring to a boil over medium-high heat, stirring occasionally to dissolve the sugar. Remove the pan from the heat and set aside to cool.

3.   Place the pecans in a medium bowl and pour the syrup over them. Toss to coat the pecans evenly with the syrup. Strain the pecans, scatter them onto the prepared sheet pan, and bake until golden brown, about 8 minutes. Set aside to cool.

PINEAPPLE CHIPS (page 345)

Make the Pineapple Chips as directed, and while they are still warm, curl them around a rolling pin.

TART SHELLS

Basic Sweet Tart Dough (page 332)

1.   Divide the dough into 2 pieces. Wrap 1 piece in plastic wrap and store it in the refrigerator. Place the other piece on a lightly floured work surface and roll it out to a thickness of ⅒ inch. Using a 4-inch pastry cutter,

cut out 4 rounds from the dough and press each into a 3-inch tart pan. Roll a rolling pin over the top of the pan and remove the excess dough. Repeat with the remaining piece of dough and tart pans. Prick the bottoms of the tart shells with the tines of a fork and arrange the shells on a sheet pan. Refrigerate the shells for 20 minutes. Meanwhile, position a rack in the center of the oven and preheat the oven to 375°F (191°C).

2.   Right before baking, line the dough in each pan with aluminum foil or parchment paper and fill with pie weights or dried beans. Bake the tart shells for 7 minutes. Carefully lift the foil, along with the weights, out of the tart pans and bake the crusts for 2 to 3 minutes longer, or until golden around the edges. Transfer the tart pans to a wire rack and cool completely.

CARAMELIZED PINEAPPLE AND SAUCE

1 medium pineapple

1 cup (340 g/12 oz) light corn syrup

1 vanilla bean, split lengthwise

1⅓ cups (350 g/12.3 oz) unfiltered apple juice

¼ cup (60 g/2.1 oz) Myers's dark rum

4¼ Tbsp (60 g/2.1 oz) unsalted butter, cut into cubes

1.   Cut the peel off the pineapple. Slice the pineapple into eight ½-inch-thick wheels. Using a 3½-inch round pastry cutter, cut the pineapple rounds into even circles. Using a 1¼-inch round pastry cutter, cut out the core from each round. Cut any remaining pineapple into ¼-inch cubes to use in the tarts.

2.   In a sauté pan, heat the corn syrup and vanilla bean pod over medium-high heat until the syrup caramelizes and turns a light amber color. Add the pineapple rounds and the apple juice and bring the liquid to a boil, stirring occasionally. Reduce the heat to low and cook for 10 minutes, until the pineapple is tender and translucent around the edges. Transfer the pineapple rounds to a plate and whisk the rum and butter into the liquid in the pan. Continue to whisk until the butter has melted. Strain the sauce through a fine-mesh sieve into a bowl and cover until ready to serve. Warm the sauce just before serving.

PECAN TARTS

Preheat the oven to 350°F (177°C). Arrange the baked Tart Shells on a half-sheet pan. Reserve about ¼ cup of the Candied Pecans to garnish the plates. Divide the remaining pecans among the baked tart shells. Place a few of the reserved pineapple cubes (from the Caramelized Pineapple) on top of the pecans in each tart. Divide the Pecan Mix equally among the tarts, filling each. Bake the tarts for 10 to 12 minutes, or until lightly browned and set.

ASSEMBLY

If the Pecan Tarts are cool, warm them in a 350°F (177°C) oven for 5 minutes. Place a tart in the center of a plate and top it with a Caramelized Pineapple round. Top with a quenelle of Brown Butter Ice Cream. Garnish the ice cream with 2 Pineapple Chips. Finish the plate with some Caramelized Pineapple Sauce and a few of the reserved Candied Pecans.

WARM CHOCOLATE TART with RASPBERRIES, CACAO NIB CRUNCH, and GIANDUJA ICE CREAM

 I SERVED THIS RICH CHOCOLATE TART AT PAYARD, and in my mind it was the perfect bistro dessert—so simple, but perfectly executed and delicious. The richness of the bittersweet chocolate filling is balanced by the acidity of fresh raspberries, which also add a fruity note. The Cacao Nib Crunch adds some much-needed crunch, and the light Gianduja Ice Cream is a refreshing, cool contrast to the warm, rich filling. Once you top them with the ice cream, serve these warm tarts immediately.

MAKES 8 SERVINGS

COMPONENTS

GIANDUJA ICE CREAM

CHOCOLATE TART SHELLS

CACAO NIB CRUNCH

CHOCOLATE FILLING

CHOCOLATE SAUCE

TUILE HOOP

SPECIAL EQUIPMENT | ice cream machine; 4-inch round pastry cutter; eight 3-inch ring molds or tart pans; pastry comb; eight 3-inch-diameter ring molds

PERFECT MATCH | 1977 Graham's Vintage Port, Douro Valley, Portugal

GIANDUJA ICE CREAM

1 oz (28 g) 72% bittersweet chocolate, chopped

0.5 oz (15 g) 64% bittersweet chocolate, chopped

2.5 oz (70 g) gianduja chocolate, chopped

1½ Tbsp (28 g/1 oz) hazelnut paste

2 cups plus 1 Tbsp (500 g/17.6 oz) whole milk

¼ cup (50 g/1.76 oz) granulated sugar

2 Tbsp (14 g/0.5 oz) unsweetened cocoa powder

5 large (93 g/3.3 oz) egg yolks

1½ Tbsp (25 g/0.88 oz) invert sugar

1. Place the chocolates and hazelnut paste in a medium stainless steel bowl, and set the bowl over a pot filled one-third of the way with barely simmering water. Heat, stirring frequently, until the chocolate has melted and the mixture is smooth. Remove the bowl from the heat and set aside.

2. In a medium saucepan, combine the milk, sugar, and cocoa powder and bring to a gentle boil over medium heat.

3. In a medium bowl, whisk together the egg yolks and invert sugar until pale. Whisk about half of the hot milk mixture into the yolks, then return this mixture to the remaining milk mixture in the saucepan and cook over medium heat, stirring constantly with a wooden

spoon, until it thickens enough to coat the back of the spoon and reaches 175°F (79°C) on an instant-read thermometer; do not let the mixture boil, or the egg yolks will curdle. Remove the pot from the heat and whisk in the melted chocolate and hazelnut paste mixture. Pass the ice cream base immediately through a fine-mesh sieve into a bowl. Set the bowl in an ice bath and stir frequently until cold.

4. Transfer the ice cream base to an airtight container and refrigerate for at least 4 hours, or overnight.

5. Process the base in an ice cream machine according to the manufacturer's instructions. (Be careful not to overchurn the ice cream or it will become grainy.) Transfer the ice cream to an airtight container and freeze until ready to serve.

CHOCOLATE TART SHELLS

Chocolate Tart Dough (page 333)

1. Divide the dough into 2 pieces. Wrap 1 piece in plastic wrap and store it in the refrigerator. Place the other piece on a lightly floured work surface and roll it out to a thickness of ⅒ inch. Using the 4-inch pastry cutter, cut out 4 rounds from the dough and press each round into a 3-inch tart pan. Roll a rolling pin over the top of the pans and remove the excess dough. Repeat with the remaining piece of dough and tart pans. Prick the bottoms of the tart shells with the tines of a fork and arrange them on a half-sheet pan. Refrigerate the shells for 20 minutes.

2. Preheat the oven to 375°F (191°C). Bake the tart shells for 8 to 10 minutes, or until the dough is no longer shiny. Cool on a wire rack and remove the tart pans.

CACAO NIB CRUNCH

7¾ Tbsp (110 g/3.8 oz) unsalted butter

2 Tbsp plus 1 tsp (36 g/1.26 oz) whole milk

1¾ Tbsp (36 g/1.26 oz) glucose or light corn syrup

½ cup plus 2½ tsp (110 g/3.8 oz) granulated sugar

2⅓ cups (225 g/8 oz) cacao nibs

1. In a small saucepan, melt the butter with the milk over low heat. Remove from the heat and set aside.

2. Pour the glucose or corn syrup into another small saucepan, and heat over medium heat until hot to the touch, about 1 minute. Gradually add the sugar one-quarter at a time, stirring it into the syrup and cooking until it has dissolved before adding more. When all the sugar is added, remove the pan from the heat and stir in the melted butter mixture until blended. Stir in the cacao nibs. Cool completely.

3. Transfer to a covered container and refrigerate for at least 6 hours, or overnight.

4. Preheat the oven to 375°F (191°C). Line a half-sheet pan with a silicone baking mat. Place a 3-inch ring mold or tart ring on the mat and spoon some of the crumbly cacao nib mixture inside the ring, just to cover the bottom. Leave the ring in place and repeat to make a total of 8 rounds, spacing them 2 inches apart. Bake for about 7 minutes, or until the rounds have browned. Cool the cacao nib rounds on the sheet pan before carefully removing the rings and releasing the rounds from the baking mat with a small, offset metal spatula. Set aside until ready to serve.

CHOCOLATE FILLING

8 oz (225 g) 72% bittersweet chocolate, finely chopped

¾ cup (175 g/6.17 oz) heavy cream

½ cup (120 g/4.2 oz) whole milk

1 large (50 g/1.76 oz) whole egg

1 large (19 g/0.65 oz) egg yolk

24 fresh raspberries

1.   Preheat the oven to 300°F (149°C). Arrange the baked Chocolate Tart Shells on a half-sheet pan.

2.   Place the chocolate in a medium bowl. In a small saucepan, combine the cream and milk and bring to a boil over medium-high heat. Pour over the chocolate and allow to stand for 1 minute to melt the chocolate. Whisk gently until smooth. Whisk the whole egg and yolk into the chocolate mixture until well blended. Divide the filling among the tart shells, filling each almost all the way. (You will have a small amount of filling left over; reserve it for another use.) Press 3 raspberries into the filling in each tart and bake for 12 to 14 minutes, or until the filling is set. Cool the tarts on a wire rack; the tarts will be rewarmed before serving.

CHOCOLATE SAUCE (page 334)

TUILE HOOPS

Vanilla Tuile batter (page 338)

1.   Preheat the oven to 375°F (191°C). Line a half-sheet pan with a silicone baking mat.

2.   Spread a thin layer of the batter into a rectangle that is roughly 3 by 10 inches (it doesn't have to be a perfect rectangle). Run a pastry comb through the batter, forming clean lines and leaving the lines connected at one of the short ends. Bake for 7 to 8 minutes, or until the tuile rectangle is beginning to turn golden brown at the edges. Remove the pan from the oven and immediately run a metal spatula under the entire length of the tuile to release it from the baking mat. While still warm, wrap the rectangle around a 3-inch ring mold (or other cylinder), lining up the lines so that one end meets the other to form complete hoops. Using a knife, disconnect the remainder of the tuile so that you have individual hoops. Let the hoops set for a couple of minutes, then store them in an airtight container until ready to serve.

ASSEMBLY

8 fresh raspberries

Preheat the oven to 300°F (149°C). Place the Chocolate Tarts in the oven for 5 minutes, or until warm. Place each tart on a plate and top with a Cacao Nib Crunch round. Place a Tuile Hoop on the plate and position a quenelle of the Gianduja Ice Cream at its base to hold the hoop up. Top with a fresh raspberry. Decorate the plate with some Chocolate Sauce.

PEACH STREUSEL UPSIDE-DOWN TART with LEMON THYME ICE CREAM

HERE'S MY TAKE ON THE AMERICAN UPSIDE-DOWN CAKE, but in tart form. This was a popular lunch dessert at Payard, and it really showcases the sweet, juicy character of peaches when they're at their peak. The tart shell is made from a simple streusel, with a layer of almond cream covering its bottom. I pair the tart with a Lemon Thyme Ice Cream, which has a mild herb flavor that's not too strong or overwhelming, lending a nice accent to the caramelized peach.

MAKES 8 SERVINGS

COMPONENTS

LEMON THYME ICE CREAM
PEACH STREUSEL TART
PEACH SAUCE
TUILE GARNISH

SPECIAL EQUIPMENT | ice cream machine; pastry comb with ¼-inch square teeth; eight 3-inch-diameter metal rings about 2 inches high; medium, plain pastry tip (Ateco #6)

PERFECT MATCH | 2004 Duché de Longueville Cidre Gros Oeillet, Normandy, France

LEMON THYME ICE CREAM

3 sprigs lemon thyme

1 cup (250 g/8.8 oz) heavy cream, plus more as needed

1 cup (250 g/8.8 oz) whole milk

6 large (112 g/4 oz) egg yolks

½ cup plus 2 Tbsp (125 g/4.4 oz) granulated sugar

1. Remove the leaves from 2 of the lemon thyme sprigs and place them in a small saucepan with the cream. Bring the cream to a gentle boil over medium heat. Remove the pan from the heat and let the cream cool. Once cool, transfer it to an airtight container and refrigerate for at least 8 hours, or overnight.

2. Strain the lemon thyme–infused cream through a fine-mesh sieve into a measuring cup. If you have less than 1 cup (250 g/8.8 oz), add as much cream as necessary to equal that amount. In a medium saucepan, combine the infused cream and the milk and bring to a gentle boil over medium heat.

3. In a medium bowl, whisk together the egg yolks and sugar until pale. Whisk about half of the hot milk mixture into the yolks, then return this mixture to the remaining milk mixture in the saucepan and cook over medium heat, stirring constantly with a wooden spoon, until it thickens enough to coat the back of the spoon and reaches 175°F (79°C) on an instant-read thermometer; do not let the mixture boil, or the egg yolks will curdle. Remove the pot from the heat and strain the ice cream base immediately into a bowl. Set the bowl in an ice bath and stir frequently until cold.

4. Transfer the ice cream base to an airtight container and refrigerate for at least 4 hours, or overnight.

5. Remove the leaves from the remaining lemon thyme sprig. Process the base in an ice cream machine according to the manufacturer's instructions, adding the lemon thyme leaves during the final minute of churning. (Be careful not to overchurn the ice cream or it will become grainy.) Transfer the ice cream to an airtight container and freeze until ready to serve.

TUILE GARNISH

Vanilla Tuile batter (page 338)

Preheat the oven to 375°F (191°C). Line a half-sheet pan with a silicone baking mat. Have a rolling pin ready. Using an offset metal spatula, spread some tuile batter on the mat in a rough 3 by 10-inch rectangle. Run a pastry comb with ¼-inch square teeth through the rectangle, making long, clean, unattached lines in the batter—leave one end of the lines connected. Bake the tuile for about 7 to 8 minutes, or until the tuile is slightly colored. Run a spatula under the entire length of the tuile to release it from the baking mat. While still warm, wrap it around the rolling pin until you have a twisted, wavy tuile. Keep the end at the bottom connected. Let it set until cool and store in an airtight container. Repeat to make a total of 8 spiral tuile garnishes.

PEACH SAUCE

¼ cup plus 1 Tbsp (62 g/2.2 oz) granulated sugar

1 Tbsp plus 1 tsp (28 g/1 oz) glucose syrup

1 cup (250 g/8.8 oz) peach purée

1 vanilla bean, split lengthwise

¼ cup (60 g/2.1 oz) water

In a medium saucepan, combine the sugar and glucose and cook over medium heat, moving the pan constantly, until the sugar caramelizes and turns a light amber color. Stir in ½ cup (125 g/4.4 oz) of the peach purée and the vanilla bean and cook, stirring, until any hardened bits of sugar are dissolved. Add the remaining ½ cup peach purée and the water and stir until blended. Strain through a fine-mesh sieve into a bowl and set aside until ready to serve.

PEACH STREUSEL TART

4 large ripe peaches

Streusel, unbaked (page 342)

Almond Cream (page 341)

1. Preheat the oven to 375°F (191°C). Fill a medium bowl halfway with ice water and set aside.

2. Fill a medium saucepan halfway with water and bring to a boil. Add the peaches and blanch for about 30 seconds. Immediately immerse them in the ice water. When cool enough to handle, peel the peaches using your fingers. The skins should peel off easily; if the peaches are not ripe, it will be impossible to remove the skins. Cut each peach in half and remove the stone.

3. Place the 3-inch rings on a half-sheet pan and brush their interiors with butter, then coat them with granulated sugar. Line the bottom of each ring with some unbaked Streusel. Make sure that the interior edges of the rings are covered by slightly pushing the Streusel up the sides.

4. Scrape the Almond Cream into a pastry bag fitted with a medium, plain tip. Pipe about ¼ cup of Almond Cream into the bottom of each ring. Place a peach half in each ring, cut side up. Bake for about 25 minutes, or until the Almond Cream is golden brown. Place the pan with the molds on a wire rack and cool before unmolding.

STREUSEL, BAKED (page 342)

ASSEMBLY

8 thyme sprigs

Preheat the oven to 300°F (149°C). Place the Peach Streusel Tarts in the oven until warmed through, about 5 minutes. Arrange a tart in the center of a plate and place some baked streusel next to it. Place a quenelle of the Lemon Thyme Ice Cream on top of the streusel. Lay a Tuile Garnish over the tart, and garnish with a small sprig of thyme. Decorate the plate with some of the Peach Sauce.

WARM HONEY TART with CANDIED ORANGE and HONEY-NOUGAT ICE CREAM

THIS DELICATE TART COMBINES THE FLA-VORS OF HONEY AND ORANGE in a warm custard filling. When you make the Honey Cream, it will appear separated when you remove it from the heat, but once it cools down, a few seconds with an immersion blender makes it come together beautifully. I serve this tart with a crunchy Honey-Nougat Ice Cream and a tuile that's fashioned after a honeycomb. Use a good local orange blossom or lavender honey from the farmers' market for this dessert.

MAKES 8 SERVINGS

COMPONENTS

CANDIED ORANGE PEEL

HONEY-NOUGAT ICE CREAM

CARAMELIZED NUTS

HONEY TART

   TART SHELLS

   HONEY CREAM

HONEYCOMB TUILE GARNISH

ORANGE SAUCE

SPECIAL EQUIPMENT | ice cream machine; 4-inch pastry cutter; 3-inch-diameter by ¾-inch-high tart rings; medium, plain decorating tip (Ateco #6); immersion blender

PERFECT MATCH | Nicolas Feuillatte Champagne Rosé, France

CANDIED ORANGE PEEL

3 oranges

2¼ cups (450 g/15.8 oz) granulated sugar

½ cup (118 g/4.2 oz) water

2 Tbsp (40 g/1.4 oz) light corn syrup

1.   Prepare the candied oranges the day before you use them. Cut the oranges into quarters and, using a paring knife, remove the pulp and as much white pith as possible. Fill a medium saucepan halfway with water and bring the water to a boil. Add the orange peel and blanch for 20 seconds. Remove and rinse the peel, change the water, and repeat the blanching two more times.

2.   Combine the sugar, water, corn syrup, and blanched peel in the saucepan and bring to a boil. Reduce the heat to low and simmer for about 1 hour, until the peel is slightly transpar-ent. Remove from the heat and set aside to cool.

3.   Transfer the peel in syrup to an airtight container and refrigerate overnight.

CARAMELIZED NUTS

1 cup (140 g/5 oz) blanched almonds

1 cup (140 g/5 oz) shelled pistachios

Finely grated zest of 1 orange

¾ cup (150 g/5.3 oz) granulated sugar

3 Tbsp (44 g/1.5 oz) water

1.   Line a half-sheet pan with a silicone bak-ing mat. In a medium bowl, toss together the nuts and orange zest and set aside.

2. In a small saucepan, combine the sugar and water and cook over medium-high heat, brushing down the sides of the pan occasionally with a wet pastry brush to prevent crystals from forming, and watching carefully, until the sugar registers 242°F (117°C) on a candy thermometer, 3 to 5 minutes. Add the nuts and zest and stir to coat the nuts with the syrup. Continue to cook, stirring constantly, until the sugar crystallizes (it will turn sandy when it does) and then caramelizes and turns golden brown. Immediately pour the caramelized nuts onto the lined sheet pan, spreading them out with a wooden spoon. Allow the nuts to cool completely.

3. Transfer the nuts to a cutting board and chop them finely.

SANGRIA PRUNES

1 vanilla bean

1 stick cinnamon

Finely grated zest of 1 grapefruit

Finely grated zest of 1 lemon

Finely grated zest of 1 orange

1 whole clove

1¼ cups (300 g/10.6 oz) red wine

1¼ cups (300 g/10.6 oz) white wine

¼ cup (50 g/1.76 oz) granulated sugar

5 cups (700 g/24.7 oz) prunes

1.   Cut a 4-inch square of cheesecloth and place the vanilla bean, cinnamon stick, citrus zests, and whole clove in the center. Using a

piece of kitchen twine, tie the cloth up into a pouch.

2.   Combine the red and white wine in a small saucepan and bring to a boil. Carefully touch a flame igniter to the surface of the liquid and flambé to allow the alcohol in the wine to burn off. Add the spice pouch, sugar, and prunes to the wine and reduce to a gentle simmer. Cover the pot and cook until the prunes are soft and the liquid has reduced by about one-third, about 20 minutes. Cool completely.

3.   Remove the prunes from the liquid with a slotted spoon and cut each one in half. Refrigerate them, along with the liquid, in an airtight container until ready to serve.

POACHED PEARS IN VANILLA SYRUP

> 2 cups (472 g/16.6 oz) water
>
> Juice of 1 lemon
>
> 2 cups (400 g/14.1 oz) granulated sugar
>
> 2 vanilla beans, split lengthwise and seeds scraped
>
> 8 Forelle pears, peeled, halved, and cored

1.   In a medium saucepan, combine the water, lemon juice, sugar, and vanilla bean pods and seeds. Place over medium-high heat and cook, stirring, until the sugar has dissolved. Add the pears and bring to a boil. Reduce the heat to a simmer, cover the pan, and simmer over low heat for 7 to 8 minutes, or until the pears are tender when pierced with a fork. Remove the pan from the heat and cool, covered.

2.   Refrigerate the pears in their liquid until ready to serve, or up to 3 days.

TEARDROP TUILE GARNISHES

> Vanilla Tuile batter (page 338)

1.   Preheat the oven to 375°F (191°C). Line a half-sheet pan with a silicone baking mat.

2.   Spread a thin layer of the batter into a rectangle that is roughly 3 by 10 inches (it doesn't have to be a perfect rectangle). Run a pastry comb that has ¼-inch square teeth through the batter, forming clean lines and leaving the lines connected at one of the short ends. Bake for 7 to 8 minutes, or until the tuile rectangle is beginning to turn golden brown at the edges. Remove the pan from the oven and immediately run a metal spatula under the entire length of the tuile to release it from the baking mat. While still warm, wrap the rectangle around a rolling pin, so that it forms a loose, teardrop shape, with the ends crossing over each other—make sure that a small pear can fit in the bend of the tuile. Using a paring knife, carefully cut the end where the tuile strips are attached so that you have individual teardrop-shaped tuiles. Let the tuiles set for a couple of minutes, then store them in an airtight container. Repeat until you have a total of 24 Teardrop Tuiles.

ASSEMBLY

Place a Red Wine Tart on a plate and arrange some Sangria Prunes around the top edge. Slice a Poached Pear half and arrange the slices on one side of the tart. Place the curved end of 3 Teardrop Tuiles in the center of the tart and place a Poached Pear half on top to hold the tuiles in place. Drizzle some of the reduced prune-poaching liquid around the dessert.

COLD DESSERT SOUPS, CRÊPES, SOUFFLÉS, and OTHER DESSERTS

THIS CHAPTER FEATURES MOSTLY COLD FRUIT SOUPS, with several miscellaneous desserts—a crêpe purse, a soufflé, a beignet, a panini, and two drinks—to round it out. The fruit soups are among my favorite desserts, because they are so refreshing and bring forward such wonderful flavors. I developed many of these while I was at Restaurant Daniel, because Daniel Boulud loved fruit so much. We served fruit soups as a palate cleanser between courses, as a pre-dessert, or as a light dessert course. I always had two or three dessert soups on the menu at a time. They are all relatively easy to make, and because they always include a sorbet or sherbet, must be assembled à la minute.

Many of the other desserts in this chapter also require some last-minute preparation. For the Chocolate Beignets with Orange Blossom Crème Anglaise, the beignet batter must be used within an hour of making, and the beignets must be deep-fried right before serving. The Brioche Panini needs to be lightly grilled before assembly, while timing is a crucial part of baking and serving the Dark Chocolate Soufflé. For the Orange Tuile Ring filled with Marshmallow and Orange Blossom Ice Cream, a rich hot chocolate is poured over the dessert's elements right before serving, creating a symphony of textures and flavors. The Plum Soda, a twist on an American classic, and the Crêpe Purse filled with Sautéed Bananas both happily require very little assembly work before serving.

PEACH SOUP with APRICOT SORBET and CRYSTALLIZED LAVENDER

LAVENDER HAS A STRONG FLORAL FLAVOR that can be overpowering, but used sparingly, it lends a delicate, almost lemony, note to desserts like this delicious peach soup. I used to serve this fruit soup at Daniel in the summer, and it was very popular because it was so refreshing and light. Make sure to use perfectly ripe peaches that have a yellow background color, are medium-soft to the touch, and that smell . . . well . . . like a peach!

MAKES 8 SERVINGS

COMPONENTS

CRYSTALLIZED LAVENDER
APRICOT SORBET
LAVENDER POACHED PEACHES

SPECIAL EQUIPMENT ice cream machine

PERFECT MATCH Champagne Perrier-Jouët Belle Époque Rosé, France

CRYSTALLIZED LAVENDER

⅓ cup (66 g/2.3 oz) granulated sugar

1 large (30 g/1 oz) egg white

8 sprigs pesticide-free, fresh lavender

Put the sugar in a small bowl and set aside. Put the egg white in a second small bowl and whisk it a little to loosen it. Place a lavender sprig on a piece of parchment or wax paper and gently brush it all over with the egg white. Toss the sprig in the sugar and place it on a plate. Repeat with the remaining sprigs. Let the sugar-coated lavender sprigs dry for at least 8 hours, or overnight.

APRICOT SORBET

2 cups (450 g/15.8 oz) apricot purée

¾ cup (175 g/6.17 oz) Simple Syrup (page 339)

¾ cup (170 g/6 oz) water

1. Combine all of the ingredients in a medium bowl. Cover the bowl and refrigerate the sorbet base for at least 4 hours, or overnight.

2. Process the base in an ice cream machine according to the manufacturer's instructions. Transfer the sorbet to an airtight container and freeze until ready to serve.

LAVENDER POACHED PEACHES

6 medium (1 kg/35.3 oz) perfectly ripe peaches

4 cups (944 g/33.3 oz) water

1¼ cups (250 g/8.8 oz) granulated sugar

1 vanilla bean, split lengthwise and seeds scraped

Finely grated zest and juice of 1 lemon

2 sprigs pesticide-free, fresh lavender

1. Fill a large bowl halfway with ice water and set aside.

2. Fill a large saucepan halfway with water and bring the water to a boil over high heat. Add 2 peaches and blanch for 30 to 45 seconds. Using a slotted spoon, transfer the peaches to the ice water. Repeat with the remaining peaches, making sure the water is at a full boil before adding the peaches. Remove the skin from the peaches with your fingers. It should peel off easily; if the peaches are not ripe, it will be impossible to remove the skin.

3. Cut each peach in half and remove the stone.

4. In a medium saucepan, combine the water, sugar, vanilla bean pod and seeds, lemon zest and juice, and the lavender sprigs and cook over medium-high heat, stirring occasionally, until the sugar has dissolved. Add the peach halves and bring to a boil. Cover the pan, reduce the heat to low, and simmer for 4 to 5 minutes, or until the peaches are tender when pierced with a fork. Remove the pan from the heat and cool, covered.

5. Store the peaches in the liquid in an air-tight container in the refrigerator until ready to serve, or for up to 3 days.

ASSEMBLY

Remove the Lavender Poached Peaches from the syrup and cut each peach half into 8 even wedges. Decoratively arrange 12 of the wedges in a shallow soup bowl. Strain the reserved syrup and pour some of it onto the peach wedges. Place a scoop of Apricot Sorbet in the center of the bowl and top it with a Crystallized Lavender sprig. Serve immediately.

CRÊPE PURSE filled with SAUTÉED BANANAS and PASSION FRUIT with CHOCOLATE–PASSION FRUIT SAUCE

SAUTÉED BANANAS ARE AN IDEAL FILLING for this little crêpe purse, as they don't give off too much juice, which would make the crêpe soggy. The crepes can be made up to a day ahead and stored, well-wrapped, in the refrigerator—just bring them to room temperature before assembling the purses. I serve these with a Chocolate–Passion Fruit Sauce, which is both rich and acidic, and complements the rum-flavored banana filling perfectly.

MAKES 10 SERVINGS

COMPONENTS

CRÊPES

BANANA FILLING

CHOCOLATE–PASSION FRUIT SAUCE

SPECIAL EQUIPMENT | 10-inch (measured across the top) crêpe pan to make 8-inch crêpes

PERFECT MATCH | 2004 Duché de Longueville Cidre Gros Oeillet, France

CRÊPES

2 cups plus 1 Tbsp (250 g/8.8 oz) all-purpose flour

Pinch of salt

½ cup (100 g/3.5 oz) granulated sugar

8 large (400 g/14.1 oz) eggs

2 cups plus 1 Tbsp (500 g/17.6 oz) whole milk

Finely grated zest of 2 oranges

10½ Tbsp (150 g/5.3 oz) Beurre Noisette (page 348)

1 cup plus 1 Tbsp (250 g/8.8 oz) heavy cream

1.   In a medium bowl, combine the flour, salt, and sugar. In another bowl, whisk together the eggs and milk until blended, then gradually stir the egg mixture into the dry ingredients. Gently stir in the orange zest and the Beurre Noisette. Stir in the cream until blended. Cover the bowl and refrigerate the batter for at least 2 hours, or up to 24 hours.

2.   Place a 10-inch nonstick crêpe pan or nonstick sauté pan over medium heat. Once heated, pour in 2 to 3 tablespoons of the crêpe batter. There should be just enough to coat the bottom of the pan. Roll the pan from side to side to coat it evenly with a thin layer of the batter. After about 2 minutes, turn the crêpe and cook on the opposite side for 20 seconds. Place the cooked crêpe on a piece of parchment paper on a plate. Continue cooking the crêpes until all of the batter has been used. Stack the crêpes, one on top of the other, as they are finished. Cover and store in the refrigerator until needed. The crêpes can be made one day ahead of time; just bring them to room temperature before using.

BANANA FILLING

5 medium ripe bananas

3½ Tbsp (50 g/1.76 oz) unsalted butter

1 Tbsp (15 g/0.5 oz) granulated sugar

3 Tbsp (45 g/1.6 oz) Myers's dark rum

¼ cup (60 g/2.1 oz) passion fruit purée

1. Peel the bananas and cut them crosswise into ¼-inch-thick slices.

2. Melt the butter in a large sauté pan. Add the bananas and sauté them while gradually adding the sugar. Add the rum and carefully touch a flame igniter to the liquid and flambé to allow the alcohol in the rum to burn off. Stir in the passion fruit purée and remove the pan from the heat.

CHOCOLATE–PASSION FRUIT SAUCE

7 oz (200 g) 72% bittersweet chocolate, chopped

8 Tbsp (1 stick/115 g/4 oz) unsalted butter, cut into ½-inch cubes

¾ cup (175 g/6.17 oz) whole milk

¼ cup (60 g/2.1 oz) passion fruit purée

1. Place the chocolate and butter in a medium bowl and set aside.

2. In a small saucepan, combine the milk and passion fruit purée and bring to a boil over medium-high heat. Pour the hot mixture over the chocolate and butter and allow to stand for 1 minute to melt the chocolate. Stir gently until the chocolate and butter have melted and the mixture is smooth.

ASSEMBLY

5 vanilla beans, quartered lengthwise

Pulp of 4 passion fruits, for garnish

Fill 20 Crêpes with a spoonful of Banana Filling each. Bring the sides of the crêpe up around the filling and use the quartered vanilla beans to tie the ends into a pouch. Place 2 of the pouches on a plate and garnish with the Chocolate–Passion Fruit Sauce and some passion fruit pulp.

DARK CHOCOLATE SOUFFLÉ with PISTACHIO ICE CREAM

YEARS AGO, when I worked at Lucas Carton in Paris, I used to make a molten chocolate cake that was very popular. When the molten chocolate cake became so fashionable in the United States in the 1990s, I adapted my Lucas Carton recipe and turned it into a soufflé that I served at Le Bernardin. This recipe is much lighter than the typical molten chocolate cake, and it requires precise timing to make it perfectly. In a restaurant, when timing soufflés can be problematic, we remove them from the oven once they've puffed up, let them cool, wrap them very tightly with plastic wrap, and freeze them. During service, the frozen soufflés are put in a warm place—on top of the oven, for example—and this revives them. The soufflés become moist and the hole in the center closes up and becomes fluid, at which point they are returned to the oven for a few minutes until they puff up and become soft and creamy in the center. This is a great technique for restaurant service, and it works perfectly every time. At Daniel, I used to make 500 of these at a time! One tip: You must use PAM Original cooking spray to coat the molds, and nothing else. Otherwise, the soufflés will stick, and that's a guarantee.

MAKES 10 SERVINGS

COMPONENTS

PISTACHIO ICE CREAM

WHITE AND DARK CHOCOLATE DISKS

CHOCOLATE SAUCE

DARK CHOCOLATE SOUFFLÉS

SPECIAL EQUIPMENT | ice cream machine; 16 by 24-inch acetate sheet; 3-inch round pastry cutter; pastry comb with pointed teeth; ten 4-ounce, 3-inch-diameter aluminum cups with straight sides; PAM Original cooking spray; medium, plain pastry tip (Ateco #6)

PERFECT MATCH | Amaretto di Saronno

PISTACHIO ICE CREAM

1 cup (250 g/8.8 oz) whole milk

1 cup (250 g/8.8 oz) heavy cream

6 large (112 g/4 oz) egg yolks

½ cup plus 2 Tbsp (125 g/4.4 oz) granulated sugar

2 Tbsp plus 1 tsp (45 g/1.58 oz) pistachio paste

1. In a medium saucepan, combine the milk and cream and bring to a gentle boil over medium heat.

2. In a medium bowl, whisk together the egg yolks and sugar until pale. Whisk about half of the hot milk mixture into the yolks, then return this mixture to the remaining milk mixture in the saucepan and cook over medium

heat, stirring constantly with a wooden spoon, until it thickens enough to coat the back of the spoon and reaches 175°F (79°C) on an instant-read thermometer; do not let the mixture boil, or the egg yolks will curdle. Remove the pot from the heat and whisk in the pistachio paste. Pass the ice cream base through a fine-mesh sieve into a medium bowl. Set the bowl in an ice bath and stir frequently until cold.

3. Transfer the ice cream base to an airtight container and refrigerate for at least 4 hours, or overnight.

4. Process the base in an ice cream machine according to the manufacturer's instructions. (Be careful not to overchurn the ice cream or it will become grainy.) Transfer the ice cream to an airtight container and freeze until ready to serve.

WHITE AND DARK CHOCOLATE DISKS

8 oz (227 g) white chocolate, tempered (see Tempered Chocolate, page 347)

8 oz (227 g) bittersweet chocolate, tempered (see Tempered Chocolate, page 347)

Spread the white chocolate thinly over a 16 by 24-inch sheet of acetate. Using a pastry comb with pointed teeth, make wavy lines in the chocolate before it sets. When the chocolate has set but is still flexible, spread a thin layer of tempered bittersweet chocolate on top. When the top layer has just set, cut out 10 rounds with a 3-inch round pastry cutter and allow to fully set at room temperature.

CHOCOLATE SAUCE (page 334)

DARK CHOCOLATE SOUFFLÉS

8 oz (228 g) 72% bittersweet chocolate, chopped

20⅓ Tbsp (286 g/10 oz) unsalted butter, cut into ½-inch chunks

5 large (93 g/3.3 oz) egg yolks (fresh, not pasteurized)

½ cup (100 g/3.5 oz) granulated sugar

1 Tbsp (7.2 g/0.25 oz) all-purpose flour

5 large (150 g/5.3 oz) egg whites (fresh, not pasteurized)

2 tsp (10.3 g/0.36 oz) freshly squeezed lemon juice

1. Prepare the soufflés no more than 2 hours before serving. Preheat the oven to 375°F (191°C). Coat the bottom and sides of ten 4-ounce, 3-inch-diameter aluminum cups with straight sides with PAM Original cooking spray. Place the cups on a half-sheet pan.

2. Put the chocolate and butter in a medium stainless steel bowl and set the bowl over a pot half filled with simmering water. Heat, stirring frequently, until the chocolate and butter are melted. Stir until well blended and smooth.

3. Meanwhile, in the bowl of a stand mixer fitted with the whisk attachment, beat the yolks on medium speed for 1 minute. Gradually add 3 tablespoons (37 g/1.3 oz) of the sugar and whip on high speed until very light and fluffy, about 10 minutes.

4. Using a handheld whisk, mix the chocolate into the beaten yolk mixture. Mix in the flour.

5. In another mixer bowl, beat the egg whites with the lemon juice on medium speed until soft peaks form. Gradually add the remaining ¼ cup plus 1 tablespoon (62 g/2.2 oz) granulated sugar and whip on high speed until stiff and glossy. Gently fold the egg whites into the chocolate and egg mixture until fully blended. Scrape the batter into a pastry bag fitted with a medium, plain tip and pipe it into the prepared cups, filling them about three-quarters full. Bake the soufflés for 9 to 11 minutes, or until puffed; they will be soft in the center, but shouldn't be too jiggly. Invert each soufflé onto a dessert plate and remove the mold.

ASSEMBLY

Finely chopped pistachios, for garnish

Immediately top each Dark Chocolate Soufflé with a White and Dark Chocolate Disk. Place a quenelle of Pistachio Ice Cream on the plate, and sprinkle some pistachios on top. Spoon some Chocolate Sauce onto the plate. Serve immediately.

PLUM SODA with VANILLA ICE CREAM STICK and ALMOND FINANCIER

ERIC ESTRELLA, the talented pastry chef who was my sous-chef at Payard for two years, created this sparkling summer dessert as a way to feature plums during their short season. Plums are rarely used in desserts anymore, which is a shame, because they are really juicy, with a lovely sweet-tart flavor. Because they are so succulent, this soda is a great way to use them. Use deeply colored plums with lots of flavor. I like to use baby plums, which are more intense than the big ones—you can usually find them at the farmers' market in July and August.

MAKES 6 SERVINGS

COMPONENTS

PLUM SODA
VANILLA ICE CREAM STICK
ALMOND FINANCIERS

SPECIAL EQUIPMENT | six 3-inch-long by 1½-inch-high acetate strips; cellophane tape; ice cream machine; 2 medium, plain pastry tips (Ateco #4); 1 by 2-inch silicone financier molds; six 4-ounce shot glasses

PERFECT MATCH | Inniskillin Icewine, Niagara Peninsula, Canada

PLUM SODA

About 25 baby or 10 medium (1 kg/2.2 lb) very ripe, deeply colored plums

1 cup (200 g/7 oz) granulated sugar

Juice of 1 lemon

1.   Cut the plums in half and remove their stones. Dice the plums and place them in a medium heatproof bowl. Add the sugar and lemon juice and toss to combine. Cover the bowl with plastic wrap. Fill a large pot halfway with water and bring the water to a boil over high heat. Reduce the heat so that the water is just simmering, and place the bowl of plums, still covered, over the water. Cook the plums, maintaining the water at a simmer and replenishing it as necessary, for 4 hours. Do not stir the plums at all during this time. Remove the bowl from the heat and let the plums cool.

2.   Strain the plum liquid through a fine-mesh sieve into a medium bowl; do not press down on the plums. Place the bowl into a larger bowl of ice water and let the plum liquid stand until chilled. Cover the bowl and refrigerate until ready to serve.

VANILLA ICE CREAM STICK

Vanilla Ice Cream (page 340), softened to piping consistency

6 chocolate cigarettes

1. Roll an acetate strip to make a tube that measures ½ inch in diameter and 1½ inches high. Secure the tube with tape and repeat to make a total of 6 acetate tubes.

2. Place some of the Vanilla Ice Cream into a pastry bag fitted with a medium, plain tip. Pipe the ice cream into each tube, filling them completely. Insert a chocolate cigarette into the center of each tube; it will stick out. Freeze the tubes until the ice cream is hard, at least 3 hours.

3. Remove the acetate from the ice cream tubes and freeze them, loosely covered, until ready to serve.

ALMOND FINANCIERS

½ cup plus 3 Tbsp (60 g/2.1 oz) almond flour

¾ cup plus 1½ Tbsp (100 g/3.5 oz) pastry flour (see Sources, page 349)

¾ cup (150 g/5.3 oz) granulated sugar

¾ tsp (3 g/0.1 oz) baking powder

4 large (125 g/4.4 oz) egg whites, at room temperature

1 tsp (3 g/0.1 oz) vanilla extract

½ cup plus 2 Tbsp (125 g/4.4 oz) Beurre Noisette (page 348), hot

1 plum, cut in half and sliced into ¼-inch wedges

1. Preheat the oven to 380°F (193°C). In a medium bowl, sift together the almond flour, pastry flour, sugar, and baking powder and whisk to combine. Stir in the egg whites and vanilla until blended. Stir in the hot Beurre Noisette until combined. Set aside to cool for 10 minutes.

2. Scrape the batter into a pastry bag fitted with a medium, plain tip and pipe it into 1 by 2-inch silicone financier molds, filling them three-quarters of the way full.

3. Top each financier with a plum slice. Bake for 8 to 10 minutes, or until golden. Cool the financiers for 5 minutes, then unmold them and cool completely.

ASSEMBLY

1 (330-ml/11-fl oz) bottle Perrier water, chilled

2 baby plums or 1 medium regular plum, cut in half and sliced into ¼-inch wedges

6 sugar cubes

Fill a 4-ounce shot glass halfway with Plum Soda. Top with Perrier. Place the glass at one end of a rectangular plate. Arrange a few plum slices on the plate next to the glass and top them with a Vanilla Ice Cream Stick. Place a financier next to the ice cream stick. Pop a sugar cube into the soda, to make it foam up, and serve immediately.

EARL GREY TEA SOUP with TAPIOCA and ORANGE SORBET

THIS CHILLED CITRUS- AND TEA-FLAVORED DES-SERT SOUP is a delicious and refreshing alternative to serving plain sorbet, and is tailor-made for a hot summer night. Each of its components can be made up to two days in advance, but the soup should be assembled right before serving.

MAKES 6 SERVINGS

COMPONENTS

ORANGE SORBET

TAPIOCA

EARL GREY TEA INFUSION

SPECIAL EQUIPMENT | ice cream machine

PERFECT MATCH | Carole Bouquet Sangue d'Oro Passito di Pantelleria, Sicily

ORANGE SORBET

¾ cup (150 g/5.3 oz) granulated sugar

½ tsp (2 g/0.07 oz) sorbet stabilizer (see Sources, page 349)

¾ cup (177 g/6.24 oz) water

2½ cups (605 g/21.34 oz) freshly squeezed orange juice

1.   In a small bowl, stir together the sugar and sorbet stabilizer.

2.   In a medium saucepan, combine the water with the sugar mixture and bring to a boil, whisking occasionally. Remove from the heat and transfer to a bowl. Add the orange juice, cover, and refrigerate the sorbet base for at least 6 hours, or overnight.

3.   Stir the mixture. Process the base in an ice cream machine according to the manufacturer's instructions. Transfer the sorbet to an airtight container and freeze for at least 3 hours before serving.

TAPIOCA

⅓ cup (60 g/2.1 oz) premium, large-pearl tapioca, such as Bob's Red Mill brand (see Sources, page 349)

1 qt (944 g/32 oz) water

1¼ cups (250 g/8.8 oz) granulated sugar

1.   Soak the tapioca in water for at least 6 hours or overnight in the refrigerator.

2.   Drain the tapioca and place it in a pot with the 1 quart (944 g/32 oz) water and the sugar. Bring to a boil, then reduce the heat and simmer until the tapioca becomes translucent, about 30 minutes. Strain the tapioca under cold running water.

3.   Store the tapioca in a container with cold water to cover by a few inches. Chill for at least 3 hours. Drain well before serving.

LEMON-ELDERFLOWER SHERBET

1 tsp (5 g/0.17 oz) sorbet stabilizer

1¼ cups (250 g/8.8 oz) granulated sugar

1 cup (236 g/8.3 oz) water

1 cup (250 g/8.8 oz) freshly squeezed lemon juice

1 cup (242 g/8.5 oz) whole milk

⅓ cup (75 g/2.6 oz) elderflower cordial

1.   In a medium saucepan, mix the stabilizer with the sugar. Stir in the remaining ingredients and bring to a boil over medium-high heat, stirring, just until the sugar has dissolved. Transfer the sherbet base to a bowl and set in a larger bowl filled one-third of the way with ice water. Stir until chilled. Cover and refrigerate the sherbet base for 24 hours.

2.   Process the base in an ice cream machine according to the manufacturer's instructions. Transfer the sherbet to an airtight container and freeze for at least 3 hours before serving.

STRAWBERRY TUILES

¾ cup (175 g/6.17 oz) strawberry purée

⅓ cup (40 g/1.4 oz) confectioners' sugar

1.   Preheat the oven to 175°F (79°C). Line a half-sheet pan with a silicone baking mat.

2.   Combine the purée and confectioners' sugar in a small saucepan and bring to a boil over medium-high heat. Pour the mixture onto the lined sheet pan and, using a small offset metal spatula, spread it out into a thin layer. Bake for 2 hours, then turn the oven off and leave the tuile sheet in the oven for another hour.

3.   Remove the pan from the oven and allow it to cool completely on a wire rack; the tuile will become crisp as it cools. Break the tuile sheet into shards and store in an airtight container until ready to serve.

ASSEMBLY

Spoon the Strawberry-Basil Soup into a bowl. Place a quenelle of Lemon-Elderflower Sherbet on top of the soup, and garnish with a shard of Strawberry Tuile.

RED BERRY and TOMATO GAZPACHO with TOMATO CHIPS

✳ EVERY CHEF HAS THEIR OWN VERSION of gazpacho, and this is mine—in dessert form. This dish shows that a tomato—which is, after all, a fruit—can be just as versatile as a berry. The gazpacho is made with fresh tomatoes, raspberries, and strawberries, puréed together with a little sugar and lemon juice in a food processor. It is served with fresh berries and an unusual Yellow Tomato Sorbet. A tomato chip, made from dried tomato skin, adds a crispy element to this refreshing summer dessert soup.

MAKES 8 SERVINGS

COMPONENTS

YELLOW TOMATO SORBET

RED BERRY AND TOMATO GAZPACHO

TOMATO CHIPS

SPECIAL EQUIPMENT | ice cream machine

PERFECT MATCH | La Zaragonza Ambar Especial Beer, Spain

YELLOW TOMATO SORBET

    1 cup plus 1 Tbsp (210 g/7.4 oz) granulated sugar

    1 tsp (5 g/0.17 oz) sorbet stabilizer

    1¾ cups (420 g/14.8 oz) water

    4 cups (600 g/21.2 oz) yellow tomato purée

    2 Tbsp plus 1 tsp (50 g/1.76 oz) glucose syrup

1. In a small bowl, combine ½ cup (100 g/3.5 oz) of the sugar with the stabilizer. In a small saucepan, combine the remaining ½ cup plus 1 tablespoon (110 g/3.8 oz) sugar with the water and place over medium-high heat. Gradually whisk in the sugar and stabilizer mixture and bring to a boil. Remove from the heat and let cool.

2. In a medium bowl, combine the sugar syrup with the remaining ingredients. Cover the bowl and refrigerate the sorbet base for at least 4 hours.

3. Process the base in an ice cream machine according to the manufacturer's instructions. Transfer the sorbet to an airtight container and freeze until ready to serve.

TOMATO CHIPS

    About 6 medium (500 g/17.6 oz) ripe tomatoes, cored

    Confectioners' sugar, for dusting

1. Preheat the oven to 175°F (79°C). Line a half-sheet pan with a silicone baking mat. Fill a large bowl halfway with ice water.

2.   Using a paring knife, make a small X at the bottom end of each tomato. Bring a large pot half full of water to a rolling boil over high heat and immerse the tomatoes in the boiling water for about 30 seconds. Remove them with a slotted spoon and immediately plunge the tomatoes into the ice water; the skins should start to come off of the tomatoes. Remove the skins with your fingers (try to remove them in one piece), and pat the skins dry with paper towels. Reserve the skinned tomatoes to use in the gazpacho. Arrange the skins on the prepared sheet pan and dust them with confectioners' sugar. Bake for 1 to 2 hours, until dry; the skins will crisp up as they cool. Store the Tomato Chips in an airtight container until ready to serve.

RED BERRY and TOMATO GAZPACHO

Skinned tomatoes (reserved from above)

2¼ cups (250 g/8.8 oz) fresh strawberries

2¼ cups (250 g/8.8 oz) fresh raspberries

¼ cup plus 1 Tbsp (60 g/2.1 oz) granulated sugar

Juice of 1 lemon

Splash of Tabasco

Cut the tomatoes into quarters and, using your fingers, remove and discard the seeds. Process the berries and tomatoes together in a food processor, working in batches, if necessary. Pass the mixture through a fine-mesh sieve into a medium bowl and stir in the sugar, lemon juice, and Tabasco. Cover and refrigerate until ready to serve.

ASSEMBLY

2 cups (226 g/8 oz) fresh strawberries, washed, hulled, and sliced

2 cups (226 g/8 oz) fresh raspberries

2 cups (226 g/8 oz) fresh blackberries

Mix together all the berries. Spoon about ½ cup of the Gazpacho into a shallow soup bowl. Place a mound of mixed berries (½ cup) in the bowl. Place a quenelle of Yellow Tomato Sorbet in the center and garnish the plate with a few more berries. Place a Tomato Chip on top of the sorbet.

CITRUS TERRINE with ELDERFLOWER-PERRIER SOUP and TANGERINE SORBET

IN THE WINTER, when fall fruits are out of season and spring berries haven't yet arrived, citrus fruits are a great choice for desserts. This dessert soup, which is refreshing and light, is made with the juice and flesh of grapefruits and blood oranges, and is flavored with a touch of elderflower. Elderflower syrup is sweet, with a grapefruit endnote, so it goes very well with citrus. To cut its sweetness, I add some Perrier water to the soup right before serving, which also gives it a pleasant effervescence.

MAKES 8 SERVINGS

COMPONENTS

CITRUS TERRINE AND SOUP
ORANGE CHIPS
TANGERINE SORBET

SPECIAL EQUIPMENT | one 9-inch round cake pan | 2-inch round pastry cutter; electric slicer; ice cream machine

PERFECT MATCH | Il Gusto della Costa Limoncello, Campania, Italy

CITRUS TERRINE AND SOUP

7 Ruby Red grapefruits

11 blood oranges (or small regular oranges)

3 sheets (6 g/0.21 oz) gelatin (silver grade)

¼ cup plus 1 Tbsp (62 g/2.2 oz) granulated sugar

1 piece star anise

1 whole clove

1 whole white peppercorn, crushed

¼ cup (64 g/2.25 oz) elderflower syrup

1. Line a 9-inch round cake pan with plastic wrap. Using a sharp paring knife, cut the peel and pith off the ends of 3 of the grapefruit. Stand the fruit upright and cut the peel and pith off the sides of the 3 grapefruit. Make a cut on each side of each segment to remove all the suprêmes. Repeat this process with 5 of the oranges. Cut the suprêmes from 1 grapefruit and 2 oranges into chunks and set aside to use for the soup. Arrange the remaining grapefruit and orange suprêmes in the lined pan, spacing them evenly apart on the pan. Set aside. Fill a medium bowl halfway with cold water and add the gelatin sheets. Allow to soften for 10 minutes.

2. Juice the remaining 4 grapefruit and the remaining 6 oranges and combine the juices with the sugar and spices in a medium saucepan. Place the pan over medium-high heat and bring to a boil, stirring to dissolve the sugar. Continue to boil the mixture until it has reduced by approximately half, about 15 minutes. Remove the pan from the heat. Pour 1 cup (240 ml/8 fl oz) of the hot juice mixture into a medium bowl. Drain the gelatin, squeezing it to remove the excess water, and add it to the juice, stirring until the gelatin has

dissolved. Strain the juice and gelatin mixture through a fine-mesh sieve onto the suprêmes in the pan. Place the pan in the freezer for at least 2 hours.

3.   Cool the reserved juice in the pan, then stir in the elderflower syrup and the reserved chunks of orange and grapefruit suprêmes. Transfer to a covered container and refrigerate the fruit soup for at least 2 hours, or until chilled.

4.   When the Citrus Terrine is frozen, unmold it and cut out at least 8 rounds using a 2-inch round pastry cutter. Place the rounds on a plate, cover, and refrigerate until ready to serve.

ORANGE CHIPS

6 medium oranges

1 qt (944 g/32 oz) water

2¼ cups (450 g/15.9 oz) granulated sugar

Confectioners' sugar, for dusting

1.   Preheat the oven to 175°F (79°C). Line four half-sheet pans with silicone baking mats.

2.   Cut the top and bottom portion of the peel off each of the oranges. Using an electric slicer, slice the oranges into rounds as thinly as possible. You will need a total of 40 slices. Arrange the slices in stacks and place toothpicks through them. Place them in a shallow pan, keeping the stacks intact.

3.   In a large saucepan, combine the water and sugar and bring to a boil over high heat, stirring, just until the sugar has dissolved. Pour the hot syrup over the orange slices in the pan. Let them stand for 30 minutes.

4.   Dust the silicone mats generously with confectioners' sugar. Remove the oranges from the syrup with a slotted spoon. Cut each stack of oranges in half so that they are crescent shaped. Unstack the orange crescents and arrange them on the prepared sheet pans, making sure they do not overlap (or they will stick together). Dust the oranges with more confectioners' sugar and let sit for 10 minutes.

5.   After the sugar has dissolved, dry the orange slices with paper towels. Place them back on the sheet pans and dust with more confectioners' sugar. Bake for 3 hours, or until they are dry. Cool completely; the chips will become crisp as they dry. Store the Orange Chips in an airtight container at room temperature until ready to serve. You will need a total of 80 chips.

TANGERINE SORBET

1½ cups (450 g/15.9 oz) tangerine purée

1½ cups (350 g/12.3 oz) Simple Syrup (page 339)

½ cup (120 g/4.2 oz) water

1.   Mix all of the ingredients together in a medium bowl, cover, and refrigerate the sorbet base for at least 4 hours, or overnight.

2.   Process the base in an ice cream machine according to the manufacturer's instructions. Transfer to an airtight container and freeze until ready to serve.

ASSEMBLY

1¼ cups (295 g/10.4 oz) Perrier water

Place a defrosted Citrus Terrine round in the center of a shallow soup bowl. Make a large ball-shaped scoop of Tangerine Sorbet and place it on top of the terrine. Insert 10 of the Orange Chips into the sorbet, cut side out, arranging them evenly around the perimeter. In a medium bowl, mix together the reserved chilled fruit soup with the Perrier water. Pour about ½ cup of the soup into the bowl.

SPICY KUMQUAT SOUP with KUMQUAT-ORANGE SORBET and STAR ANISE

KUMQUATS ARE NOT USED VERY OFTEN by pastry chefs because they are full of little seeds, and which take time and patience to remove. But I love their sour orange flavor, and they go wonderfully with sweet oranges, particularly in this refreshing dessert soup. The soup itself is made with fresh orange juice, white wine, and sliced kumquats, and subtly flavored with star anise and cracked peppercorns. I serve it with a block of Kumquat-Orange Sorbet and a chiffonade of fresh mint leaves. Make this soup the day before you serve it to allow the flavors to blend and develop.

MAKES 8 SERVINGS

COMPONENTS

KUMQUAT SOUP
KUMQUAT-ORANGE SORBET

SPECIAL EQUIPMENT | ice cream machine; 8-inch square baking pan

PERFECT MATCH | 2004 Duché de Longueville Cidre Gros Oeillet, France

KUMQUAT SOUP

1 tsp (3 g/0.1 oz) cornstarch

½ cup (121 g/4.2 oz) freshly squeezed orange juice

2 cups (510 g/17.9 oz) white wine

½ cup (100 g/3.5 oz) granulated sugar

3 pieces star anise

5 whole black peppercorns, cracked

12 (108 g/3.8 oz) kumquats

1. In a small bowl, combine the cornstarch and 2 tablespoons (30 g/1 oz) of the orange juice until smooth and set aside. In a small saucepan, combine the wine, the remaining 6 tablespoons orange juice, the sugar, and spices and bring to a boil over medium-high heat.

Remove from the heat and let stand, covered, for 10 minutes to allow to infuse.

2. Slice the kumquats into thin wheels, removing and discarding the seeds as you slice. Place the kumquat wheels in a medium bowl and set aside.

3. Place the pan containing the wine mixture over medium-high heat and whisk in the cornstarch mixture. Bring to a boil, whisking constantly, and boil for 1 minute. Remove from the heat and pour the hot liquid through a fine-mesh sieve over the kumquats. Cool completely.

4. Cover the bowl and refrigerate the soup for at least 24 hours before serving.

KUMQUAT-ORANGE SORBET

About 26 (200 g/7 oz) kumquats

2 cups (475 g/16.75 oz) water

1 cup (200 g/7 oz) granulated sugar

1¼ cups (300 g/10.6 oz) freshly squeezed orange juice

1½ cups (350 g/12.34 oz) Simple Syrup (page 339)

1. Cut the kumquats in half. Fill a medium saucepan halfway with water and bring the water to a boil over high heat. Add the kumquat halves and boil for 5 minutes. Drain and repeat, then drain again.

2. Combine 1½ cups (350 g/12.3 oz) of the water with the sugar in the saucepan and bring to a boil over medium-high heat. Add the blanched kumquats, reduce the heat to medium-low, and simmer until the kumquats are translucent, about 20 minutes. Drain, then purée in a food processor or blender until smooth.

3. In a bowl, combine the kumquat purée with the orange juice, Simple Syrup, and remaining ½ cup (125 g/4.4 oz) water. Cover and refrigerate the sorbet base for at least 4 hours.

4. Line an 8-inch square baking pan with plastic wrap. Process the sorbet base in an ice cream machine according to the manufacturer's instructions. Scrape the sorbet into the prepared pan, cover with plastic wrap, and freeze until firm, about 2 hours.

5. Cut the block of sorbet into 2-inch square blocks and return to the freezer until ready to serve.

ASSEMBLY

Chiffonade of fresh mint leaves

8 pieces star anise

Pour some of the Kumquat Soup into a shallow serving bowl. Place a square of Kumquat-Orange Sorbet in the center, and garnish with the chiffonade of mint and a piece of star anise.

BRIOCHE PANINI with RASPBERRY JAM and PEANUT BUTTER CRUNCH ICE CREAM

ONE DAY AT PAYARD I was eating a panini for lunch and Eric Estrella, one of my pastry chefs, came up with the idea for a dessert panini that was a play on a classic peanut butter and jelly sandwich. In it, slices of brioche are spread with pastry cream and then grilled. A scoop of Peanut Butter Crunch Ice Cream is served alongside, and a dollop of home-made Raspberry Jam tops the Brioche Panini. If you don't have a panini press, you can use a reg-ular grill pan instead—just top the panini with a bacon press or small pan to weigh it down.

MAKES 8 SERVINGS

COMPONENTS

BRIOCHE

PASTRY CREAM

PEANUT BUTTER CRUNCH ICE CREAM

RASPBERRY JAM

SPECIAL EQUIPMENT | ice cream machine; candy thermometer; panini press

PERFECT MATCH | Di Majo Norante Moscato del Molise Apianae, Italy

---

1 LOAF BRIOCHE (page 342) OR STORE-BOUGHT BRIOCHE OR CHALLAH

PASTRY CREAM (page 341)

PEANUT BUTTER CRUNCH ICE CREAM

1 cup (125 g/4.4 oz) unsalted peanuts

⅓ cup Simple Syrup (page 339)

1 cup (250 g/8.8 oz) whole milk

1 cup (250 g/8.8 oz) heavy cream

1 vanilla bean, split lengthwise and seeds scraped

6 large (112 g/4 oz) egg yolks

½ cup plus 2 Tbsp (125 g/4.4 oz) granulated sugar

¾ cup (180 g/6.3 oz) creamy peanut butter

1. Preheat the oven to 350°F (177°C). Line a half-sheet pan with a silicone baking mat.

2. In a medium bowl, toss the peanuts with the Simple Syrup. Scatter the nuts on the pan and bake for 10 minutes, stirring the nuts once or twice during baking, until they are golden brown. Cool completely. Transfer the nuts to a cutting board and chop them finely. Set aside.

3. In a medium saucepan, combine the milk, cream, and vanilla bean pod and seeds and bring to a gentle boil over medium heat.

4. In a medium bowl, whisk together the egg yolks and sugar until pale. Whisk about half of the hot milk mixture into the yolks, then return this mixture to the remaining milk mixture in the saucepan and cook over medium heat, stirring constantly with a wooden spoon, until it thickens enough to coat the back of the spoon and reaches 175°F (79°C) on an instant-read thermometer; do not let the mixture boil, or the egg yolks will curdle. Remove the pot from the heat and strain the mixture immediately into a bowl. Whisk in the peanut butter. Set the bowl in an ice bath and stir frequently until cold.

5. Transfer the ice cream base to an airtight container and refrigerate for at least 4 hours, or overnight.

6. Process the base in an ice cream machine according to the manufacturer's instructions, adding the chopped peanuts during the final minute of churning. (Be careful not to over-churn the ice cream or it will become grainy.) Transfer the ice cream to an airtight container and freeze until ready to serve.

RASPBERRY JAM

1¾ cups (350 g/12.3 oz) granulated sugar

½ cup (120 g/4.2 oz) water

2⅔ cups (300 g/10.5 oz) fresh raspberries

Finely grated zest of 1 lemon

In a medium saucepan, combine the sugar and water and cook over medium-high heat until the syrup registers 246°F (119°C) on a candy thermometer. Add the raspberries and lemon zest and continue to cook over medium heat, stirring occasionally, until the fruit begins to break down and some of the liquid has evaporated, about 5 minutes; the finished jam should appear looser than a typical jam. Cool completely.

ASSEMBLY

Melted Clarified Butter (page 348), for brushing the brioche

Finely chopped peanuts, for garnish

Whole peanuts, for garnish

Preheat a panini press. Cut sixteen ½-inch-thick slices of Brioche. Spread a layer of Pastry Cream (about ⅓ cup) on half of the brioche slices and top with the remaining slices to form sandwiches. Coat the outside of each of the brioche slices lightly with Clarified Butter. Grill the sandwiches in the panini press until the bread is toasted. Cut each panini in half on the diagonal and arrange on a plate. Spoon a small mound of chopped peanuts next to the panini, and place a quenelle of Peanut Butter Crunch Ice Cream on top. Garnish the plate with a few whole peanuts. Spoon some of the Raspberry Jam on the brioche and serve warm.

CHOCOLATE BEIGNETS with ORANGE BLOSSOM CRÈME ANGLAISE

A BEIGNET IS A PASTRY made from a yeast-leavened batter that is deep-fried. These beignets are made with a beer-based batter that surrounds a frozen chocolate ganache center. As the beignets fry, the ganache center melts, so that when you cut into them, a pool of chocolate comes gushing out. I serve them here with an Orange Blossom Crème Anglaise, which has a floral note that stands up to the chocolate. Because the beignet batter is made with yeast and beer, it doesn't hold for more than an hour, so make sure you use it soon after you make it.

MAKES 8 SERVINGS

COMPONENTS

CHOCOLATE BEIGNETS
  CHOCOLATE GANACHE BEIGNET CENTERS
  BEIGNET BATTER
ORANGE BLOSSOM CRÈME ANGLAISE

SPECIAL EQUIPMENT | deep, straight-sided saucepan or deep fryer

PERFECT MATCH | 2008 Zind-Humbrecht Riesling Brand Grand Cru, France

CHOCOLATE GANACHE BEIGNET CENTERS

5.3 oz (151 g) 64% bittersweet chocolate, finely chopped

¾ cup (166 g/5.8 oz) heavy cream

1. Place the chopped chocolate in a medium bowl and set aside. In a small saucepan, bring the cream to a gentle boil over medium heat. Pour the hot cream over the chocolate. Let stand for 1 minute to melt the chocolate, then gently whisk until the mixture is thoroughly blended and smooth. Cover the bowl and refrigerate the ganache until firm, about 45 minutes.

2. Line a half-sheet pan with parchment paper. Spoon out some ganache and shape it into a ¾-inch ball. Place the ball on the sheet pan and repeat to make at least 24 ganache balls. Freeze the balls until firm, at least 1 hour.

ORANGE BLOSSOM CRÈME ANGLAISE

Crème Anglaise (page 335)

2 Tbsp (30 g/1.05 oz) orange blossom water

Stir the orange blossom water into the chilled Crème Anglaise and refrigerate, covered, until ready to serve.

BEIGNET BATTER

¾ cup plus 1 Tbsp (195 g/6.8 oz) beer (any kind)

3 Tbsp (25 g/0.88 oz) fresh yeast

1⅔ cups (200 g/7 oz) all-purpose flour

1 Tbsp plus 2 tsp (20 g/0.87 oz) granulated sugar

Pour the beer into a medium bowl and add the fresh yeast. Let stand for 5 minutes, then stir to dissolve the yeast. Gradually whisk in the flour until blended. Whisk in the sugar. Cover the bowl and refrigerate until ready to use. You must use the batter within 1 hour while the yeast is still active.

ASSEMBLY

4 cups (858 g/30.26 oz) vegetable oil

2 large (100 g/3.5 oz) eggs, lightly whisked

1 cup (90 g/3.17 oz) fine bread crumbs

1. In a deep, straight-sided saucepan or deep fryer, begin heating the oil to 380°F (193°C). Line a half-sheet pan with paper towels. Place the eggs and bread crumbs in two separate bowls. Dip a frozen ganache ball in the egg, then completely coat it in the bread crumbs. Dip it in the Beignet Batter, coating it completely (this is a little messy) and fry in the hot oil, keeping it submerged with a spider or slotted spoon, until browned, 2 to 3 minutes. Remove with a spider and set on the paper towels to drain. Repeat to make the remaining beignets.

2. Serve 3 or 4 hot Chocolate Beignets on a plate with the Orange Blossom Crème Anglaise.

WATERMELON and VODKA SOUP with a "LIMESICLE" and LIME SYRUP

❋ ❋ THIS IS ONE OF THE MOST REFRESHING summer dessert soups you'll find, and one of the few I make that has alcohol in it. Accented with citrus, ginger, and cinnamon and spiked with a shot of vodka, it features cubes of zesty Lime Gelée and a frozen "Limesicle." It's a very different way to present a soup, and it's an ideal dessert for a hot summer night. If you prefer, you can leave out the vodka.

MAKES 8 SERVINGS

COMPONENTS

WATERMELON SOUP
LIME GELÉE
LIME SHERBET
LIMESICLES
LIME SYRUP
PHYLLO STRIPS

SPECIAL EQUIPMENT 8-inch square baking pan; ice cream machine; 8-inch square nonreactive baking pan

PERFECT MATCH Crop Organic Cucumber Vodka with freshly squeezed lime juice

WATERMELON SOUP

½ (2.5 kg/ 5.5 lb) seedless watermelon

¼ cup plus 3 Tbsp (87 g/3 oz) granulated sugar

Finely grated zest of 2 limes

Finely grated zest of 2 oranges

1 (3-inch) piece (45 g/1.6 oz) fresh ginger, peeled and sliced

1 stalk fresh lemongrass

1 vanilla bean, split lengthwise and seeds scraped

1 stick cinnamon

¼ cup (60 g/2.1 oz) vodka

1.   Cut the watermelon in half and remove the flesh from the rind. Cut half of the flesh into ¼-inch cubes, and place the remaining flesh in a blender and purée until smooth.

Place the cubed watermelon and watermelon purée in separate containers, cover, and refrigerate overnight.

2.   Remove the water from the purée (the mixture will have separated into 2 layers) by spooning it off with a ladle into a medium saucepan. Add the sugar, citrus zests, ginger slices, lemongrass, vanilla bean pod and seeds, and the cinnamon stick to the saucepan with the watermelon water and bring to a boil over medium-high heat. Remove from the heat and cool completely.

3.   Strain the cooled watermelon liquid and combine it with the watermelon purée and vodka. Cover and refrigerate until ready to serve.

LIME GELÉE

6 sheets (12 g/0.42 oz) gelatin (silver grade)

1 cup (250 g/8.8 oz) Simple Syrup (page 330)

1 cup (250 g/8.8 oz) freshly squeezed lime juice

Finely grated zest of 2 limes

1.   Line an 8-inch square baking pan with plastic wrap, leaving a 2-inch overhang on all sides. Fill a medium bowl halfway with cold water and add the gelatin sheets. Allow to soften for 10 minutes.

2.   Place the Simple Syrup in a small saucepan over medium heat and heat until hot. Remove the pan from the heat. Drain the gelatin and squeeze it to remove the excess water. Add the gelatin to the hot syrup, and stir until the gelatin has dissolved. Stir in the lime juice and pass the syrup through a fine-mesh sieve into a bowl. Stir in the lime zest. Pour the mixture into the lined pan and freeze until firm, at least 2 hours.

3.   Using the plastic wrap as handles, gently lift the gelée out of the pan. Cut the gelée into ¼-inch cubes. Cover and refrigerate the cubes until ready to serve.

LIME SHERBET

½ cup (125 g/4.4 oz) water

½ cup plus 2 Tbsp (125 g/4.4 oz) granulated sugar

½ cup (125 g/4.4 oz) whole milk

½ cup (125 g/4.4 oz) freshly squeezed lime juice

1.   In a small saucepan, combine the water and sugar and bring to a boil over medium-high heat. Remove from the heat, stir in the milk, and cool completely.

2.   Stir in the lime juice, transfer the sherbet base to an airtight container, and refrigerate for at least 4 hours.

3.   Process the base in an ice cream machine according to the manufacturer's instructions. Transfer the sherbet to an airtight container and freeze until ready to use.

LIMESICLES

½ recipe Vanilla Ice Cream (page 340)

Lime Sherbet (above)

1.   Line an 8-inch square nonreactive baking pan with plastic wrap. Spread the Vanilla Ice Cream into the pan in an even layer. Top with the Lime Sherbet, spreading it out into an even layer. Cover with plastic wrap and freeze for at least 2 hours, or overnight.

2.   Cut ten 1½ by 3-inch rectangles from the square, cover, and freeze until ready to serve.

LIME SYRUP

2 sheets (4 g/0.14 oz) gelatin (silver grade)

¾ cup (180 g/6.3 oz) freshly squeezed lime juice

1½ cups (300 g/10.6 oz) granulated sugar

Finely grated zest of 2 limes

1 sprig fresh mint

1.   Fill a small bowl halfway with cold water and add the gelatin sheets. Allow to soften for 10 minutes.

2.   In a small saucepan, combine the lime juice, sugar, lime zest, and mint and bring to a boil over medium-high heat, boiling until the sugar is dissolved. Drain the gelatin and squeeze it to remove the excess water. Add the gelatin to the lime syrup, stirring until the gelatin has dissolved. Set aside to cool.

3.   Remove the mint sprig and transfer the syrup to a covered container. Refrigerate until ready to serve.

PHYLLO STRIPS

4 (13 by 18-inch) sheets phyllo dough

17¾ Tbsp (250 g/8.8 oz) unsalted butter, melted

Confectioners' sugar, for dusting

1.   Preheat the oven to 350°F (177°C). Line a half-sheet pan with a silicone baking mat. Place a sheet of phyllo dough on a piece of parchment paper and brush it with some of the melted butter. Dust with confectioners' sugar. Repeat the layering process until you have used all 4 phyllo sheets. Brush the last sheet with butter and dust with confectioners' sugar. Refrigerate the phyllo layers for 30 minutes, or until the butter has firmed up.

2.   Using a pastry wheel, cut the layered sheet into sixteen 6 by ½-inch strips. Arrange the strips on the prepared sheet pan and cover with another baking mat to keep the phyllo flat. Bake for 8 to 10 minutes, or until crisp. Cool the strips on the sheet pan, set on a wire rack.

ASSEMBLY

Confectioners' sugar, for dusting

In a soup bowl, arrange a mixed mound of diced watermelon (about ⅓ cup) and Lime Gelée (about 2 tablespoons). Pour some of the Watermelon Soup over the fruit. Dust two Phyllo Strips with confectioners' sugar, place them on the rim of the bowl, and place a Limesicle on top. Spoon some of the Lime Syrup over the dessert and serve immediately.

ORANGE TUILE RING filled with MARSHMALLOW and ORANGE BLOSSOM ICE CREAM

THIS WAS A DESSERT WE SERVED AT PAYARD, and I developed it at a time when hot chocolate—the really rich and thick kind—was all the rage in New York. I decided to pair my version with orange, using segments, Orange Marshmallows, Orange Gelée, an Orange Blossom Ice Cream, and a lacy Orange Tuile Ring as elements in an elegant, hot chocolate–inspired plated dessert. When it was served, the waiter poured the rich hot chocolate on top of the oranges, marshmallows, and ice cream at the table, and the orange and chocolate and marshmallow flavors all came together to create a wonderful combination of flavors and textures.

MAKES 8 SERVINGS

COMPONENTS

ORANGE MARSHMALLOWS

ORANGE BLOSSOM ICE CREAM

ORANGE TUILE RINGS

ORANGE GELÉE

BITTERSWEET HOT CHOCOLATE

SPECIAL EQUIPMENT | 9 by 13-inch baking pan; candy thermometer; ice cream machine; 1 by 9-inch rectangular plastic tuile stencil; four 2½-inch ring molds; 8½ by 4½-inch loaf pan; blowtorch

PERFECT MATCH | Grand Marnier Cuvée du Cent Cinquantenaire

ORANGE MARSHMALLOWS

5 cups (1.18 kg/41.6 oz) cold water

8 sheets (16 g/0.56 oz) gelatin (silver grade)

Confectioners' sugar, for dusting the pan and marshmallows

2¼ cups (450 g/15.87 oz) granulated sugar

⅓ cup (100 g/3.5 oz) light corn syrup

6 large (180 g/6.34 oz) egg whites

Finely grated zest of 1 orange

1 tsp (5 g/0.17 oz) orange oil (see Sources, page 349)

1. Place 4 cups (944 g/33.3 oz) of the water in a medium bowl and add the gelatin sheets. Submerge them completely and allow to soften.

2. Spray the bottom and sides of a 9 by 13-inch baking pan with nonstick cooking spray and line it with plastic wrap. Dust the plastic liberally with sifted confectioners' sugar.

3. In a medium, heavy-bottomed saucepan, combine the sugar, the remaining 1 cup (236 g/8.3 oz) water, and the corn syrup and place over medium-high heat. Bring to a boil,

occasionally brushing down the sides of the pan with a wet pastry brush to prevent crystals from forming, and continue to boil until the syrup registers 248°F (120°C) on a candy thermometer. Remove from the heat, and immediately drain the gelatin, squeezing it to remove the excess water, and add it to the hot syrup, stirring to dissolve the gelatin.

4.   Place the egg whites in the bowl of a stand mixer fitted with the whisk attachment and whip on high speed until they are opaque and doubled in volume. Reduce the speed to medium and gradually add the hot syrup in a slow stream. Add the orange zest and orange oil and beat on high speed until cool, about 8 minutes. Spread out the meringue in an even layer on the prepared pan. Dust the top of the meringue with sifted confectioners' sugar. Let stand at room temperature, uncovered, for 24 hours.

5. Dust a cutting board with confectioners' sugar. Turn out the marshmallows onto the cutting board. Dust a sharp knife with confectioners' sugar to prevent the marshmallow from sticking to it and cut the marshmallow into ½-inch cubes. Once the cubes are cut, dust with more confectioners' sugar to keep the pieces separate. Store the marshmallows in an airtight container.

ORANGE BLOSSOM ICE CREAM

2 cups (484 g/17 oz) whole milk

⅓ cup plus 1 Tbsp (50 g/1.76 oz) milk powder

½ cup plus 1 Tbsp (110 g/3.8 oz) granulated sugar

¼ cup plus 1 Tbsp (50 g/1.76 oz) powdered glucose (see Sources, page 349)

4 extra-large (80 g/2.8 oz) egg yolks

⅔ cup (150 g/5.3 oz) heavy cream

1 Tbsp plus 1 tsp (20 g/0.7 oz) orange blossom water

Finely grated zest of 2 oranges

5 oz (142 g) bittersweet chocolate, finely chopped

½ cup (78 g/2.75 oz) chopped candied orange peel

1. In a medium saucepan, combine the milk, milk powder, sugar, and powdered glucose and bring to a boil over medium-high heat.

2. In a medium bowl, whisk the yolks until smooth. Whisk in half of the hot milk mixture, then return this mixture to the remaining milk mixture in the saucepan, take off the heat, and strain through a fine-mesh sieve into a bowl.

Stir in the cream, orange blossom water, and orange zest. Set the bowl in an ice bath and stir frequently until cold.

3. Transfer the ice cream base to an airtight container and refrigerate for at least 4 hours, or overnight.

4. Process the base in an ice cream machine according to the manufacturer's instructions. (Be careful not to overchurn the ice cream or it will become grainy.) Fold in the chocolate and candied orange peel. Transfer the ice cream to an airtight container and freeze until ready to serve.

ORANGE TUILE RINGS

¾ cup plus 3 Tbsp firmly packed (200 g/7 oz) light brown sugar

1 cup (200 g/7 oz) granulated sugar

1⅔ cups (200 g/7 oz) all-purpose flour

¾ cup plus 1 Tbsp (200 g/7 oz) freshly squeezed orange juice

14 Tbsp (200 g/7 oz) unsalted butter, softened

1. Preheat the oven to 350°F (177°C). Line a half-sheet pan with a silicone baking mat and set a 1 by 9-inch rectangular stencil on the mat.

2. Sift the brown sugar, granulated sugar, and flour together in a medium bowl. Place in a food processor with the orange juice and process until smooth. Add the butter and process until smooth.

3. Spread the tuile batter over the stencil. Repeat to form 3 more tuiles on the mat. Bake the tuiles for about 8 minutes, or until golden brown around the edges. While the tuiles are still hot, wrap each one around a 2½-inch ring

mold, pressing the overlapping ends against the side to form a clean ring. Allow the tuiles to cool on a wire rack. Repeat to make at least 4 more tuile rings (though you may want to make a few more in case of breakage).

ORANGE GELÉE

1 pint (472 g/16.6 oz) cold water

4 sheets (8 g/0.28 oz) gelatin (silver grade)

1 cup (250 g/8.8 oz) orange juice concentrate, thawed

1.   Line the bottom and sides of an 8½ by 4½-inch loaf pan with plastic wrap, leaving a 2-inch overhang on all sides. Place the water in a medium bowl and add the gelatin sheets. Submerge them completely and allow to soften for 10 minutes.

2.   Place ½ cup (125 g/4.4 oz) of the orange juice concentrate in a small saucepan over medium-high heat and heat until it just begins to bubble. Drain the gelatin and squeeze it to remove the excess water. Add the gelatin to the hot orange concentrate and stir until the gelatin has dissolved. Stir in the remaining ½ cup (125 g/4.4 oz) orange concentrate. Pour the mixture into the prepared pan and freeze until firm, at least 1 hour.

3.   Using the plastic wrap as handles, gently lift the gelée out of the pan. Cut the gelée into ¼-inch cubes, place in an airtight container and refrigerate until ready to serve.

BITTERSWEET HOT CHOCOLATE

5.3 oz (150 g) 72% bittersweet chocolate, chopped

1 cup (232 g/8.18 oz) heavy cream

1 cup (242 g/8.5 oz) whole milk

1.   Place the chocolate in a medium heatproof bowl and set aside.

2.   Combine the cream and milk in a small saucepan and bring to a boil over medium-high heat. Pour the hot cream mixture over the chopped chocolate and allow it to stand for 1 minute to melt the chocolate. Stir until the mixture is smooth and the chocolate has completely melted. Serve warm.

ASSEMBLY

24 orange suprêmes (page 348)

¼ cup firmly packed (54 g/31.9 oz) light brown sugar

16 chocolate cigarettes (see Sources, page 349)

Place an Orange Tuile Ring in the center of a soup plate. Place three orange suprêmes inside the tuile to anchor it to the plate. Sprinkle the orange suprêmes with ½ tablespoon (7 g/0.24 oz) of the brown sugar and caramelize them with a blowtorch. Arrange about 6 Orange Gelée cubes and 6 Orange Marshmallow cubes inside the ring. Balance 2 chocolate cigarettes parallel on the tuile and place a quenelle of the Orange Blossom Ice Cream on the chocolate. Pour some warm Bittersweet Hot Chocolate on top of the ice cream.

THE CHEESE COURSE: SAVORY DESSERTS

MANY OF THE DESSERTS IN THIS CHAPTER were created for a special menu I developed when I first opened Payard Patisserie at Caesars Palace in Las Vegas. I wanted to do something a little different, something that would shake up the Las Vegas dining scene, so I created a savory dessert menu that featured desserts that paired cheese with fruit. All the food writers in Las Vegas loved it, giving it glowing reviews because it was so refreshingly new. Macarons were just taking off, so we developed a Black Olive Macaron that was colored with squid ink, then filled with a cream cheese and olive tapenade filling and served with a Gorgonzola Ice Cream. We also did a couple of savory cheesecakes that were popular, one made with feta and one with chèvre. We made an Apple Tatin without any added sugar, and served it with a piece of aged white cheddar cheese and a frisée salad with walnuts. We also had a Seckel pear that really was incredible. It was poached in pomegranate juice and served with a piece of Cabrales cheese from Spain, a Szechuan Pepper Ice Cream, and baked almond cream. Every dessert in this chapter is a little unusual, but you know, people really only open their minds to these unusual flavors when they go to fancy restaurants, where the desserts have a high price tag. Diners say, "Tonight is a special night," and their minds are open to just about anything the chef or pastry chef suggests. And that's what makes it all worthwhile.

BLACK OLIVE MACARON with GORGONZOLA ICE CREAM

✳ SQUID INK IS THE SECRET INGREDIENT that gives this savory-sweet macaron its striking jet black hue. It also lends a briny and slightly earthy flavor to the meringue shell, an ideal complement to its cream cheese and tapenade filling. The ice cream is made with a creamy Gorgonzola that's just sharp enough to cut through the richness of the cream, without overwhelming your palate.

MAKES 8 SERVINGS

COMPONENTS

GORGONZOLA ICE CREAM
BLACK MACARONS
BLACK OLIVE–CREAM CHEESE FILLING
STREUSEL

SPECIAL EQUIPMENT | Pacojet or standard ice cream machine; immersion blender; candy thermometer; large pastry bag fitted with a ⅜-inch, plain tip (Ateco #4); 3-inch round pastry cutter (optional)

PERFECT MATCH | Vin d'Orange de Provence, France

GORGONZOLA ICE CREAM

¾ cup (150 g/5.3 oz) granulated sugar

2½ tsp (8 g/0.28 oz) ice cream stabilizer

4 cups plus 2 Tbsp (1 kg/35.27 oz) whole milk

1¾ cups (400 g/14 oz) heavy cream

¼ cup plus 2½ Tbsp (140 g/5 oz) honey

⅔ cup (170 g/6 oz) Gorgonzola cheese, crumbled

1.   In a small bowl, mix together the sugar and ice cream stabilizer.

2.   In a large saucepan, combine the milk, cream, honey, and sugar and bring to a boil, stirring occasionally to dissolve the sugar. Remove the pan from the heat, add the Gorgonzola cheese and, using an immersion blender, blend until smooth. Pass the ice cream base through a fine-mesh sieve into a medium bowl. Set the bowl in an ice bath and allow to stand, stirring occasionally, until chilled. If you are using a Pacojet, pour the ice cream base into the Pacojet canisters and freeze until ready to use, then process in the Pacojet as directed. If you are using a standard ice cream machine, cover the bowl and refrigerate the ice cream base for at least 4 hours.

3.   Process the base in the ice cream machine according to the manufacturer's instructions. (Do not overchurn it or the ice cream will become grainy.) Transfer the ice cream to an airtight container and freeze until ready to serve.

BLACK MACARONS

4 cups (450 g/15.8 oz) confectioners' sugar

4½ cups (400 g/14 oz) almond flour

9½ large (285 g/9.96 oz) egg whites

1 Tbsp plus 1 tsp (0.7 oz/20 g) squid ink (see Sources, page 349)

Black food coloring paste, as needed

2 cups (400 g/14 oz) granulated sugar

⅓ cup (78 g/2.75 oz) water

1.   Position two racks near the center of the oven and preheat the oven to 325°F (163°C). Line two half-sheet pans with silicone baking mats.

2.   In the bowl of a stand mixer fitted with the paddle attachment, mix together the confectioners' sugar, almond flour, 5 (150g/5.2 oz) of the egg whites, and the squid ink on low speed until blended. Mix in enough black food coloring paste to turn the mixture jet black.

3. In a medium saucepan, cook the sugar and water over medium-high heat, occasionally washing down the sides of the pan with a wet pastry brush to prevent crystals from forming, and watching carefully, until the syrup registers 240°F (116°C) on a candy thermometer. While the syrup is cooking, put the remaining 4½ (135 g/4.76 oz) egg whites in a clean mixer bowl and begin beating them with a clean whisk attachment on medium-high speed. The timing is a little tricky, but you ideally want the egg whites to just reach soft peaks when the syrup reaches the proper temperature. If the eggs reach the soft peak stage before the syrup is ready, turn the mixer off until the syrup reaches the proper temperature. When both are ready, reduce the mixer speed to low and slowly pour the hot syrup into the whites. Increase the speed to high and mix the whites until they are glossy, but still warm. Remove the bowl of meringue from the mixer stand and stir about one-third of the meringue into the almond flour mixture until blended. Gently fold in the remaining meringue in two additions. Fold the meringue several more times, pressing the batter against the side of the bowl, until it drips slowly from the spatula as you scoop it.

4. Scrape some of the mixture into a large pastry bag fitted with a ⅜-inch, plain tip and pipe 3-inch rounds onto the prepared sheet pans. Drop the pans onto the countertop a few times to eliminate any air pockets. Let the macaron shells dry at room temperature for 20 to 30 minutes, or until a skin forms over them; when you lightly touch them they should feel dry, not wet. Put each sheet pan on another empty sheet pan and bake the macaron shells for 12 to 14 minutes, or until they are crisp on the outside. Cool the macaron shells on the sheet pans, set on wire racks. Repeat with the remaining batter. You will need a total of 16 macaron shells for this recipe.

5. Carefully remove the macaron shells from the baking mats and store in an airtight container until ready to serve.

BLACK OLIVE–CREAM CHEESE FILLING

3½ cups (680 g/24 oz) cream cheese, softened

½ cup (100 g/3.5 oz) black olive tapenade (see Sources, page 349)

In the bowl of a stand mixer fitted with the paddle attachment, mix the cream cheese on medium-low speed until smooth. Add the olive tapenade and mix just until combined. The filling should be used when it is soft.

STREUSEL, BAKED (page 342)

ASSEMBLY

Extra-virgin olive oil, for drizzling

Scrape the Black Olive–Cream Cheese Filling into a pastry bag fitted with a medium, plain tip. Pipe a mound of filling onto a Black Macaron shell. Top with another macaron shell, gently pressing down on it to squeeze the filling toward the edge. Repeat with the remaining shells and filling. (Note: If you want the filling to be a perfect round, as in the photo (on page 305), spread it onto a sheet pan and refrigerate it for 30 minutes, then cut out rounds of filling with a 3-inch pastry cutter.) Pipe a small dollop of filling onto a plate and lean a macaron against it, so that it is standing up on the plate. Sprinkle some Streusel in a mound next to the macaron and top with a quenelle of Gorgonzola Ice Cream. Drizzle a little olive oil on the plate and serve immediately.

APPLE TATIN with AGED WHITE CHEDDAR CHEESE, FRISÉE SALAD, and TOASTED WALNUTS

This is not a classic Apple Tatin—in this savory-sweet version the apples aren't cooked in caramel on the stovetop, but are baked in the oven until the apples' natural sugars turn brown and caramelize. After baking, I compress each apple by pressing down on it with a sugar shaker or a mug, and then chill it for several hours to set its shape. Right before serving, I top the apple with a strong-flavored, aged white cheddar and bake it just long enough to melt the cheese. The Baked Apple is served on a puff pastry round with a Frisée Salad and toasted walnuts. If you have some walnut oil on hand, you can substitute it for half of the olive oil in the dressing for the salad. Make sure you use a strong-flavored cheddar here, otherwise its flavor will be overpowered by the apple.

MAKES 10 SERVINGS

Components

PUFF PASTRY ROUNDS
BAKED APPLES
FRISÉE SALAD

Special Equipment | 2¾-inch round pastry cutter; ten 4-ounce aluminum cups

Perfect Match | Étienne Dupont Organic Cidre Bouché Brut de Normandie, France

PUFF PASTRY ROUNDS

1 lb (454 g) Puff Pastry (page 343) or store-bought puff pastry

1 egg, whisked with a fork with a small amount of water, for egg wash

1.   Preheat the oven to 375°F (191°C). Line a half-sheet pan with a silicone baking mat.

2.   On a lightly floured work surface, roll out the puff pastry to a thickness of ⅛ inch. Using a 2¾-inch round pastry cutter, cut out 10 rounds from the dough and prick them at ½-inch intervals with the tines of a fork. Refrigerate the rounds for 15 minutes.

3.   Place the rounds on the prepared sheet pan and brush with the egg wash. Bake for 9 to 12 minutes, or until the rounds are golden brown and crispy. Transfer to a wire rack and cool completely. Reduce the oven temperature to 350°F (177°C).

BAKED APPLES

5 medium Fuji apples

1. Preheat the oven to 350°F (177°C). Brush the bottom and sides of ten 4-ounce disposable aluminum cups generously with the softened butter and place them on a half-sheet pan.

2. Peel and core the apples and cut each in half crosswise. Place each apple half in a prepared cup and bake for 45 to 60 minutes, or until lightly browned. Allow the apples to cool for 30 minutes.

3. Wrap the bottom of a sugar shaker or mug with plastic wrap and press it down firmly onto each apple to compress it. Unmold the apples, then refrigerate them, covered, for at least 4 hours.

FRISÉE SALAD

3 Tbsp (45 g/1.6 oz) balsamic vinegar

½ cup (128 g/4.5 oz) extra-virgin olive oil (or use half walnut oil, half olive oil)

Salt

Freshly ground black pepper

2 heads (300 g/10.5 oz) frisée (French curly endive), leaves washed and spun dry

1. Place the vinegar in a small bowl, and pour in the oil in a slow steady stream, whisking constantly. Season with salt and pepper to taste.

2. When ready to serve, in a medium bowl, combine the frisée leaves with the dressing and toss to combine.

ASSEMBLY

5 oz (142 g) aged white cheddar cheese, thinly sliced

25-year-old balsamic vinegar, for garnish

½ cup (50 g/1.76 oz) walnuts, toasted (see Toasting Nuts, page 346)

1. Preheat the oven to 350°F (177°C). Line a half-sheet pan with a silicone baking mat or parchment paper.

2. Arrange the baked apples on the lined half-sheet pan. Top each apple with a slice or two of the cheese, covering the top. Bake the apples for about 4 minutes, or until the cheese has melted. Remove the pan from the oven and place a Puff Pastry Round on top of the cheese. Flip each apple over and arrange it on one side of a plate. Arrange some Frisée Salad on the other side. Garnish the salad with some toasted walnuts, and dot the plate with some of the balsamic vinegar.

WARM RICOTTA TART with CITRUS-MINT SALAD

For the tart, I blend fresh ricotta and mascarpone cheese with honey to yield a creamy and slightly tangy filling that has the consistency of cheesecake. I top the tart with a salad made from blood orange and grapefruit suprêmes tossed with a light vinaigrette, a few turns of white pepper, and fresh mint. A Parmesan tuile, known in Italy as a *frico*, adds another savory note to this uncommonly good tart.

MAKES 8 SERVINGS

COMPONENTS

WARM RICOTTA TARTS
   TART SHELLS
   RICOTTA FILLING
CITRUS-MINT SALAD
PARMESAN TUILES

SPECIAL EQUIPMENT | pepper mill; 4-inch round pastry cutter; eight 3-inch tart pans

PERFECT MATCH | Di Majo Norante Moscato del Molise Apianae, Italy

---

CITRUS-MINT SALAD

4 pink grapefruit

6 blood oranges

10 fresh mint leaves, cut into thin ribbons

1 Tbsp (15 g/0.5 oz) white balsamic vinegar

3 Tbsp (48 g/1.7 oz) extra-virgin olive oil

3 to 5 turns of freshly ground white pepper

Using a sharp knife, cut the peel off the top and bottom of each grapefruit and orange so that it stands up without wobbling. Cutting from top to bottom, remove the peel from each fruit, exposing the flesh. Make a cut on each side of each segment to free it from the fruit. Continue until all the suprêmes are removed. Set aside 8 grapefruit suprêmes and 16 orange suprêmes for the tarts. Combine the remaining suprêmes in a medium bowl with the mint, vinegar, olive oil, and white pepper and stir gently just to combine. Refrigerate until ready to use.

TART SHELLS

Basic Sweet Tart Dough (page 332)

1.   Divide the dough into 2 pieces. Wrap 1 piece in plastic wrap and store it in the refrigerator. Place the other piece on a lightly floured work surface and roll it to a thickness of ⅒ inch. Using a 4-inch pastry cutter, cut out 4 rounds from the dough and press each into a 3-inch tart pan. Roll a rolling pin over the top of the pan and remove the excess dough. Repeat with the remaining piece of dough and tart pans. Prick the bottoms of the tart shells with the tines of a fork and arrange them on a sheet pan. Refrigerate the shells for 20 minutes. Meanwhile, position a rack in the center of the oven and preheat the oven to 375°F (191°C).

2. Right before baking, line the dough in each pan with aluminum foil or parchment paper and fill with pie weights or dried beans. Bake the tart shells for 7 minutes. Carefully lift the foil, along with the weights, out of the tart pans and bake the crust for 2 to 3 minutes longer, until golden around the edges. Transfer the tart pans to a wire rack and cool completely, then remove the tart shells from the pans.

RICOTTA FILLING

¾ cup (350 g/12.3 oz) fresh ricotta cheese

¼ cup plus 2½ Tbsp (100 g/3.5 oz) mascarpone cheese

3 large (56 g/2 oz) egg yolks

1 large (50 g/1.76 oz) whole egg

1 Tbsp (25 g/0.88 oz) honey

1. Preheat the oven to 250°F (121°C). Arrange the tart shells on a half-sheet pan and place one of the reserved grapefruit suprêmes and two of the reserved orange suprêmes in the bottom of each tart shell.

2. In a medium bowl, stir the ricotta cheese with a rubber spatula until smooth. Add the mascarpone cheese and stir until smooth. Add the egg yolks, whole egg, and honey and whisk until combined. Divide the mixture equally among the tart shells and bake for about 8 minutes, or until the filling is just set.

PARMESAN TUILES

1 cup (57 g/2 oz) grated Parmesan cheese

Position a rack in the center of the oven and preheat the oven to 350°F (177°C). Line a half-sheet pan with a silicone baking mat. Sprinkle the cheese evenly onto the mat into a rough rectangular shape about 12 by 6 inches. Bake until the cheese melts together and is a golden brown color, 5 to 7 minutes. While the tuile is still hot, using a sharp knife, carefully cut out eight 6 by 6 by 1½-inch triangles from the rectangle. Allow to cool completely.

ASSEMBLY

The Ricotta Tarts should be served warm, so if you need to heat them up, place them in a preheated 250°F (121°C) oven for about 10 minutes. Place a warm tart on a plate and top with some of the Citrus-Mint Salad. Top the salad with a Parmesan Tuile. Spoon a drizzle of the liquid from the salad onto the plate.

POACHED SECKEL PEAR with POMEGRANATE, CABRALES CHEESE, and SZECHUAN PEPPER ICE CREAM

HERE'S ANOTHER DESSERT THAT WAS INSPIRED BY a wine-tasting dinner. It's often hard to come up with a dessert that pairs well with wine, but this savory-sweet dessert does. At its center is a Seckel pear, a small, reddish pear with a slightly spicy flavor. It has a firm flesh that makes it perfect for poaching. In this dessert I poach the pears in pomegranate juice with some ground black pepper. A chunk of Cabrales cheese, a strong blue cheese from northern Spain, is sandwiched between the top and bottom halves of the pear, and a Szechuan Ice Cream is served with it, sitting on a diamond of baked almond cream.

MAKES 8 SERVINGS

COMPONENTS

SZECHUAN PEPPER ICE CREAM

POACHED PEARS WITH POMEGRANATE

POMEGRANATE SAUCE

BAKED ALMOND DIAMONDS

SPECIAL EQUIPMENT | ice cream machine; pepper mill; 9-inch square baking pan; 2-inch-long by 1-inch-wide diamond-shaped pastry cutter

PERFECT MATCH | Carole Bouquet Passito di Pantelleria Sangue d'Oro, Sicily

SZECHUAN PEPPER ICE CREAM

3 cups (750 g/26.4 oz) whole milk

1 cup plus 1 Tbsp (250 g/8.8 oz) heavy cream

3 Tbsp plus 1 tsp (20 g/0.7 oz) Szechuan peppercorns

8½ large (160 g/5.6 oz) egg yolks

¾ cup plus 2 Tbsp (180 g/6.3 oz) granulated sugar

1. In a medium saucepan, combine the milk, cream, and peppercorns and cook over medium-high heat until the mixture comes to a gentle boil. Remove the pan from the heat, cover, and allow to infuse for 20 minutes.

2. Strain the milk mixture and return it to the saucepan. Reheat until the mixture just begins to boil. Remove from the heat.

3. In a medium bowl, whisk together the egg yolks and sugar vigorously until pale. Whisk about ½ cup of the hot milk mixture into the yolks, then return this mixture to the saucepan with the remaining milk mixture and cook over medium heat, stirring constantly with a wooden spoon, until it thickens enough to coat the back of the spoon and reaches 175°F (79°C) on an instant-read thermometer;

do not let the mixture boil, or the egg yolks will curdle. Remove the pot from the heat. Pass the ice cream base through a fine-mesh sieve into a bowl. Set the bowl in an ice bath and stir frequently until cold. Cover the bowl and refrigerate the ice cream base for at least 4 hours.

4.   Process the base in an ice cream machine according to the manufacturer's instructions (be careful not to overchurn the ice cream or it will become grainy). Transfer the ice cream to an airtight container and freeze until ready to serve.

POACHED PEARS WITH POMEGRANATE

4 cups (1 kg/2.2 lb) pomegranate juice

3 to 5 turns freshly ground black pepper

8 Seckel pears, peeled (you will core them after they are poached)

1.   In a medium saucepan, bring the pomegranate juice and black pepper to a boil over medium-high heat. Add the pears and reduce the heat to medium-low. Poach the pears in the simmering juice until tender, about 15 minutes. Cool completely at room temperature.

2.   Transfer the pears, still in the liquid, to an airtight container and refrigerate until ready to serve.

POMEGRANATE SAUCE

2 cups (500 g/17.6 oz) poaching liquid from Poached Pears with Pomegranate (left)

Pour the poaching liquid in a small saucepan and bring to a boil over medium-high heat. Continue to boil the liquid until it has reduced by half, about 15 minutes. Pass the syrup through a fine-mesh sieve into a bowl and cool.

BAKED ALMOND DIAMONDS

8¾ Tbsp (125 g/4.4 oz) unsalted butter

½ cup plus 2 Tbsp (125 g/4.4 oz) granulated sugar

1⅓ cups (125 g/4.4 oz) almond flour

2 large (100 g/3.5 oz) eggs

1 Tbsp plus 1 tsp (10 g/0.35 oz) all-purpose flour

1.   Preheat the oven to 375°F (191°C). Coat the bottom and sides of a 9-inch square baking pan with nonstick cooking spray.

2.   In the bowl of a stand mixer fitted with the paddle attachment, mix together the butter and sugar on medium speed until creamy and well blended, about 2 minutes. Add the almond flour and mix until blended. Reduce the mixer speed to medium-low and add the eggs, one at a time, mixing well after each addition and scraping down the sides of the bowl as necessary. Add the flour and mix until blended. Scrape the almond mixture into the prepared pan, smoothing it into an even layer. Bake for 18 to 22 minutes, or until golden brown. Place the pan on a wire rack and cool completely.

3.   Using a 2-inch-long by 1-inch-wide diamond-shaped pastry cutter, cut out 8 diamonds of baked almond cream. Store in an airtight container until ready to use.

ASSEMBLY

4 oz (113 g) Cabrales cheese, cut into eight ½-inch-thick slices

Cut each Poached Pear with Pomegranate in half crosswise and remove the cores from the bottom halves. Place each pear bottom standing up on a plate and top with a slice of Cabrales cheese. Replace the pear tops. Glaze the pears with some of the Pomegranate Sauce, letting some of the sauce drip onto the plates. Place a Baked Almond Diamond on each plate and top with a scoop of Szechuan Pepper Ice Cream.

BUTTERMILK PANNA COTTA with CITRUS TERRINE, MÂCHE SALAD, and PARMESAN TUILE

⬥⬥ I DEVELOPED THIS DESSERT, which features a savory topping of mâche salad, for a magazine that was doing a story on microgreens. They wanted a dessert that used microgreens as more than just a garnish, and this dish, with a crispy Parmesan Tuile on top, was the perfect combination of savory and sweet. Mâche, also known as "lamb's lettuce," has a buttery, sweet flavor that balances the acidity of the Buttermilk Panna Cotta and the Citrus Terrine. The panna cotta uses only enough gelatin to bind it; too much and it will be rubbery. It should be soft, creamy, and a little jiggly.

MAKES 8 SERVINGS

COMPONENTS

BUTTERMILK PANNA COTTA
CITRUS TERRINE
BASIL-MÂCHE OLIVE OIL
PARMESAN TUILES

SPECIAL EQUIPMENT | eight 3-ounce oval- or dome-shaped silicone molds; 9-inch round cake pan; 2-inch round pastry cutter; squeeze bottle

PERFECT MATCH | 2007 Carole Bouquet Passito di Pantelleria Sangue d'Oro, Sicily

BUTTERMILK PANNA COTTA

4 sheets (8 g/0.28 oz) gelatin (silver grade)

1⅓ cups (308 g/10.8 oz) heavy cream

1⅔ cups (400 g/14 oz) buttermilk

½ cup (100 g/3.5 oz) granulated sugar

1 vanilla bean, split lengthwise and seeds scraped

1. Fill a medium bowl one-third of the way with ice-cold water and add the gelatin sheets, submerging them completely. Allow to soften for 10 minutes.

2. In a small saucepan, combine the cream, buttermilk, and sugar and bring to a gentle boil over medium-high heat. Remove the pan from the heat. Drain the gelatin and squeeze it to remove the excess water. Add the gelatin to the hot cream mixture and stir until the gelatin has dissolved. Strain the cream mixture into a pourable cup measure and refrigerate the mixture until it is chilled, but not set, about 40 minutes (this will prevent the vanilla seeds from sinking to the bottom of the molds).

3. Scrape the vanilla bean seeds into the chilled cream mixture and stir to combine. Divide the mixture equally among eight 3-ounce oval- or dome-shaped silicone molds. Freeze the desserts until firm, about 2 hours.

4. Unmold the panna cottas and defrost in the refrigerator for about 2 hours before serving.

CITRUS TERRINE

7 (1.59 kg/3.5 lb) grapefruit

10 (1.5 kg/3 lb, 5 oz) oranges

3 cups (708 g/25 oz) cold water

3 sheets (6 g/0.21 oz) gelatin (silver grade)

⅓ cup (66 g/2.3 oz) granulated sugar

1 piece star anise

1 whole clove

1 whole white peppercorn, crushed with the bottom of a pan

1. Line a 9-inch round cake pan with plastic wrap, leaving a 2-inch overhang on all sides.

2. Using a paring knife, slice off the bottom and top of 3 of the grapefruit so that they stand upright. Slicing from top to bottom, cut away the peel, including the white pith, in strips. Remove the grapefruit segments, slicing between the translucent membranes to release them. Repeat this process with 4 of the oranges. Arrange the orange and grapefruit suprêmes, evenly spaced, in the prepared pan and set aside.

3. Place the cold water in a medium bowl and add the gelatin sheets, submerging them completely. Allow to soften for 10 minutes.

4. Juice the remaining 4 grapefruit and 6 oranges and place the juice in a medium, nonreactive saucepan. Add the sugar, star anise, whole clove, and white peppercorn and bring to a boil over high heat. Continue to boil until the liquid has reduced by half, 30 to 45 minutes. Measure out 1 cup (240 ml/8½ fl oz) of the reduced liquid into a bowl. Drain the gelatin and squeeze it to remove the excess water. Add the gelatin to the hot liquid, stirring until the gelatin has dissolved. Strain the liquid through a fine-mesh sieve onto the citrus suprêmes in the pan. Place the pan in the freezer for at least 2 hours, or until the liquid is firm.

5. Using the plastic wrap as handles, lift out the frozen terrine. Using a 2-inch round pastry cutter, cut out 8 rounds from the terrine. Store the rounds in an airtight container in the refrigerator until ready to use.

BASIL-MÂCHE OLIVE OIL

1 cup packed (60 g/2.1 oz) mâche (lamb's lettuce) leaves

½ cup packed (30 g/1 oz) fresh basil leaves

1 cup plus 2 Tbsp (250 g/8.8 oz) extra-virgin olive oil

1. Fill a large bowl halfway with ice water and set aside.

2. Fill a saucepan halfway with water and bring the water to a boil over high heat. Add the mâche and basil to the water and, once the water returns to a boil, drain the leaves and plunge them into the ice water. Once they are cold, remove them and pat them with paper towels to absorb any excess water.

3. Place the blanched mâche and basil in a blender with the olive oil and blend until smooth. Transfer to a squeeze bottle and set aside until ready to serve.

PARMESAN TUILES

1 cup (57 g/2 oz) finely grated Parmesan cheese

Position a rack in the center of the oven and preheat the oven to 350°F (177°C). Line a half-sheet pan with a silicone baking mat. Sprinkle the cheese evenly onto the mat into a rough rectangular shape about 12 by 6 inches. Bake until the cheese melts together and is a golden brown color, about 10 minutes. While the tuile is still hot, using a knife, carefully cut the rectangle into eight 6 by 1½-inch strips. Allow to cool completely.

ASSEMBLY

Mâche (lamb's lettuce) leaves

Extra-virgin olive oil, as needed

Place a Citrus Terrine round in the center of a plate. Place a Buttermilk Panna Cotta on top of the terrine. Decorate the plate with the Basil-Mâche Olive Oil. Arrange a Parmesan Tuile at an angle against the panna cotta and top with some mâche dressed with a few drops of olive oil.

FETA CHEESECAKE with RED WINE– POACHED DATES and WHITE PEPPER ICE CREAM

The Mediterranean flavors of feta cheese, dates, orange, and almond come together marvelously in this dessert. My sous-chef Eric Estrella and I developed it for the menu at InTent, a Middle Eastern Mediterranean restaurant I opened in downtown Manhattan in 2006. The cheesecake is made with a combination of feta cheese, cream cheese, and crème fraîche, which gives it a slightly tangy, complex character that tempers the sweetness of the dates. The White Pepper Ice Cream adds a spicy note, while the Orange Tuile adds a nice crunch.

MAKES 8 SERVINGS

COMPONENTS

WHITE PEPPER ICE CREAM
FETA CHEESECAKES
RED WINE–POACHED DATES
ALMOND ROUNDS
PHYLLO ROUNDS
ORANGE TUILES
STREUSEL

SPECIAL EQUIPMENT | pepper mill; 9-inch springform pan; 9-inch round cake pan; 2-inch round pastry cutter; 3-inch round tuile stencil

PERFECT MATCH | Alphonse Mellot Red Sancerre, France

WHITE PEPPER ICE CREAM

Vanilla Ice Cream (page 340), prepared through step 2

3 to 5 turns freshly crushed white pepper

Add the white pepper to the ice cream base, then proceed with the recipe as directed. Transfer the ice cream to an airtight container and freeze until ready to serve.

FETA CHEESECAKES

¾ cup (100 g/3.5 oz) feta cheese

1 cup firmly packed (200 g/7 oz) cream cheese, at room temperature

¾ cup (150 g/5.25 oz) granulated sugar

1 Tbsp (7.5 g/0.26 oz) all-purpose flour

1½ large (75 g/2.6 oz) whole eggs

½ large (9 g/0.31 oz) egg yolk

2 tsp (10 g/0.35 oz) crème fraîche

1. Preheat the oven to 300°F (149°C). Spray a 9-inch springform pan with nonstick cooking spray and line it with a round of parchment paper. Wrap the outside of the pan with aluminum foil to prevent leakage.

2. In the bowl of a stand mixer fitted with the paddle attachment, mix together the feta cheese and cream cheese on medium-low speed until blended. Add the sugar and flour and beat on medium speed until the mixture is well blended, about 2 minutes. Add the whole eggs and egg yolk, mixing until they are incorporated and scraping down the sides of the bowl with a rubber spatula as necessary. Add the crème fraîche and mix until blended. Pour the cheesecake mixture into the prepared pan. Set the pan in a slightly larger pan, such as a 10-inch cake pan, and pour water into the larger pan so that it comes halfway up the sides of the pan containing the cheesecake mixture. Bake the cake for about 40 minutes, or until just set in the center. Remove the pan from the water bath and cool the cake completely on a wire rack.

3. Place the cheesecake in the freezer until firm, about 2 hours.

4. Using a 2-inch round pastry cutter, cut out 8 rounds from the cheesecake. Refrigerate the cake rounds until ready to serve.

RED WINE–POACHED DATES

1 cup (250 g/8.8 oz) red wine

⅓ cup plus 2 Tbsp (90 g/3.17 oz) granulated sugar

1 vanilla bean, split lengthwise and seeds scraped

Juice of 1 lemon

20 (about 425 g/15 oz) Medjool dates, pitted

1. In a medium saucepan, combine the red wine, sugar, and vanilla bean pod and seeds and bring to a boil over medium-high heat. Add the lemon juice and dates, reduce to a simmer, and simmer until the dates are softened, about 5 minutes. Remove the dates with a slotted spoon and reserve in a container. The remaining liquid should be syrupy; if it's not, boil until it is slightly reduced and syrupy. Remove the pan from the heat and strain the sauce into a container. Set aside to cool.

2. Cover the containers holding the dates and the sauce and set aside until ready to serve.

ALMOND ROUNDS

4 cups (640 g/22.57 oz) Almond Cream (page 341)

1. Preheat the oven to 375°F (191°C). Spray a 9-inch round cake pan with nonstick cooking spray.

2. Spread out the almond cream in the prepared pan. Bake for about 17 minutes, or until golden brown. Cool completely in the pan, set on a wire rack.

3. Unmold the cake and, using a 2-inch round pastry cutter, cut out 8 rounds from the baked almond cream.

PHYLLO ROUNDS

4 (13 by 18-inch) sheets phyllo dough

17¾ Tbsp (250 g/8.8 oz) unsalted butter, melted

Confectioners' sugar, for dusting

1.   Preheat the oven to 350°F (177°C). Line a half-sheet pan with a silicone baking mat.

2.   Place a sheet of phyllo dough on a piece of parchment paper and brush it with some of the melted butter. Dust with confectioners' sugar. Repeat the layering process until you have used all 4 phyllo sheets. Brush the top sheet with butter and dust with confectioners' sugar. Refrigerate the phyllo layers for 30 minutes, or until the butter has firmed up.

3.   Using a 2-inch round pastry cutter, cut out 16 rounds from the phyllo layers. Arrange the rounds on the prepared sheet pan and place another silicone baking mat on top to keep them flat. Bake the rounds for about 10 minutes, or until crisp. Cool the rounds on the pan, set on a wire rack.

ORANGE TUILES

Orange Tuile batter (page 339)

Preheat the oven to 350°F (177°C). Line a half-sheet pan with a silicone baking mat. Spread some of the tuile batter over a 3-inch round tuile stencil onto the baking mat. Repeat to form as many tuiles as possible. Bake for about 8 minutes, or until golden brown. Let the tuiles cool for a couple of minutes, then transfer to a wire rack to cool completely. Repeat to make more tuiles. You will need a total of 8 tuiles for this recipe.

STREUSEL, BAKED (page 342)

ASSEMBLY

Freshly ground white pepper, for garnish

Place a Phyllo Round on a dessert plate and top with an Almond Round, then another Phyllo Round, and then a Feta Cheesecake. Top the cheesecake with 2 Red Wine–Poached Dates. Sprinkle some Streusel on the plate and top it with a quenelle of White Pepper Ice Cream. Top the ice cream with a sprinkling of white pepper. Spoon some of the red wine reduction over the dates, allowing it to drip on the plate, and garnish with an Orange Tuile.

PLUM TOMATO NAPOLEON with ROSEMARY DIPLOMAT CREAM and TOMATO-BASIL SORBET

[decorative symbols] I CREATED THIS SAVORY DESSERT while I was at Daniel, for a tomato festival that I participated in to benefit local food pantries. Surprisingly, I had no problem coming up with a dessert for this event, because tomatoes are such a versatile fruit. This is a classic napoleon with not-so-classic flavors. It consists of caramelized Puff Pastry Rectangles layered with oven-dried plum tomatoes, rosemary cream, and a Tomato-Basil Sorbet. I serve it with a Raisin-Tomato Sauce made with diced tomatoes, golden raisins, and pine nuts. Make sure to use smooth-skinned, firm, weighty plum tomatoes at their peak of ripeness, in late summer.

MAKES 8 SERVINGS

COMPONENTS

TOMATO-BASIL SORBET
PUFF PASTRY RECTANGLES
OVEN-DRIED TOMATOES
ROSEMARY DIPLOMAT CREAM
RAISIN-TOMATO SAUCE

SPECIAL EQUIPMENT | ice cream machine; pepper mill; immersion blender; medium, plain pastry tip (Ateco #6)

PERFECT MATCH | 2011 Château Fontcreuse Vin Blanc de Provence Cassis

TOMATO-BASIL SORBET

2 Tbsp (30 g/1 oz) water

½ cup plus 1½ Tbsp (120 g/4.2 oz) granulated sugar

10 medium (620 g/22 oz) plum tomatoes

2 fresh basil leaves, cut into thin ribbons

Juice of 1 lime

1. In a small saucepan, combine the water and sugar and bring to a boil over medium-high heat, stirring, just until the sugar has dissolved. Remove the pan from the heat and cool for 10 minutes.

2. Coarsely chop the plum tomatoes, place them in the bowl of a food processor along with the sugar syrup and basil, and process until puréed. Strain the purée through a fine-mesh sieve into a medium bowl and stir in the lime juice. Cover the bowl with plastic wrap and refrigerate the sorbet base for at least 4 hours, or until well chilled.

3. Process the base in an ice cream machine according to the manufacturer's instructions. Transfer the sorbet to an airtight container and freeze until ready to use.

PUFF PASTRY RECTANGLES

1 lb (454 g) Puff Pastry (page 343) or store-bought puff pastry

Confectioners' sugar, for dusting

1.   Preheat the oven to 375°F (191°C). Line two half-sheet pans with silicone baking mats.

2.   On a lightly floured work surface, roll out the puff pastry into two 11 by 16-inch rectangles about ⅛ inch thick. Prick the dough all over using a pastry docker or the tines of a fork. Place each rectangle on a prepared pan and top with another silicone baking mat and another sheet pan. Bake for about 17 minutes, or until the pastry is lightly browned. Remove the top sheet pans and baking mats. Preheat the broiler and dust the pastry liberally with confectioners' sugar. Place the pastry under the broiler until it is caramelized. Cool completely.

3.   Cut the pastry into 2 by 4-inch rectangles. You will need a total of 24 rectangles.

OVEN-DRIED TOMATOES

16 medium (1.5 kg/3.3 lb) ripe plum tomatoes

Extra-virgin olive oil, for drizzling

3 to 5 turns freshly ground white pepper

1.   Preheat the oven to 175°F (79°C).

2.   Cut the tomatoes in half and, using your fingertips, remove and discard the seeds. Place the halved tomatoes cut side up on a half-sheet pan. Drizzle with some olive oil, then grind a few turns of white pepper on top. Dry the tomatoes in the oven for 3½ to 4 hours, or until they are withered and have given up some of their juice. Set aside to cool completely.

ROSEMARY DIPLOMAT CREAM

1 cup (250 g/8.8 oz) heavy cream

Rosemary Pastry Cream (page 341)

1.   In the bowl of a stand mixer fitted with the whisk attachment, whip the cream on high speed to soft peaks.

2.   Whisk the chilled Rosemary Pastry Cream until smooth and gently fold in the whipped cream. Cover the bowl and refrigerate until ready to serve.

RAISIN-TOMATO SAUCE

6 medium (375 g/13.2 oz) plum tomatoes, cored

¼ cup plus 2 Tbsp (60 g/2.1 oz) golden raisins

3 Tbsp (30 g/1 oz) pine nuts

1 to 2 Tbsp (15 to 30 g/0.5 to 1 oz) water, as needed

1.   Fill a medium bowl halfway with ice water and set aside. Fill a medium saucepan halfway with water and bring the water to a boil. Using a paring knife, cut a small X in the pointed end of each tomato. Add the tomatoes to the boiling water and, once the water returns to a boil, boil them for 20 to 30 seconds. Using a slotted spoon, transfer the tomatoes to the ice water.

2.   Peel off and discard the skin from each tomato. Cut each tomato in half lengthwise and, using your fingertips, scoop out and discard the seeds. Cut the tomatoes into ¼-inch dice.

3.   Place the diced tomatoes in a medium saucepan and cook over medium heat, stirring frequently, until the tomatoes begin to break down, about 5 minutes. Remove the pan from the heat and, using an immersion blender, purée the sauce so that it is half smooth, half chunky. Add the raisins and pine nuts and cook over medium heat until the sauce is hot, adding the water as needed to thin the sauce a bit. Remove the pan from the heat and set aside to cool.

ASSEMBLY

Confectioners' sugar, for dusting

8 yellow cherry tomatoes, for garnish

Scrape the Rosemary Diplomat Cream into a pastry bag fitted with a medium, plain tip. Place one of the Puff Pastry Rectangles on a plate. Halve two of the dried tomatoes and place them on the rectangle. Pipe the Rosemary Diplomat Cream on top of the tomatoes and place another rectangle on top. Place a quenelle of the Tomato-Basil Sorbet on the second puff layer. Dust half of another rectangle with confectioners' sugar and place it on top of the sorbet at an angle. Spoon some Raisin-Tomato Sauce around the plate and garnish with a yellow cherry tomato.

WARM BARTLETT PEAR with CHÈVRE CHEESECAKE, WALNUT CAKE, and FRIED SAGE LEAVES

※ ※ ※ ONE OF MY FANTASTIC SOUS-CHEFS, Alessandra Altieri, created this plated dessert for a special event in Las Vegas. It combines a beautiful Bartlett pear, roasted in butter and honey, with a tangy Chèvre Cheesecake and a spicy Walnut Cake made with maple syrup and walnut oil. A Sage Syrup and deep-fried sage leaves add a slightly earthy, lemony note that gives this special dessert a very interesting flavor profile.

MAKES 8 SERVINGS

COMPONENTS

WALNUT CAKE

CHÈVRE CHEESECAKE

PEAR GELÉE

SAGE SYRUP

WALNUT CRUMBLE

ROASTED PEAR

TUILES

FRIED SAGE LEAVES

SPECIAL EQUIPMENT | two 9 by 13-inch cake pans; medium, plain pastry tip (Ateco #6); 9-inch square baking pan; cheesecloth; 5-inch-diameter cylinder; 2 by 7 by 7-inch triangle stencil

PERFECT MATCH | 2010 Domaine Alain Graillot Crozes-Hermitage, Rhône, France

WALNUT CAKE

2¾ cups plus 2 Tbsp (287 g/10.14 oz) walnuts

¾ cup (150 g/5.25 oz) granulated sugar

¾ cup plus 2 Tbsp (113 g/4 oz) all-purpose flour

2½ Tbsp (18 g/0.6 oz) cornstarch

¾ tsp (3.7 g/0.13 oz) baking powder

¾ tsp (1.3 g/0.04 oz) ground cinnamon

½ tsp (1 g/0.03 oz) freshly grated nutmeg

½ tsp (1 g/0.03 oz) ground cloves

12 Tbsp (170 g/6 oz) unsalted butter, softened

1½ Tbsp (30 g/1 oz) maple syrup

1½ Tbsp (23 g/0.81 oz) walnut oil

3 large (150 g/5.25 oz) eggs

1. Preheat the oven to 350°F (177°C). Spray the bottom and sides of a 9 by 13-inch baking pan with nonstick cooking spray. Line the bottom of the pan with parchment paper and spray the paper with cooking spray.

2. In the bowl of a food processor, combine 1 cup plus 2 Tbsp (113 g/4 oz) of the walnuts with the sugar and process until the mixture is ground and almost a powder. Transfer to a large bowl and sift over the flour, cornstarch, baking powder, and spices. Whisk gently to combine.

3. In the bowl of a stand mixer fitted with the paddle attachment, beat the butter, maple syrup, and walnut oil on high speed until creamy, about 3 minutes. Reduce the speed to medium and add the eggs, one at a time, mixing well after each addition and scraping down the sides of the bowl as necessary. Reduce the speed to low and add the dry ingredients, one-third at a time, mixing just until blended.

Remove the bowl from the mixer stand and fold in the remaining 1¾ cups (175 g/6.17 oz) walnuts. Scrape the batter into the prepared pan, level the top, and bake for about 27 minutes, or until a toothpick inserted into the center of the cake comes out clean. Cool in the pan, set on a wire rack, for 15 minutes. Unmold onto the rack and cool completely.

4. Cut eight 1½ by 4-inch rectangles from the cake and set them aside in an airtight container until ready to serve (you will have cake left over, but it makes an excellent snack).

CHÈVRE CHEESECAKE

1 cup plus 2½ Tbsp (283 g/10 oz) soft goat cheese

1¼ cups plus 2 Tbsp (340 g/12 oz) cream cheese

¼ cup plus 2 Tbsp (75 g/2.6 oz) granulated sugar

½ vanilla bean, split lengthwise and seeds scraped

Finely grated zest of ½ orange

1½ large (75 g/2.6 oz) whole eggs

2 large (37 g/1.3 oz) egg yolks

¾ cup plus 2 Tbsp (200 g/7 oz) heavy cream

1. Preheat the oven to 300°F (149°C).

2. In the bowl of a stand mixer fitted with the paddle attachment, beat the goat cheese and cream cheese on medium speed until smooth. Gradually add the sugar, vanilla bean seeds, and orange zest and beat on high speed until creamy and light, about 2 minutes.

3. In a medium bowl, whisk together the whole eggs, egg yolks, and cream until blended. While mixing on medium speed, gradually add the egg mixture to the goat cheese mixture and mix until well blended and smooth, scraping down the sides of the bowl with a rubber spatula as necessary. Pour the batter into a 9 by

13-inch baking pan. Place the pan in a larger roasting pan and pour hot water into the larger pan so that it comes ¾ inch up the sides of the baking pan. Cover the baking pan with aluminum foil and bake the cake for about 1 hour, until set. Cool in the pan, set on a wire rack.

4. Scrape the cheesecake into a pastry bag fitted with a medium, plain tip, and refrigerate until ready to use.

PEAR GELÉE

11 sheets (22 g/0.77 oz) gelatin (silver grade)

3 cups (1 kg/2.2 lb) pear purée

1. Line a 9-inch square baking pan with plastic wrap, leaving 2 inches hanging over on all sides. Fill a large bowl halfway with cold water and add the gelatin sheets. Allow to soften for 10 minutes.

2. In a medium saucepan, bring the purée to a boil over medium heat. Remove the pan from the heat. Drain the gelatin, squeezing it to remove the excess water, and add it to the hot purée, stirring until the gelatin is completely dissolved. Pour the gelée into the prepared pan and freeze until solid, about 2 hours.

3. Using the plastic wrap as handles, remove the gelée from the pan and cut it into eight 1½ by 4-inch rectangles. Refrigerate, loosely covered, until ready to serve.

SAGE SYRUP

½ cup (30 g/1 oz) fresh sage leaves

1 cup (200 g/7 oz) granulated sugar

2 Tbsp (30 g/1 oz) hot water

1 Tbsp (20 g/0.7 oz) light corn syrup

1.   Fill a medium bowl halfway with ice water and set aside.

2.   Fill a medium saucepan halfway with water and bring the water to a boil. Add the sage leaves and boil for 15 seconds. Using a slotted spoon, transfer the sage leaves to the bowl of ice water to shock them and stop the cooking.

3.   Once the leaves are cold, blot them dry with paper towels and place them in the bowl of a food processor with the sugar. Process for a few seconds until the leaves are finely chopped. Gradually add the 2 tablespoons (30 g/1 oz) hot water and process until the mixture forms a thick paste. Strain through a cheesecloth-lined sieve into a small bowl and whisk in the corn syrup. Place in a squeeze bottle and refrigerate until ready to serve.

WALNUT CRUMBLE

½ cup plus 2 Tbsp (125 g/4.4 oz) granulated sugar

1 cup (125 g/4.4 oz) all-purpose flour

1⅓ cups plus 1 Tbsp (125 g/4.4 oz) almond flour

9 Tbsp (125 g/4.4 oz) unsalted butter, cut into tablespoon-size pieces and softened

1 tsp (4 g/0.14 oz) kosher salt

2½ cups (250 g/8.8 oz) walnuts

1.   Preheat the oven to 350°F (177°C). Line a half-sheet pan with a silicone baking mat.

2.   Place all of the ingredients in the bowl of a stand mixer fitted with the paddle attachment and mix on low speed until the mixture comes together. Crumble up the mixture with your hands and scatter it onto the prepared sheet pan. Bake for about 8 minutes, until browned. Cool completely.

ROASTED PEAR

2 Tbsp (28 g/1 oz) unsalted butter

3 Tbsp (60 g/2.1 oz) honey

2 small (440 g/15.5 oz) Bartlett pears, peeled, cored, and cut lengthwise into quarters

1.   Preheat the oven to 375°F (191°C).

2.   Melt the butter in an ovenproof sauté pan over medium-high heat. Add 2 tablespoons (40 g/1.4 oz) of the honey to the pan and add the pears, cut side down. Cook, basting the pears with butter, until they are browned on both sides. Drizzle the pears with the remaining 1 tablespoon (20 g/0.7 oz) honey, place the pan in the oven, and bake them until they are tender, about 20 minutes.

TUILES

Vanilla Tuile batter (page 338)

1.   Preheat the oven to 350°F (177°C). Line a half-sheet pan with a silicone baking mat. Have a 5-inch-diameter cylinder at the ready.

François Payard and photographer Rogério Voltan

2.   Using a small, offset metal spatula, spread a thin layer of the tuile batter onto the prepared sheet pan over a 2 by 7 by 7-inch triangle stencil. Repeat to form a total of 4 tuile triangles on the sheet. Bake for about 8 minutes, or until just beginning to turn golden in spots. Immediately curl the warm tuiles around the cylinder, forming an arch shape. Repeat to make a total of 8 tuiles.

FRIED SAGE LEAVES

(page 346)

ASSEMBLY

If necessary, warm the pears in a 350°F (177°C) oven for 5 minutes. Place a rectangle of the Pear Gelée on top of the Walnut Cake. Pipe 2 lengthwise logs of Chèvre Cheesecake on top of the gelée. Place the cake on a rectangular plate. Arrange a small piece of leftover Walnut Cake on the plate next to the dessert and lean a Roasted Pear quarter against it. Arrange the wide end of the Tuile underneath the Walnut Cake. Sprinkle some Walnut Crumble on top of the dessert. Drizzle some Sage Syrup on the plate and garnish the dessert with 2 Fried Sage Leaves.

BASIC RECIPES

BASIC SWEET TART DOUGH

THIS VERSATILE SWEET DOUGH, or *pâte sucrée*, is used for many of the tarts in this book. The recipe will generally yield more dough than you'll need, but you can freeze the remaining dough, well-wrapped, for up to a month.

MAKES 618 G/21.7 OZ, ENOUGH DOUGH FOR TWO 12-INCH TART SHELLS OR TWENTY 3-INCH TART SHELLS

9 Tbsp (125 g/4.4 oz) unsalted butter

½ cup plus 2 Tbsp (125 g/4.4 oz) granulated sugar

1 large (50 g/1.76 oz) egg

2 cups (250 g/8.8 oz) all-purpose flour

¾ cup (62 g/2.2 oz) almond flour

¼ plus ⅛ tsp (2.5 g/0.08 oz) salt

½ Tbsp (6 g/0.21 oz) cold water

1.   Place the butter and sugar in the bowl of a stand mixer fitted with the paddle attachment and beat on medium speed until smooth, about 2 minutes. Add the egg and mix until blended. Add the flour, almond flour, and salt and mix on low speed until combined. Add the water and mix until just combined.

2.   Transfer the dough to a work surface and shape it into 2 disks. Wrap each disk in plastic wrap and refrigerate for at least 2 hours, or for up to 3 days. The dough can be frozen for up to 3 months.

CHOCOLATE TART DOUGH

THIS CHOCOLATE COOKIE CRUST is made with a combination of all-purpose and almond flour. The almond flour makes it tender, flaky, and slightly crisp, and also gives it a subtle almond flavor, which complements the chocolate nicely.

MAKES 1.13 KG/2 LB 7.8 OZ, ENOUGH DOUGH FOR FOUR 12-INCH TART SHELLS OR FORTY 3-INCH TART SHELLS

3½ cups plus 1⅓ Tbsp (430 g/15.16 oz) all-purpose flour

⅔ cup (65 g/2.3 oz) unsweetened alkalized cocoa powder

17¾ Tbsp (250 g/8.8 oz) unsalted butter, at room temperature

1¼ cups (250 g/8.8 oz) granulated sugar

1 tsp (5 g/0.17 oz) salt

2 large (100 g/3.5 oz) eggs

1½ cups (125 g/4.4 oz) almond flour

1 Tbsp (15g/0.5 oz) water

1. In a medium bowl, combine the flour and cocoa powder and set aside.

2. In the bowl of a stand mixer fitted with the paddle attachment, mix the butter, sugar, and salt on medium speed until well blended and light, about 3 minutes. Add the eggs, one at a time, and mix on low speed until well blended, scraping down the sides of the bowl as needed. Add the almond flour and mix until blended. Add the flour and cocoa powder mixture and mix just until combined. Add the water and mix until blended. Divide the dough into 2 disks, wrap each disk in plastic wrap, and refrigerate for at least 1 hour before using. The dough may also be frozen, well wrapped, for up to 1 month.

SABLÉ BRETON DOUGH

SABLÉ IS THE FRENCH WORD FOR "SANDY," which reflects the crumbly texture of this sweet dough when baked. It is similar to American shortbread, but is made with hard-boiled egg yolks as well as butter, which makes it exceptionally tender. I also add a touch of dark rum to give the dough a warm note.

MAKES 830 G/29.3 OZ, ENOUGH DOUGH FOR THREE 11-INCH TART SHELLS OR THIRTY 3-INCH TART SHELLS

4 (74 g/2.6 oz) hard-boiled egg yolks

5 Tbsp (280 g/10 oz) unsalted butter

1 cup (120 g/4.2 oz) confectioners' sugar

½ tsp (2 g/0.07 oz) salt

2½ cups (300 g/10.6 oz) all-purpose flour

½ cup plus 1 Tbsp (50 g/1.76 oz) almond flour

2 tsp (10 g/0.35 oz) light or Myers's dark rum

1. Pass the cooked yolks through a fine-mesh sieve onto a piece of wax or parchment paper.

2. In the bowl of a stand mixer fitted with the paddle attachment, beat the butter, confectioners' sugar, and salt on medium speed until well blended and smooth. Add the flour, egg yolks, almond flour, and rum and mix on low speed until the mixture comes together and forms a dough. Remove from the bowl, form the dough into a disk, wrap in plastic wrap, and refrigerate for at least 1 hour. The dough may also be frozen, well wrapped, for up to 1 month.

CHOCOLATE SAUCE

BECAUSE THIS CHOCOLATE SAUCE IS MADE with cocoa powder instead of chocolate, it's great for production, because it doesn't separate and remains shiny even when it's been on the plate for three hours. It's best served warm.

MAKES 1 CUP (240 G/8.5 OZ) SAUCE

> 1½ cups (300 g/10.5 oz) granulated sugar
>
> 1⅓ cups (125 g/4.4 oz) unsweetened alkalized cocoa powder
>
> 1 cup (232 g/8.18 oz) heavy cream
>
> 1 cup (236 g/8.3 oz) water

1. In a small bowl, combine the sugar and cocoa powder and set aside.

2. In a medium saucepan, combine the cream and water. Place the pan over medium heat. Whisk the sugar and cocoa powder into the liquid and continue to heat, continuing to whisk, until it comes to a boil. Reduce the heat to medium-low and cook, stirring frequently, until the liquid has reduced by half. Pass the sauce through a fine-mesh sieve into a bowl and let cool. The sauce can be made ahead and refrigerated, covered, for up to 3 days. Reheat in the microwave before serving.

CARAMEL SAUCE

I LIKE TO THINK OF THIS as the kind of sauce that chefs—as opposed to pastry chefs—like to make, because its focus is more on flavor than technique. The flavor here is caramel, which has a deep and slightly bitter character, and it is enhanced by a good deal of butter, whisked in at the end. To allow the flavor to develop, you must refrigerate this sauce for at least 24 hours before serving.

MAKES ABOUT 2 CUPS (576 G/20.3 OZ) SAUCE

> 1 cup plus 1 Tbsp (250 g/8.8 oz) heavy cream
>
> 1¼ cups (250 g/8.8 oz) granulated sugar
>
> 2 Tbsp (30 g/1 oz) water
>
> 10½ Tbsp (150 g/5.3 oz) unsalted butter, cut into tablespoon-size pieces

1. In a small saucepan, bring the cream to a boil over medium-high heat. Remove from the heat.

2. In a small, heavy-bottomed saucepan, combine the sugar with the water and cook over medium-high heat, occasionally washing down the sides of the pan with a wet pastry brush to prevent crystals from forming, and watching carefully, until the syrup caramelizes and turns a dark amber color, 3 to 5 minutes. Slowly add the hot cream and stir over the heat until any hardened bits of sugar have dissolved and the mixture is smooth, about 2 minutes. Whisk in the butter, 1 tablespoon (14 g/ 0.5 oz) at a time, whisking well after each addition, until completely incorporated. Let cool and refrigerate, covered, for at least 24 hours before using, or for up to 5 days. Reheat gently over low heat before using.

CRÈME ANGLAISE

THIS RICH CUSTARD SAUCE, a pastry chef's staple, is served with many of the desserts in this book. It can be made up to 3 days in advance, as long as it's stored in an airtight container in the refrigerator.

MAKES 2¼ CUPS (550 G/19.4 OZ) SAUCE

> 1 cup (242 g/8.5 oz) whole milk
>
> 1 cup (232 g/8.18 oz) heavy cream
>
> 1 vanilla bean, split lengthwise and seeds scraped
>
> 6 large (110 g/3.8 oz) egg yolks
>
> ¼ cup plus 2 Tbsp (75 g/2.6 oz) granulated sugar

1. In a medium saucepan, combine the milk, cream, and vanilla bean pod and seeds and cook over medium-high heat until the mixture comes to a gentle boil. Remove the pan from the heat.

2. In a medium bowl, whisk together the egg yolks and sugar vigorously until pale. Whisk about ½ cup of the hot milk mixture into the yolks, then return this mixture to the saucepan with the remaining milk mixture and cook over medium heat, stirring constantly with a wooden spoon, until it thickens enough to coat the back of the spoon and reaches 175°F (79°C) on an instant-read thermometer; do not let the mixture boil, or the egg yolks will curdle. Remove the pot from the heat and pass the mixture through a fine-mesh sieve into a bowl. Set the bowl in an ice bath and stir frequently until cold. Transfer to an airtight container and refrigerate for at least 3 hours before using, or for up to 3 days.

Pistachio Crème Anglaise: Whisk 2 tablespoons (40 g/1.4 oz) pistachio paste into the hot custard right after passing it through the sieve in step 2.

CARAMEL CRÈME ANGLAISE

THIS SAUCE IS A BASIC CARAMEL, cooked to a dark amber to develop its flavor and then combined with cream, milk, sugar, and eggs and cooked until thickened, as in a classic crème anglaise. A pinch of fleur de sel heightens the caramel's flavor and balances its sweetness. I serve this sauce with my Kugelhopf Caramel Glacé on page 31.

MAKES 2½ CUPS (600 G/21.2 OZ) SAUCE

> 1 cup plus 1 Tbsp (250 g/8.8 oz) heavy cream
>
> 1 cup (250 g/8.8 oz) whole milk
>
> 1 cup (200 g/7 oz) granulated sugar
>
> Pinch of fleur de sel
>
> 2 Tbsp (30 g/1 oz) water
>
> 8½ large (160 g/5.6 oz) egg yolks

1. In a small saucepan, combine the cream and milk and cook over medium-high heat until it almost comes to a boil. Reduce the heat to low to keep it warm.

2. In a medium, heavy-bottomed saucepan, combine ½ cup (100 g/3.5 oz) of the sugar, the salt, and the water and cook over medium-high heat, occasionally washing down the sides of the pan with a wet pastry brush to prevent crystals from forming, and watching carefully, until the

sugar caramelizes and turns a dark amber color, 3 to 5 minutes; it should begin to smoke a little at this point. Remove the pan from the heat and gradually stir in the warm cream and milk mixture. Return the pan to the heat and stir until any hardened bits of caramel have dissolved, about 2 minutes. Remove the pan from the heat.

3.   In a medium bowl, whisk together the egg yolks and the remaining ½ cup (100 g/3.5 oz) sugar until pale. Whisk about ½ cup of the hot caramel mixture into the yolks, then return the entire mixture to the saucepan. Cook over medium heat, stirring constantly with a wooden spoon until it thickens enough to coat the back of the spoon and reaches 175°F (79°C) on an instant-read thermometer; do not let the mixture boil, or the egg yolks will curdle. Remove the pot from the heat and pass the mixture through a fine-mesh sieve into a bowl. Set the bowl in an ice bath and stir frequently until cold. Transfer to an airtight container and refrigerate until ready to use, or for up to 3 days.

CARAMEL GARNISHES

THOUGH NOT AS FASHIONABLE AS THEY ONCE WERE, caramel garnishes are among the simplest to make, and they add color, shine, and a complex sweetness to plated desserts. If the caramel cools too much as you're making the garnishes, return it to low heat for a short time to thin it out slightly. If necessary, cool it again until it reaches the proper consistency.

MAKES ABOUT 1 CUP (304 G/10.7 OZ) CARAMEL; ENOUGH FOR TWELVE 3-INCH GARNISHES

1 cup (200 g/7 oz) granulated sugar

2 Tbsp (30 g/1 oz) water

1.   Line a half-sheet pan with a silicone baking mat. Fill a large stainless steel bowl halfway with ice water.

2.   In a medium, heavy-bottomed saucepan, combine the sugar and water and cook over medium-high heat, occasionally washing down the sides of the pan with a wet pastry brush to prevent crystals from forming, and watching carefully, until the sugar caramelizes and turns a medium amber color, 3 to 5 minutes. Remove the pan from the heat and immediately plunge the bottom of the pan into the ice water to stop the cooking process and cool the caramel slightly. Remove the pan from the ice water and stir the caramel to even out the temperature.

3.   Dip a thick wooden spoon in the caramel and drizzle the caramel onto the prepared sheet in whatever shape you like—spirals, lacy circles, zigzags, or wavy lines. Let the caramel garnishes cool completely, about 10 minutes. Using an offset metal spatula or pancake turner, carefully remove each garnish from the sheet. Store the garnishes in an airtight container in a dry place for up to 5 days.

CHOCOLATE MOUSSE

THIS DARK CHOCOLATE MOUSSE is an element in many of the desserts in this book. There are several ways to make chocolate mousse, and the method you choose depends on its application. Sometimes you want a mousse that's dense and rich; other times you may want a mousse that is light. This method is very traditional and involves making a pâte à bombe base, an aerated mixture of egg yolks and hot sugar syrup. The pâte à bombe is blended with melted 72% chocolate, and then a generous amount of softly whipped cream is folded in. This technique yields a very light mousse with a beautiful, creamy texture, ideal for using in multicomponent desserts.

MAKES ABOUT 4 CUPS (1 KG/2.2 LB) MOUSSE

> 2 cups (450 g/15.87 oz) heavy cream
>
> 10.5 oz (300 g) 72% bittersweet chocolate, chopped
>
> 2 large (100 g/3.5 oz) eggs
>
> ½ cup plus 1½ Tbsp (120 g/4.2 oz) granulated sugar
>
> ¼ cup (60 g/2.1 oz) water

1. In the bowl of a stand mixer fitted with the whisk attachment, whip the cream on medium-high speed to soft peaks. Cover the bowl and set aside in the refrigerator.

2. Place the chocolate in a medium, microwave-safe glass bowl and microwave on 50 percent power, stirring every 30 seconds, until melted. Set aside.

3. Place the eggs in the bowl of a stand mixer fitted with the whisk attachment and begin whipping on medium speed. Meanwhile, combine the sugar and water in a small saucepan and cook over high heat until it comes to a full boil. Allow to boil for 1 minute. Remove from the heat and very slowly add it to the whipping eggs. Increase the speed to high and whip the eggs until they have doubled in volume and are completely cool, about 6 minutes. Remove the bowl from the mixer stand and whisk in one-third of the melted chocolate. Ideally, the chocolate should be at 104°F (40°C) when it is folded in; if it's too cool, rewarm it gently. Gently fold in the remaining chocolate. Fold in the whipped cream, one-third at a time. Cover and refrigerate until ready to serve, or for up to 3 days.

FRUIT TUILES

WITH ONLY TWO INGREDIENTS, this may be the simplest tuile you'll ever make. The flavor of the fruit is foremost here, so make sure you use a high-quality purée with no more than 10 percent sugar content. If you feel the purée is lacking in acidity, add a little bit of fruit powder to bump up the flavor of the finished tuile.

MAKES 1 HALF-SHEET PAN TUILES

> ¾ cup plus 2 Tbsp (250 g/8.8 oz) fruit purée (10% sugar content)
>
> ¾ cup (85 g/3 oz) confectioners' sugar

1. Preheat the oven to 200°F (93°C). Line a half-sheet pan with a silicone baking mat.

2. In a small saucepan, mix together the purée and the confectioners' sugar and cook over medium heat, stirring, until the sugar has dissolved. Pour onto the center of the baking mat. Shake and tilt the pan to spread the loose mixture evenly. Bake for 2 to 3 hours, or until the tuile is crisp and dry. Cool completely.

3. Break off pieces of tuile as needed. Store in an airtight container at room temperature for up to a week.

VANILLA TUILES

THESE THIN, CRISP COOKIES add a bit of sweetness and crunch to many of the desserts in this book. Fresh out of the oven, the warm tuiles can be rolled up or curled around a rolling pin, or cut into a variety of different shapes. I developed this recipe at Daniel, and lots of pastry chefs requested it, because it's very different from the standard one. Here I warm the egg whites and sugar in a bowl set over simmering water before combining them with the other ingredients. I also use clarified butter instead of melted butter. These two deviations from the classic recipe make the tuiles more stable, so they stay dry and don't break as much during production.

MAKES 1½ CUPS (456 G/1 LB) TUILE BATTER

> 5 large (150 g/5.25 oz) egg whites
>
> 1 cup plus 2 Tbsp (125 g/4.4 oz) confectioners' sugar
>
> ¼ vanilla bean, split lengthwise and seeds scraped
>
> ¾ cup plus 1 Tbsp plus 1 tsp (100 g/3.5 oz) all-purpose flour, sifted
>
> ¾ cup (150 g/5.3 oz) melted Clarified Butter (page 348)

Fill a small saucepan halfway with water and bring the water to a simmer. In a medium, stainless steel bowl, whisk together the egg whites, confectioners' sugar, and vanilla bean seeds and place the bowl over the pot of simmering water. Continue to whisk gently until the mixture is warm to the touch and the sugar has dissolved. Remove the bowl and whisk in the flour until blended. Mix in the Clarified Butter. Transfer the batter to an airtight container and refrigerate for at least 2 hours, or up to 3 days, before using. Follow instructions for baking as directed in each recipe.

ORANGE TUILES

THESE THIN, CRISP COOKIES are flavored with freshly squeezed orange juice and add sweetness, crunch, and a subtle acidity to a variety of desserts.

MAKES 2 CUPS (608 G/21.4 OZ) TUILE BATTER

> 1 cup lightly packed (200 g/7 oz) light brown sugar
>
> 1 cup (200 g/7 oz) granulated sugar
>
> 1⅓ cups (200 g/7 oz) all-purpose flour
>
> ¾ cup plus 1 Tbsp (200 g/7 oz) freshly squeezed orange juice
>
> 14 Tbsp (200 g/7 oz) unsalted butter, at room temperature

In a bowl, sift together the brown sugar, granulated sugar, and flour. Place the dry ingredients in a food processor fitted with the blade attachment. With the machine running, gradually add the orange juice and process until well blended. Turn off the machine and add the butter. Process the batter just until the butter is incorporated and there are no large lumps. Transfer to an airtight container and chill for at least 6 hours, or overnight, before using. Bake as directed in each recipe.

Orange-Almond Tuiles: Sift ⅓ cup (30 g/ 1 oz) almond flour into the flour mixture in step 1.

SIMPLE SYRUP

THIS CLASSIC SYRUP has a number of applications in the pastry world, but its main purpose in this book is as an ingredient in sorbets.

MAKES 2 CUPS (500 G/17.6 OZ) SYRUP

> 2¼ cups (450 g/15.8 oz) granulated sugar
>
> 1¾ cups plus 2 Tbsp (450 g/15.8 oz) water

Combine the sugar and water in a saucepan. Bring the mixture to a boil over high heat, occasionally washing down the sides of the pan with a wet pastry brush to remove any clinging sugar crystals. Boil for 1 minute, then remove from the heat. Cool, then transfer to an airtight container and refrigerate until ready to use, or for up to 1 month.

VANILLA ICE CREAM

Vanilla ice cream accompanies many of the recipes in this book. Make sure to use a fresh, plump vanilla bean—I prefer to use either Mexican or Bourbon vanilla beans from the French island Île Bourbon. This recipe can easily be doubled.

Special Equipment: ice cream machine

MAKES 1½ PINTS (720 ML) ICE CREAM

> 1 cup (250 g/8.8 oz) whole milk
>
> 1 cup (250 g/8.8 oz) heavy cream
>
> 1 vanilla bean, split lengthwise and seeds scraped
>
> 6 large (112 g/4 oz) egg yolks
>
> ½ cup plus 2 Tbsp (125 g/4.4 oz) granulated sugar

1. In a medium saucepan, combine the milk, cream, and vanilla bean pod and seeds and bring to a gentle boil over medium heat.

2. In a medium bowl, whisk together the egg yolks and sugar until pale. Whisk about half of the hot milk mixture into the yolks, then return this mixture to the remaining milk mixture in the saucepan and cook over medium heat, stirring constantly with a wooden spoon, until it thickens enough to coat the back of the spoon and reaches 175°F (79°C) on an instant-read thermometer; do not let the mixture boil, or the egg yolks will curdle. Remove the pot from the heat and immediately pass the ice cream base through a fine-mesh sieve into a bowl. Set the bowl in an ice bath and stir frequently until cold.

3. Transfer the ice cream base to an airtight container and refrigerate for at least 4 hours, or overnight.

4. Process the base in an ice cream machine according to the manufacturer's instructions. (Be careful not to overchurn the ice cream or it will become grainy.) Transfer the ice cream to an airtight container and freeze until ready to serve.

Whole Milk Ice Cream: For the milk, use organic, cream-top milk from a local creamery.

ALMOND CREAM

ALSO KNOWN AS FRANGIPANE, baked almond cream is used as a filling or base for several of the desserts in this book. To make this we use California almonds, which lack the sharp, bitter notes of more expensive Valencia almonds, so I always add a little dark rum to our recipe—it adds some depth without overwhelming the almond flavor. To store, seal the unbaked almond cream tightly in an airtight container. It can be refrigerated for up to a week, or frozen for up to a month.

MAKES 4¾ CUPS (1.4 KG/3 LB) ALMOND CREAM

> 17¾ Tbsp (250 g/8.8 oz) unsalted butter, at room temperature
>
> 1¼ cups (250 g/8.8 oz) granulated sugar
>
> 2¾ cups (250 g/8.8 oz) almond flour
>
> 5 large (250 g/8.8 oz) eggs
>
> 3 Tbsp plus 1 tsp (25 g/0.88 oz) all-purpose flour
>
> 1 tsp (5 g/0.17 oz) vanilla extract
>
> 2 tsp (10 g/0.35 oz) dark rum, such as Myers's

In the bowl of a stand mixer fitted with the paddle attachment, beat the butter and sugar together on medium speed until well combined and smooth, about 2 minutes. Add the almond flour and mix until combined. Add the eggs in three additions, making sure that each addition is incorporated before adding the next. Add the flour, vanilla extract, and rum and mix until combined. Place in an airtight container and refrigerate until ready to use. Bake as directed in the recipe.

PASTRY CREAM

A CLASSIC FILLING FOR FRUIT TARTS AND ÉCLAIRS, pastry cream is also used as a component in many of the desserts in this book, from napoleons to panini.

MAKES 2½ CUPS (605 G/21.3 OZ) PASTRY CREAM

> 2 cups (484 g/17 oz) whole milk
>
> ½ cup (100 g/3.5 oz) granulated sugar
>
> 5 large (93 g/3.3 oz) egg yolks
>
> ⅓ cup (40 g/1.4 oz) cornstarch
>
> 1 Tbsp (14 g/0.5 oz) unsalted butter

1. In a medium saucepan, bring the milk to a boil over medium heat. Remove from the heat.

2. In a medium bowl, whisk together the sugar and egg yolks until pale. Sift the cornstarch into the mixture and whisk to combine. Whisk about one-quarter of the milk into the yolk mixture, then whisk the yolk mixture into the pan with the remaining milk. Cook over medium-high heat, whisking constantly, until the custard thickens and boils. Remove the pan from the heat and whisk in the butter until it has completely melted. Scrape the pastry cream through a fine-mesh sieve into a stainless steel bowl, set the bowl in an ice bath, and stir frequently until cold. Cover the surface of the pastry cream with plastic wrap pressed directly on the surface to prevent a skin from forming, and refrigerate until ready to use.

Vanilla Pastry Cream: Add a vanilla bean, split lengthwise with a paring knife and seeds scraped, to the milk in step 1. Remove the vanilla bean pod after the pastry cream has cooked.

Rosemary Pastry Cream: Add the finely chopped leaves from 1 sprig fresh rosemary to the milk in step 1 and proceed as directed.

STREUSEL

THIS CRUMBLY MIXTURE is used as a topping or filling for many desserts. In this book, it's also used frequently as a base for a scoop of ice cream—it prevents the ice cream from sliding and also from melting too quickly.

MAKES 1 CUP (90 G/3.17 OZ) STREUSEL

> 4 Tbsp (57 g/2 oz) unsalted butter, slightly softened
>
> 5 Tbsp (62 g/2.2 oz) granulated sugar
>
> ½ cup (60 g/2.1 oz) all-purpose flour
>
> ⅔ cup (58 g/2 oz) almond flour

1. In the bowl of a stand mixer fitted with the paddle attachment, beat the butter and sugar together on medium-low speed until smooth. Add the all-purpose and almond flours and mix until blended; the dough will be crumbly. Gather the dough into a disk, wrap in plastic wrap, and refrigerate until firm, about 1 hour.

2. Unwrap the dough and grate it on the large holes of a box grater (or, alternatively, using a crosshatched wire cooling rack and, holding it at an angle, "grate" the dough through its holes).

3. For baked Streusel, preheat the oven to 375°F (191°C) and line a half-sheet pan with a silicone baking mat. Scatter the pieces of streusel onto the prepared sheet pan and bake for about 8 minutes, or until golden brown. Cool completely.

BRIOCHE

THIS LIGHT AND TENDER FRENCH BREAD is made with yeast and enriched with eggs and lots of butter. In my recipe, I slow down the proofing of the dough by refrigerating it during its second rise, which yields an exceptionally fluffy brioche. Brioche is used in several of the recipes in this book, including the Apricot Charlotte (page 43), Brioche Panini (page 289), and Roasted Summer Apricots (page 81). This recipe yields three loaves of brioche—if you don't need that much, wrap any leftover bread well and freeze it for up to 3 months.

MAKES THREE 8½ BY 4½-INCH LOAVES (1.4 KG/3 LB)

> 5 cups (660 g/23.3 oz) bread flour
>
> 3 Tbsp (25 g/0.88 oz) fresh yeast
>
> ¼ cup plus 1½ tsp (56 g/1.9 oz) granulated sugar
>
> 6 large (300 g/10.6 oz) eggs
>
> ½ cup (125 g/4.4 oz) water
>
> 2 tsp (10 g/0.35 oz) salt
>
> 12 Tbsp (170 g/6 oz) unsalted butter, cold but malleable, plus more for buttering bowl
>
> 1 egg, whisked with a little water, for egg wash

1. In the bowl of a stand mixer fitted with the paddle attachment, mix together the flour, yeast, and sugar on low speed. Add the eggs, one at a time, mixing well after each addition and scraping down the sides of the bowl with a rubber spatula as necessary. Add the water

and salt and mix until combined. Continue mixing until the dough forms a ball, about 2 minutes. While continuing to mix on low speed, add the butter, 1 tablespoon at a time, and mix until well blended. Continue to mix until the dough is smooth and no longer sticks to the side of the bowl. Transfer the dough to a buttered, medium bowl, cover with a damp cloth, and let rise in a warm, dry place until the dough has doubled in volume, about 1 hour.

2.   Punch down the dough to release the air, cover the bowl again, and let rise in the refrigerator for 2 hours, or for up to 8 hours.

3.   Butter the bottom and sides of three 8½ by 4½-inch loaf pans (alternatively, you can use 9 by 5-inch pans). Punch the dough down again and divide the dough into 3 equal pieces. Shape each piece into a smooth ball. Elongate each ball and roll it into a tight 8-inch log. Arrange each log in a prepared loaf pan. Brush the top of the dough logs with egg wash, loosely cover with plastic wrap, and allow the dough to rise until it comes three-quarters of the way up the side of each pan, about 1 hour.

4.   Preheat the oven to 350°F (177°C). Brush the top of the dough again with egg wash. Using a clean razor blade or serrated knife, cut a shallow slit down the length of each loaf. Bake the loaves for about 30 minutes, rotating the pans once during baking, until the brioche is golden and a knife inserted into the center of each loaf comes out clean. Unmold and cool the loaves on a wire rack.

PUFF PASTRY

THIS RICH, BUTTERY PASTRY is used to create a variety of pastries and baked goods. I use it in many of my plated desserts, such as for napoleon layers and as the base for multicomponent desserts. This particular recipe is my favorite, because it makes an ultra-flaky, very airy pastry in which you can actually see the layers. I give the dough a total of five turns—two double turns and one single turn—to achieve this lightness.

MAKES 5 POUNDS (2.25 KG) DOUGH

BUTTER INSERT

3⅓ cups (750 g/1 lb 10.4 oz) unsalted butter

2⅔ cups (300 g/10.5 oz) all-purpose flour

Place the butter in the bowl of a stand mixer fitted with the paddle attachment and beat on low speed until it is pliable. Add the flour and mix until combined. Scrape the mixture out onto a work surface and shape it into a 6-inch square about ½ inch high. Wrap the butter in plastic wrap and place it in a cool place (not the refrigerator) until ready to use.

ENROBING DOUGH

½ cup plus 2 Tbsp (150 g/5.3 oz) water

1 Tbsp plus 1½ tsp (30 g/1.05 oz) salt

1¾ cups (200 g/7 oz) all-purpose flour

3¾ cups plus 1½ Tbsp (500 g/17.6 oz) bread flour

10½ Tbsp (150 g/5.3 oz) unsalted butter, melted

Put the water in the bowl of a stand mixer and stir the salt into it. Place the bowl on the mixer stand fitted with the dough hook. Begin mixing on low speed, gradually adding the all-purpose and bread flours. Add the melted butter and mix until a dough begins to form and just comes together; do not overmix. Shape the dough into a tight ball and, using a serrated knife, cut a cross halfway into the ball and wrap it in plastic wrap. Let the dough rest in the refrigerator for 30 minutes.

ROLLING AND FOLDING

1.   Pull out the corners of the cut edges in the dough ball to make it square shaped. On a lightly floured work surface, using a rolling pin, roll out the opened dough to an 8-inch square. Place the butter square diagonally in the center of the dough and fold over the dough points so that they meet in the center. Pinch the edges of the dough to seal the butter in the dough. Roll the dough out into a 10 by 20-inch rectangle, dusting very lightly with flour, as necessary, to prevent the dough from sticking. Make an impression with the rolling pin in the center of the rectangle. Brush off any excess flour from the dough and, with a short end facing you, fold the two short ends of the dough so that they meet in the center, leaving a slight gap. Fold the dough together as if you were closing a book—this is a double turn. Place the dough on a half-sheet pan, cover with plastic wrap, and refrigerate for 30 minutes.

2.   For the next turn, place the unwrapped dough rectangle on the work surface so that the folded edges are facing you; the open ends will be on the left and right. Roll out the dough to a 10 by 20-inch rectangle and repeat the folding, rolling, and resting as directed in step 1.

3.   Remove the dough from the refrigerator and place the unwrapped dough rectangle on the work surface so that the folded edges are facing you; the open ends will be on the left and right. Roll it out again to a 10 by 20-inch rectangle, dusting it lightly with flour as necessary. Brush off the excess flour and fold the bottom third of the dough up over the center, then fold the top third over, as if you were folding a business letter—this is a single turn. The dough is now ready to use.

NOUGATINE

NOUGATINE IS A CLASSIC CONFECTION that adds texture and crunch to a variety of desserts. I make mine with lots of good butter and a little milk, which gives it a rich and somewhat complex flavor. You can also add a chocolate character to this nougatine by sprinkling it with some cacao nibs just before baking. Many of the recipes in this book call for crushed nougatine; just chop the nougatine on a cutting board to the consistency you need.

SPECIAL EQUIPMENT: candy thermometer

MAKES 2 POUNDS (907 G) NOUGATINE

22 Tbsp (310 g/11 oz) unsalted butter, cut into tablespoon-size pieces

1¾ cups plus 2 Tbsp (375 g/13.2 oz) granulated sugar

½ cup (125 g/4.4 oz) whole milk

2 tsp (6 g/0.21 oz) pectin powder

¼ cup plus 2 Tbsp (125 g/4.4 oz) glucose syrup

3½ cups (300 g/10.6 oz) sliced almonds

1.   Preheat the oven to 350°F (177°C) and position two racks near the center of the oven. Line two half-sheet pans with silicone baking mats.

2.   Put all of the ingredients except for the sliced almonds in a medium saucepan and bring to a boil over medium-high heat, occasionally washing down the sides of the pan with a wet pastry brush to prevent crystals from forming. Cook until the mixture registers 239°F (115°C) on a candy thermometer, stirring occasionally. Stir in the sliced almonds and pour the mixture onto the two prepared half-sheet pans, dividing it evenly. Using a small, offset metal spatula, spread out the mixture evenly. Bake the nougatine for 12 to 14 minutes, or until it is evenly golden brown. Cool in the pan, set on a wire rack. Use the nougatine as directed in the recipe.

PINEAPPLE CHIPS

THESE DELICATE, CRISPY CHIPS garnish several desserts in this book. For best results, the pineapple must be sliced very thinly. Because the diameter of the pineapple is wider than a mandoline, you will need to use an electric slicer to accomplish this. Also, don't substitute parchment paper for the silicone mat—the chips will stick to the paper. The finished chips should be golden brown; if you undercook them, they will lack the roasted pineapple flavor that makes them so wonderful.

SPECIAL EQUIPMENT: electric slicer

MAKES ABOUT 20 CHIPS

⅓ medium pineapple

Confectioners' sugar, for dusting

1.   Position two racks near the center of the oven and preheat the oven to 200°F (93°C). Line two half-sheet pans with a silicone baking mats and dust the mats generously with confectioners' sugar.

2.   Using a sharp knife, cut the peel off the pineapple; do not remove the core. Slice the pineapple on an electric slicer into very thin

rounds. Place the rounds on the prepared sheet pans and dust them generously with more confectioners' sugar. Bake for 2 hours, rotating the sheet pans halfway through baking, or until they are just beginning to turn golden brown. While the chips are still warm, shape them as directed in the recipe. Cool completely; the chips will become crisp as they cool. Carefully remove them from the mat using a metal spatula; the chips are extremely delicate. Store in an airtight container between layers of parchment paper.

TOASTED NUTS

TOASTING BRINGS OUT THE FULL FLAVOR OF NUTS. Watch the nuts carefully as they toast as they can overbrown and burn easily.

Preheat the oven to 350°F (177°C). Spread out the nuts in a single layer on a half-sheet pan and toast for 5 to 12 minutes (the time will vary depending on the nut variety; see guide below) shaking the pan once or twice during baking, until they are golden (if they have skins, look beneath the skin) and fragrant. Transfer to a plate to cool. The nuts can be stored in an airtight container for up to 1 day.

TOASTING TIMES

Slivered or sliced almonds: 5 to 10 minutes

Whole almonds: 10 to 15 minutes

Walnuts and pecans: 5 to 10 minutes

Hazelnuts: 8 to 12 minutes

Pistachios: 5 to 7 minutes

FRIED HERBS

FRIED HERBS make an unexpected and beautiful garnish for many desserts. Because of the size and shape of their leaves, basil, sage, and mint are all excellent candidates for frying.

1 cup (224 g/8 oz) grapeseed oil

Fresh herb leaves, removed from stem

Superfine granulated sugar, as needed

1.   Line a plate with paper towels. Place the oil in a small sauté pan over medium heat and heat until it registers 300°F (149°C) on an instant-read thermometer. Make sure the herb leaves are dry. Using a slotted spoon, gently place 8 to 10 leaves into the oil; be careful, as the oil may spatter. Fry for 5 to 10 seconds, until they are evenly colored. Transfer the fried leaves to the plate to drain.

2.   Roll the herbs lightly in the superfine sugar.

TEMPERED CHOCOLATE

TEMPERING IS WHAT GIVES CHOCOLATE its glossy sheen and snap. Since it's difficult to temper small quantities of chocolate, it's best to work with a minimum of one pound. Any leftover chocolate can be allowed to set and retempered at a later date. Though there are a few ways to temper chocolate, this is the easiest, and my preferred way.

1 pound (450 g) couverture chocolate of any type, finely chopped

1.   Put one-third of the chocolate in a bowl and set aside.

2.   Have an instant-read thermometer at hand. Fill a medium pot one-third full with water and bring the water to a gentle simmer over medium heat. Place the chopped chocolate in a heatproof bowl that will fit snugly over the top of the pot but not touch the water. Reduce the heat to low and place the bowl over the pot. Heat until the chocolate has completely melted, stirring occasionally with a silicone spatula. Check the temperature frequently to make sure you don't go above the desired temperature (see the Temperature Guide below). Once the chocolate reaches the proper temperature, stir in the reserved chocolate to lower the temperature of the chocolate to its proper cooling temperature for its type. Once that temperature is reached, return the bowl of chocolate to the pot of simmering water and briefly heat it so that it reaches its proper working temperature.

3.   Use the tempered chocolate as directed in the recipe.

TEMPERATURE GUIDE

Type of Chocolate	Melting Temperature	Cooling Temperature	Working Temperature
Dark	122–131°F (50–55°C)	82–84°F (28–29°C)	87°F (30°C)
Milk	113–118°F (45–48°C)	80–82°F (28–29°C)	86°F (30°C)
White	113–118°F (45–48°C)	78–80°F (26–27°C)	84°F (29°C)

CLARIFIED BUTTER and BEURRE NOISETTE

CLARIFYING BUTTER is a process that removes the milk solids from butter. Clarified butter has a much higher smoking point than regular butter. For browned butter, or *beurre noisette*, continue cooking the clarified butter until the milk solids turn dark brown and the butter has a nutty fragrance.

> Unsalted butter, as needed (use 33 percent more solid butter than you need of clarified butter; for example, if you need 225 g/8 oz clarified butter, start with 300 g/10.5 oz solid butter)

1. Cut the butter into tablespoons and place it in a heavy saucepan over medium heat, partially covered to prevent spattering. When the butter is melted, reduce the heat to low and cook, uncovered, until the solids drop to the bottom of the pan and begin to turn brown, about 20 minutes for 454 g/1 lb of butter. (For Beurre Noisette, cook the clarified butter until the solids turn dark brown.)

2. Strain the butter through a fine-mesh sieve or cheesecloth-lined strainer. Cool and store in an airtight container in the refrigerator for up to 3 months.

CITRUS FRUIT SUPRÊMES

CITRUS FRUIT, AS NEEDED

Using a sharp paring knife, cut the peel and pith off the ends of the citrus fruit. Stand the fruit upright and cut the peel and pith off the sides of the fruit. Make a cut on each side of each segment to remove all the suprêmes.

SOURCES

ALBERT USTER IMPORTS

Hundreds of chocolate and pastry products for the pastry chef, from chocolate couvertures to fruit purées to decorative marshmallow sheets and crystallized rose petals. They also carry Albert & Ferran Adrià's Texturas line of products for molecular gastronomy.

800-231-8154

www.auiswiss.com

AMADEUS VANILLA BEANS

Bulk vanilla beans and extracts from Madagascar, Tahiti, Indonesia, and other exotic locales.

310-670-9731

www.amadeusvanillabeans.com

AMORETTI

A large variety of pastry flavorings and ingredients including extracts, compounds, pastes, flavor sprays, pralines, and nut flours.

800-266-7388

www.amoretti.com

ATECO

Cake decorating supplies and an assortment of pastry tools, including pastry tips and the iconic Ateco cake turntable.

800-645-7170

www.atecousa.net

BOB'S RED MILL

A variety of grains and flours, including almond flour, hazelnut flour, and semolina.

800-349-2173

www.bobsredmill.com

THE CHEFS' WAREHOUSE

This online source has an excellent selection of professional baking ingredients, including chocolate, cacao nibs, vanilla beans, elderflower cordial, clotted cream, praline and other nut pastes, extracts, and ice cream and sorbet stabilizers.

718-842-8700

www.chefswarehouse.com

CHOCOSPHERE

This online source offers a great selection of products from high-quality chocolate brands, including Valrhona, Scharffen Berger, Guittard, and Felchlin.

877-992-4626

www.chocosphere.com

GOURMET FOOD STORE

This online source carries an impressive selection of gourmet food products, including French butters, fruit purées (Ravifruit brand), crème fraîche, fleur de sel, spices, candied oranges, chestnuts, and European chocolates.

877-220-4181

www.gourmetfoodstore.com

GUITTARD CHOCOLATE

This American-based chocolate maker produces chocolate in syrups, blocks, large chips, and powders for pastry chefs. The E. Guittard Collection vintage product line contains blends and single bean varietal chocolates, including the Quevedo, a varietal couverture chocolate from Ecuador, the Chucuri from northwest Colombia, the Sur del Lago couverture chocolate from western Venezuela, and the Ambanja from Madagascar.

800-468-2462

www.guittardchocolate.com

JB PRINCE

Professional-grade bakeware, silicone molds, chocolate molds, tart pans, and other pastry equipment.

36 E. 31st Street, 11th floor
New York, NY 10016
800-473-0577
www.jbprince.com

KEREKES

Full line of professional pastry, baking, and cake decorating supplies, including chocolate molds and supplies, silicone molds, and large and small bakery equipment.

6103 Fifteenth Avenue
Brooklyn, NY 11219
800-525-5556
www.bakedeco.com

KING ARTHUR FLOUR

This consumer site offers a full line of flours, including pastry, bread, cake, whole wheat, and organic varieties. They also have nut flours, spices, extracts, chocolate, cocoa powder, and baking pans and equipment.

800-827-6836

www.kingarthurflour.com

L'ÉPICERIE

Excellent line of high-end pastry ingredients, including powdered glucose, fruit purées (Boiron brand), nut flours, chocolate, and hard-to-find extracts and flavorings, such as licorice powder. As a bonus, L'Épicerie allows you to order their products in small quantities.

866-350-7575

www.lepicerie.com

NIELSEN MASSEY VANILLAS

High-quality vanilla beans, paste, powder, and extracts in Madagascan Bourbon, Tahitian, Mexican, and organic varieties. They also have a line of pure extracts in a variety of flavors, including coffee, chocolate, almond, and rose.

847-578-1550

www.nielsenmassey.com

PARIS GOURMET

A leading specialty food importer and distributor, Paris Gourmet carries a wide range of pastry ingredients including chocolate from Cacao Noel, Weiss, Valrhona, and Cacao Barry; pastry ingredients from Pastry 1; molecular gastronomy ingredients from Cuisine Tech; Gahara vanilla beans and extracts; Ravifruit fruit purées; and Mec 3 gelato and pastry ingredients.

800-727-8791
201-939-5656
www.parisgourmet.com

PASTRY CHEF CENTRAL

This online site offers a large line of professional-grade baking tools (molds and rings), small equipment (scales, knives, and cake decorating equipment), and pastry ingredients and garnishes (chocolate cigarettes).

www.pastrychef.com

SWISS CHALET

Large selection of pastry ingredients, including Felchlin chocolate, fondant, marzipan, flavorings and extracts, fruit purées, gels, and glazes.

800-347-9477
www.scff.com

THE PERFECT PUREE OF NAPA VALLEY

A large line of excellent quality fruit purées and concentrates for use in pastry components, from sauces to mousses to ice creams and sorbets.

2700 Napa Valley Corporate Dr., Suite L
Napa, CA 94558
800-556-3707
707-261-5100
www.perfectpuree.com

TUILE TIME CULINARY TEMPLATES

A large selection of excellent-quality half-sheet pan–size tuile templates made of high-density polyethylene. The templates are stain-proof and meet FDA and USDA certification for food processing.

www.culinarytemplates.com

VALRHONA

This French chocolate maker produces a line of premium chocolate favored by top pastry chefs around the world, including me. Valrhona pioneered the production of high-quality chocolate from carefully controlled sources and started the trend of featuring the percentage of cocoa solids in chocolate. They also have led the way toward chocolate from known origins and quality beans. The product line includes chocolate confectionery, flavored and plain chocolate bars, and bulk chocolate in bars or pellets.

888-682-5746
www.valrhona.com

ACKNOWLEDGMENTS

I want to give special thanks to Philippe Bertineau, Hervé Poussot, Enrique Aranda, Adil Slassi, Nancy Kershner, Eric Estrella, David Carmichael, Lincoln Carson, Pierre Gatel, Gregory Gourreau, Craig Harzewski, Christopher Hereghty, Johnny Iuzzini, Nicolas Néant, Simon Veauvy, Simon Dupin, Garry Laurdinat, and Alex Zamora. I also want to thank Eric Ripert, Daniel Boulud, Jean-Georges Vongerichten, David Burke, Wolfgang Puck, Alain Ducasse, Laurent Gras, Laurent Tourondel, Thomas Keller, and Michael Mina. You guys are not only incredible chefs, but great friends who never cease to inspire me.

A special thanks to Tish Boyle, without whom this book wouldn't have been possible. Thank you so much for your hard work and dedication—it never went unnoticed.

And to my wife, Fernanda, thank you for always supporting me and my career, and pushing me to go above and beyond.

—François Payard

Many thanks to François Payard, a great pastry chef and friend, for asking me to help him with this book. I had the pleasure of working with François on his first book, *Simply Sensational Desserts,* and loved every sweet second of it. This project turned out to be even more fun, particularly since I got to work in the amazing Payard kitchen every day for almost three months. Thanks to all the great people at Payard who made my stay so happy, especially Garry Larduinat, Julien Khalaf, Youssef Aderdou, and Diego Chino, who were always ready to share their considerable pastry knowledge and good cheer. I'd also like to thank my other friends at Payard who made this project such a pleasurable one: Alex Zamora, Rebecca Dorfman, Abby Klausner, Simon Veauvy, Mandy Pan, Jeremy Dumaine, John Espinal, Erika Garcia, Irene Rodriguez, Heidi Gunlocke, Yvette Hakim, Martin Ventura, Anthony Le Mezec, Felipe Coronado, and Cesar Navarro. A very special thanks also to my fabulous interns from The Institute of Culinary Education, Betsy Green, Rita Chou, and Shari Tanaka.

Thanks to Christine McKnight, an amazing hands-on editor who is as delightful as she is smart and professional. She was there every step of the way on this project, along with Jillian Saland, who seamlessly took over for Christine while she was on maternity leave. Also thanks to Tim Moriarty, great friend and colleague, and Dick Eggleston, my wonderful husband, for reading this manuscript and (gently) suggesting improvements.

—Tish Boyle

INDEX

A

Almond(s)
  Black Macarons, 305–6
  Cream, 341
  Crispy Meringue, 115 16
  Croustine Tuile Rounds, 35
  Dacquoise, 124
  Diamonds, Baked, 314
  Financiers, 272
  Maple Syrup Nougat Glacé, 27–28
  Nougatine, 345
  Rectangles, 102
  Rounds, 78–79, 322
Anise Cream, 236
Apple Cider Sauce, 47
Apple(s)
  Caramelized, 254
  Croustade, *212,* 213–14
  Cups, 128
  Four-Hour Baked, 110
  Spiral Tempura with Apple Cider Reduction, *46,* 47–48
  Tatin with Aged White Cheddar Cheese, Frisée Salad, and Toasted Walnuts, 307–8, *309*
  Winter Fruit Medley, 66
Apricot(s)
  Charlotte with Rum-Soaked Raisins, Chamomile Crème Anglaise, and Whole Milk Ice Cream, 43–45, *45*
  Roasted Summer, with Honey Pain Perdu and Saffron Ice Cream, *80,* 81–83

  Sauce, 82
  Sorbet, 263
Armagnac, 5
Armagnac-Prune Ice Cream, 100 101
Avocado Purée, 157

B

Banana Leaf Boat with Lemongrass Chiboust and Citrus Sauce, *166,* 167 69
Banana(s)
  Chips, 256
  -Chocolate Beignet, Quince Cooked in Caramel with, 88–90, *89*
  Exotic Sorbet, 57
  Ravioli with Exotic Sorbet and Passion Fruit, 57–58, *59*
  –Rum Raisin Ice Cream, 256
  Sautéed, and Passion Fruit, Crêpe Purse filled with, with Chocolate–Passion Fruit Sauce, 265–67, *266*
  Tart with White Chocolate Cream and Passion Fruit Sauce, 220, 221–23
Basil
  -Lemon Sherbet, 216
  -Mâche Olive Oil, 318
  Oil, 216
  -Strawberry Soup, 277
  -Tomato Sorbet, 324
Bavarian, Pear, 155
Bavarian Cream, Praline, 172

Beet and Mint Crème Brûlée—A Market Inspiration, 142, *143*
Beignets
  Chocolate, with Orange Blossom Crème Anglaise, 292–93, *293*
  Chocolate-Banana, Quince Cooked in Caramel with, 88–90, *89*
Berries. *See specific berries*
Blackberry(ies)
  Hibiscus Berry Gelée, 198
  Sauce, 37
Blueberry(ies)
  Berries in Vanilla Syrup, 185
  Coulis, 18
  Ice Cream, Fried, with Blueberry Coulis, 17–18, *19*
  Marmalade, 228–29
  Mixed Berries, 165
  Sauce, 116
  Sorbet, 115
Brioche, 342–43
  Apricot Charlotte, 44–45
  Honey Pain Perdu, 83
  Panini with Raspberry Jam and Peanut Butter Crunch Ice Cream, 289–90, *291*
Butter, 5
  Beurre Noisette, 348
  Brown, Ice Cream, 239–40
  Clarified, 348
Buttermilk
  Crème Anglaise, 98
  Ice Cream, 97–98
  Panna Cotta, 148, 317

C

Cacao Nib(s), 5
    Crunch, 244
    –Espresso Tuile, 152
Café Liégeois, Reconstruction of,
        with Cacao Nib–Espresso
        Tuile and Meringue
        Sticks, *150,* 151–52
Cakes
    Carrot, 225–26
    Chocolate Chiffon, 21–22
    Chocolate Génoise, 207–8
    Chocolate Sacher, 191–92
    Lemon–Poppy Seed, 55–56
    Pain d'Épices, 127–28
    Walnut, 327–29
    Yogurt, 52–53
Caramel
    Balsamic Sauce, 163
    Butter Sauce, 129–30
    Chantilly, 110
    Crème Anglaise, 194, 335–36
    Garnishes, 336
    Ice Cream, 31–32
    Passion Fruit, 73–74
    Sauce, 334
Cardamom Ice Cream, 49–50
Carré Payard with Caramel
        Anglaise, Fleur de Sel,
        and Caramel Ice Cream,
        190, 191–94
Carrot
    Cakes, 225–26
    Fried, Garnish, 226
    -Honey Emulsion, 226
    Jus, 227
Cassis
    Chantilly, 138
    Japonaise with Japonaise
        Noodles and Cassis Port
        Sauce, *136,* 137–39
    Poached Pears, 63
    Port Sauce, 139
Chamomile Crème Anglaise, 43
Chantilly
    Caramel, 110
    Cassis, 138
    Chocolate, 176

Milk Chocolate and Peanut
        Butter, 133–34
    Vanilla, 146
Cheese. *See also* Cream Cheese;
        Mascarpone
    Aged White Cheddar, Frisée
        Salad, and Toasted
        Walnuts, Apple Tatin
        with, 307–8, *309*
    Cabrales, Pomegranate, and
        Szechuan Pepper Ice
        Cream, Poached Seckel
        Pear with, 313–15, *315*
    Chèvre Cheesecake, 329
    Feta Cheesecakes, 321–22
    Gorgonzola Ice Cream, 304
    Parmesan Tuiles, 312
    Ricotta Tart Filling, 312
Cheesecake
    Chèvre, 329
    Feta, with Red Wine–Poached
        Dates and White Pepper
        Ice Cream, *320,* 321–23
    Rosemary-Scented, 69–70
Cherries
    Fricassée of, with Hyssop,
        Pistachio Crumble, and
        Pistachio Ice Cream, *60,*
        61–62
    Poached, 54
    Sautéed, 53
Chestnut(s), 5
    Candied, Garnish, 107
    Ice Cream, 105–6
    Purée, 146
Chocolate. *See also* White Chocolate
    -Banana Beignet, Quince
        Cooked in Caramel with,
        88–90, *89*
    Bittersweet Hot, 301
    brands, 5
    Chiffon Cake, 21–22
    cigarettes, about, 5
    Dark, Soufflés, 270
    Decorations, 189

Dome with Vanilla Crème
        Brûlée and Hazelnut
        Dacquoise, *202,* 203–4
    Earl Grey Tea Mousse, 208
    Filling for Tart, 245
    Ganache Beignet Centers, 292
    Garnish, 205
    Génoise, 207–8
    Gianduja Ice Cream, 243–44
    Gianduja Mousse, 200
    -Ginger Sauce, 106
    Glaze, 189
    Hazelnut Wafers, 187–88
    Milk, and Peanut Butter
        Chantilly, 133–34
    Milk, Cube Filled with Earl
        Grey Tea Mousse and
        Grapefruit and Orange
        Gelée, 206–9, *207*
    Milk, Rice Crispy, 134
    Mousse, 188, 193, 337
    –Passion Fruit Sauce, 267
    Pastry Cream Tuile, 22–23
    Phyllo, 176
    Phyllo Triangles, 197
    Raspberry Ganache, 138
    Rice Crispy Disks, 175
    Sablé Breton, 192
    Sacher Cake, 191–92
    Sauce, 334
    Shell Filled with Coconut
        Sorbet and Star Anise
        Sabayon, *24,* 25–26
    Sorbet, 156
    Spray, 201
    Tart Dough, 333
    Tart Shells, 244
    Tempered, 347
Cinnamon Ice Cream, 159–60
Citrus Suprêmes, 348
Clotted Cream, Whipped, 56
Cocoa butter, 6
Cocoa powder, 5
Coconut, 6
Coconut Sorbet, 25, 85
Coffee
    Granité, 195
    Pastry Cream, 196–97

**Cranberry Gelée filled with Pear
	Bavarian, Nougatine, and
	Poached Pear,** 153–55,
	154
Cream, 6. *See also* Chantilly
	Anise, 236
	Crème Fraîche, 50
	Honey, 253
	Rosemary Diplomat, 326
	Whipped, 105, 116
	White Chocolate, 221
Cream Cheese
	Black Olive Macaron Filling,
		306
	Chèvre Cheesecake, 329
	Feta Cheesecakes, 321–22
	Ice Cream, 227
	Rosemary-Scented Cheesecake,
		69–70
**Crema Catalana, Deconstruction
	of: Blood Orange Gelée,
	Foamed Crème Brûlée,
	and Cinnamon Ice Cream,**
	158, 159–61
Crème Anglaise, 335
	Buttermilk, 98
	Caramel, 194, 335–36
	Chamomile, 43
	Orange Blossom, 292
	Pistachio, 335
	Poire William, 92
	Szechuan Peppercorn, 164
Crème Brûlée
	**Beet and Mint—A Market
		Inspiration,** 142, *143*
	**Pumpkin, with Vanilla
		Chantilly, Crispy
		Meringue, and Chestnut
		Purée,** *144,* 145–46
	Vanilla, 203–4
Crème fraîche, 6
Crème Fraîche Cream, 50
Crêpes, 265
**Croustine filled with Fromage
	Blanc Sorbet and
	Blackberry Sauce,** *34,*
	35–37
Currant Garnish, 138

D

Dacquoise
	Almond, 124
	Hazelnut, 134, 171, 200, 204
Dates, Red Wine–Poached, 322
**Dulce de Leche Coulant with
	Avocado Purée and
	Chocolate Sorbet,**
	156–57
**Duo of Coffee and Chocolate with
	a Mascarpone-Espresso
	Shot,** 195–97, *196*

E

Earl Grey Tea
	Infusion, 276
	Mousse, Chocolate, 208
	Syrup, 208
Elderflower-Lemon Sherbet, 278
Equipment notes, 8–11
Espresso–Cacao Nib Tuile, 152

F

Fennel, Poached, 236
Fennel Chips, 237
**Feuille de Brick filled with Sautéed
	Apples, Pain d'Épices,
	and Caramel Sauce,** *126,*
	127–28
Feuilles de brick, about, 6
Feuilletine, 6
Fig(s)
	Mascarpone Cream, 232–33
	Pulp, Spiced, 218
	Roasted, 233
Financiers, Almond, 272
Fleur de sel, 6
Flour, for recipes, 6
Flours, nut, about, 7
Fondant, 6
Frisée Salad, 308
Fromage Blanc
	Sorbet, 36, 52

**Soufflé Tart with Blueberry
	Marmalade and Fromage
	Blanc Sorbet with Cumin,**
	228–30, *229*
Fruit(s). *See also specific fruits*
	Citrus Suprêmes, 348
	purées, 6
	Tuiles, 338
	**Winter, Fricassée of, with
		Vanilla Ice Cream,** 66–67,
		67
	Winter, Medley, 66

G

Gelatin, 6
Gelées
	Blood Orange, 161
	Cranberry, 155
	Grapefruit and Orange, 209
	Hibiscus Berry, 198
	Lime, 296
	Orange, 301
	Pear, 329–30
	Pineapple, 86
Gianduja
	Ice Cream, 243–44
	Mousse, 200
Ginger
	-Chocolate Sauce, 106
	Ice Cream, 42
	Poached, 40–41
	Syrup, 40
Glucose syrup, 6
Granité, Coffee, 195
Grapefruit
	Citrus-Mint Salad, 311
	Citrus Suprêmes, 348
	Citrus Terrine, 318
	Citrus Terrine and Soup, 283–84
	and Orange Gelée, 209

H

Hazelnut(s)
	Caramelized, 173
	Dacquoise, 134, 171, 200, 204
	Japonais Disks, 137–38

Hazelnut(s), *continued*
  Praline Dome with Ganache
    Citron and Honeyed
    Phyllo Leaves, *170,*
      171–73
  Succès Biscuits, 186
  Wafers, 187–88
Herbs, Fried, 346. *See also specific*
    herbs
Hibiscus Berry Gelée, 198
Hibiscus Sauce, 200
Honey
  Cream, 253
  and Nougat Ice Cream, 74
  -Nougat Ice Cream, 252
  Pain Perdu, 83
Hyssop, Cherries in, 62

I

Ice Cream
  Banana–Rum Raisin, 256
  Blueberry, 17–18
  Brown Butter, 239–40
  Buttermilk, 97–98
  Caramel, 31–32
  Cardamom, 49–50
  Chestnut, 105–6
  Cinnamon, 159–60
  Cream Cheese, 227
  Gianduja, 243–44
  Ginger, 42
  Gorgonzola, 304
  Honey and Nougat, 74
  Honey-Nougat, 252
  Lemon Thyme, 247–48
  Lychee Crème Glacé, 124–25
  Mascarpone, 231
  Orange Blossom, 300
  Peanut Butter Crunch, 289–90
  Pistachio, 61, 268–69
  Prune-Armagnac, 100–101
  Rosemary, 70–71
  Saffron, 81
  stabilizers, about, 7
  Stick, Vanilla, 272
  Szechuan Pepper, 63, 313–14

Vanilla, 340
Vanilla-Prune, 78
White Pepper, 321
Whole Milk, 340
Ingredient notes, 5–7
Invert sugar, 7

J

Japonais Bean Thread Noodles, 139
Japonais Disks, 137–38

K

Kugelhopf Caramel Glacé with
    Rum-Raisin Parfait,
    Caramel Crème Anglaise,
    and Chocolate Sauce, *30,*
      31–33
Kumquat
  -Orange Sorbet, 288
  Soup, 287

L

Lavender
  Crystallized, 263
  -Poached Peaches, 264
Lemongrass, 7
Lemongrass Chiboust with
    Pomegranate Pineapple,
    178, 179–81
Lemon(s)
  -Basil Sherbet, 216
  Cream, 215
  -Elderflower Sherbet, 278
  Ganache Citron, 172
  Meyer, Sherbet, 235
  -Poppy Seed Cake filled with
    Red Wine–Poached
    Cherries and Clotted
    Cream, 54–56, *55*
  Tuiles, 216
Lemon Thyme Ice Cream, 247–48
Licorice Meringue Rounds, 15–16

Lime
  Gelée, 296
  Peel, Candied, 42
  Sherbet, 296
  Syrup, 297
Limesicles, 296
Lychee Crème Glacé, 124–25

M

Macaron, Black Olive, with
    Gorgonzola Ice Cream,
    304–6, *305*
Mâche-Basil Olive Oil, 318
Mango
  Carpaccio with Ginger Syrup,
    Poached Ginger, and
    Ginger Ice Cream with
    Candied Lime Peel,
    40–42, *41*
  Sautéed, with Tarragon, 148
  Maple Syrup Nougat Glacé with
    Almond and Pistachio,
    and Pistachio Crème
    Anglaise, 27–28, *29*
Marshmallows, Orange, 298–300
Mascarpone
  Fig Cream, 232–33
  Ice Cream, 231
  Mousse, 195–96
Meringue(s)
  Almond Dacquoise, 124
  Crispy, 115–16
  Disks and Sticks, 146
  Hazelnut Dacquoise, 134, 171,
    200, 204
  Japonais Disks, 137–38
  Orange Blossom, 227
  Rounds, Licorice, 15–16
  Steamed, and Rhubarb Cream
    with Berries in Vanilla
    Bean Syrup, *182,* 183–85
  Succès Biscuits, 186
Mint
  Leaves, Crystallized, 23
  Syrup, 99

Mousse
    Chocolate, 188, 337
    Chocolate Earl Grey Tea, 208
    Gianduja, 200
    Mascarpone, 195–96
    Rose, 123

N

Napoleons
    Almond-Prune, with Prune-
        Armagnac Ice Cream,
        100–103, *101*
    Chestnut Ice Cream, with
        Whipped Cream and
        Chocolate-Ginger Sauce,
        104, 105–7
    Four-Hour Baked Apple, with
        Caramel Chantilly and
        Caramel Sauce, *108,*
        109–11
    Peanut Butter and Milk
        Chocolate Crispy, *132,*
        133–35
    Plum Tomato, with Rosemary
        Diplomate Cream and
        Tomato-Basil Sorbet,
        324–26, *325*
    Red Currant, with Peppered
        Nougatine, 112–14, *113*
    Rhubarb, filled with Braised
        Rhubarb, *118,* 119–21
    White Chocolate Rose Water,
        with Lychee Crème Glacé,
        122, 123–25
Noodles, Japonais Bean Thread, 139
Nougat and Honey Ice Cream, 74
Nougatine, 345
Nougatine Rectangles, Peppered,
    112–13
Nut flours, 7
Nuts. *See also specific nuts*
    Caramelized, 177, 250–51
    Toasted, 346

O

Oil, Basil, 216
Oil, Olive, Basil-Mâche, 318
Olive, Black, Cream Cheese Macaron
    Filling, 306
Orange blossom (water), 7
    Crème Anglaise, 292
    Ice Cream, 300
    Meringue, 227
Orange(s)
    Blood, Gelée, 161
    Chips, 147–48, 284
    Citrus-Mint Salad, 311
    Citrus Sauce, 169
    Citrus Suprêmes, 348
    Citrus Terrine, 318
    Citrus Terrine and Soup, 283–84
    Gelée, 301
    and Grapefruit Gelée, 209
    -Kumquat Sorbet, 288
    Marshmallows, 298–300
    Peel, Candied, 250
    Sauce, 253
    -Scented Pastry Cream, 129
    -Scented Streusel, 161
    Sorbet, 275
    Tuile filled with Marshmallow
        and Orange Blossom Ice
        Cream, 298–301, *299*
    Tuiles, 339

P

Palet d'Or, Big, filled with Hazelnut
    Wafer and Manjari
    Mousse, 186–89, *187*
Panna Cotta, Buttermilk with
    Citrus Terrine, Mâche
    Salad, and Parmesan
    Tuile, *316,* 317–19
    Shot of, with Tarragon-Scented
    Mango, 147–49, *149*

Passion Fruit
    Caramel, 73–74
    -Chocolate Sauce, 267
    Exotic Sorbet, 57
    Sauce, 222–23
    and Sautéed Bananas, Crêpe
        Purse filled with, with
        Chocolate–Passion Fruit
        Sauce, 265–67, *266*
    Tuiles, 57–58
Pastry Cream, 341
    Coffee, 196–97
    Orange-Scented, 129
    Prune, 103
    Red Currant, 113–14
    Rhubarb, 120, 184
    Rosemary, 341
    Vanilla, 341
    Walnut, 92
Pavlova, Blueberry, with Warm
    Blueberry Coulis, 115–16,
    117
Peach(es)
    Lavender-Poached, 264
    Sauce, 248
    Streusel Tart, 249
Peanut Brittle, 135
Peanut Butter
    Crunch Ice Cream, 289–90
    and Milk Chocolate Chantilly,
        133–34
    Milk Chocolate Rice Crispy, 134
Pear(s)
    Bavarian, 155
    Brown Butter Roasted, with
        Maple Syrup and Vanilla-
        Prune Ice Cream, *76,*
        77–79
    Gelée, 329–30
    Poached, 92, 153
    Poached, in Port and Black
        Currant with Julienned
        Black Truffle and
        Szechuan Pepper Ice
        Cream, 63–65, *64*
    Poached, in Vanilla Syrup, 259
    Poached, with Pomegranate, 314

Pears(s), *continued*
    Poached in Passion Fruit
        Caramel, Arlette, and
        Honey and Nougat Ice
        Cream, *72,* 73–75
    Roasted, 330
    Warm Bartlett, with Chèvre
        Cheesecake, Walnut Cake,
        and Fried Sage Leaves,
        327–31, *328*
    Winter Fruit Medley, 66
Pecans, Candied, 130, 240
Pecan Tarts, 241
Peppered Nougatine Rectangles,
    112–13
Peppermint Parfait Glacé with
    Chocolate Pastry Cream
    Tuile, *20,* 21–23
Phyllo
    Chocolate, 176
    Crescents, 185
    dough, about, 7
    Leaf Shards, 173
    Pears, 91
    Rectangles, 102
    Rounds, 89–90
    Strips, 214
    Tarts, 222
    Triangles, 106–7
    Triangles, Chocolate, 197
Pineapple
    Caramelized, and Sauce, 241
    Carpaccio, 26
    Chips, 345–46
    Gelée, 86
    Pomegranate, 181
    Seared with Thyme with
        Tapioca Parfait Wrapped
        in Pineapple Gelée and
        Coconut Sorbet, *84,*
        85–87
Pistachio(s)
    Candied, 53
    Crème Anglaise, 335
    Crumble, 62
    Ice Cream, 61, 268–69

Maple Syrup Nougat Glacé,
    27–28
Plum(s)
    Soda with Vanilla Ice Cream
        Stick and Almond
        Financier, 271–72, *273*
    Steamed Baby, in Extra-Virgin
        Olive Oil, Fleur de Sel,
        and Cardamom Ice
        Cream, 49–50, *51*
    Tuiles, 50
Poire William Crème Anglaise, 92
Pomegranate
    Pineapple, 181
    Poached Pears with, 314
    Sauce, 314
Port Sauce, 65
Port Sauce, Cassis, 139
Praline paste, 7
    Hazelnut Wafers, 187–88
    Praline Bavarian Cream, 172
    Rice Crispy Disks, 175
Prune(s)
    -Armagnac Ice Cream, 100–101
    Pastry Cream, 103
    Sangria, 77, 102–3, 258
    -Vanilla Ice Cream, 78
Pudding, Rice, with Szechuan
    Peppercorn Anglaise and
    Caramel Balsamic Sauce,
    162, 163–65
Puff Pastry, 343–44
    Arlette, 74–75
    Rectangles, 325
    Rounds, 78
Pumpkin Crème Brûlée, 145–46
Pyramid of Gianduja with Hibiscus
    Berry Gelée and Hibiscus
    Sauce, 198–201, *199*

Q

Quince Cooked in Caramel with
    Chocolate-Banana
    Beignet, 88–90, *89*

R

Raisin(s)
    Rum, –Banana Ice Cream, 256
    -Rum Parfait Centers, 32–33
    Rum-Soaked, 44
    -Tomato Sauce, 326
Raspberry(ies)
    Berries in Vanilla Syrup, 185
    Caramelized, 125
    Chocolate Ganache, 138
    Fresh, Lemon-Basil Sherbet, and
        Basil Oil, Warm Lemon Tart
        with, 215–16, *217*
    Hibiscus Berry Gelée, 198
    Jam, 290
    Mixed Berries, 165
    Red Berries in Vanilla Syrup,
        114
    Red Berry and Tomato Gazpacho,
        282
Red Currant(s)
    Berries in Vanilla Syrup, 185
    Hibiscus Sauce, 200
    Pastry Cream, 113–14
    Red Berries in Vanilla Syrup,
        114
    Sauce, 114
Rhubarb
    Braised, 121
    Pastry Cream, 120, 184
    Sauce, 119–20, 183
Rice cereal, crispy
    Milk Chocolate Rice Crispy, 134
    Rice Crispies with Milk
        Chocolate and Crispy
        Chocolate Phyllo, *174,*
        175–77
    White Chocolate Rice Crispy,
        124
Rice Pudding, 164
Rosemary
    Diplomat Cream, 326
    Ice Cream, 70–71
    Pastry Cream, 341
    -Scented Cheesecake with Oven-
        Roasted Strawberries and
        Rosemary Ice Cream, *68,*
        69–71

Rose Mousse, 123
Rose water, 7
Rum, 7
  Raisin–Banana Ice Cream, 256
  -Raisin Parfait Centers, 32–33
  -Soaked Raisins, 44

S

Sabayon, Star Anise, 26
Sablé Breton, Chocolate, 192
Sablé Breton Dough, 333
Saffron Ice Cream, 81
Sage Syrup, 330
Salt, 6
Sauces
  Apple Cider, 47
  Apricot, 82
  Blackberry, 37
  Blueberry, 116
  Blueberry Coulis, 18
  Caramel, 334
  Caramel Balsamic, 163
  Caramel Butter, 129–30
  Caramelized Pineapple, 241
  Cassis Port, 139
  Chocolate, 334
  Chocolate-Ginger, 106
  Chocolate–Passion Fruit, 267
  Citrus, 169
  Hibiscus, 200
  Orange, 253
  Passion Fruit, 222–23
  Peach, 248
  Pomegranate, 314
  Port, 65
  Raisin-Tomato, 326
  Red Currant, 114
  Red Wine, 233
  Rhubarb, 119–20, 183
  Strawberry, 16
  Tapioca, 86–87
**Scones, Buttermilk, with
    Strawberry and Tomato
    Jam,** *96,* 97–99

Sherbet
  Lemon-Basil, 216
  Lemon-Elderflower, 278
  Lime, 296
  Meyer Lemon, 235
Simple Syrup, 339
**Soda, Plum, with Vanilla Ice
    Cream Stick and Almond
    Financier,** 271–72, *273*
Sorbet
  Apricot, 263
  Blueberry, 115
  Chocolate, 156
  Coconut, 25, 85
  Exotic, 57
  Fromage Blanc, 36, 52
  Fromage Blanc, with Cumin, 230
  Kumquat-Orange, 288
  Orange, 275
  stabilizers, about, 7
  Strawberry, 15
  Tangerine, 284
  Tomato-Basil, 324
  Yellow Tomato, 281
Soufflés
  **Dark Chocolate, with Pistachio
      Ice Cream,** 268–70, *269*
  **of Puff Pastry with Orange-
      Scented Pastry Cream,
      Candied Pecans, and
      Caramel Butter Sauce,**
      129–30, *131*
Soups
  **Citrus Terrine with Elderflower-
      Perrier, and Tangerine
      Sorbet,** 283–85, *285*
  **Earl Grey Tea, with Tapioca
      and Orange Sorbet,** *274,*
      275–76
  **Farm Strawberry–Basil, with
      Lemon-Elderflower
      Sherbet and Strawberry
      Tuile,** 277–78, *279*

**Peach, with Apricot Sorbet and
    Crystallized Lavender,**
    262, 263–64
**Red Berry and Tomato
    Gazpacho with Tomato
    Chips,** *280,* 281–82
**Spicy Kumquat, with Kumquat-
    Orange Sorbet and Star
    Anise,** *286,* 287–88
**Watermelon and Vodka, with
    a "Limesicle" and Lime
    Syrup,** *294,* 295–97
Star Anise Sabayon, 26
Strawberry(ies)
  -Basil Soup, 277
  Berries in Vanilla Syrup, 185
  Hibiscus Berry Gelée, 198
  Oven-Roasted, 70
  Red Berries in Vanilla Syrup,
      114
  Red Berry and Tomato Gazpacho,
      282
  Sauce, 16
  Sorbet, 15
  and Tomato Jam, 98
  Tuiles, 278
Streusel, 342
Streusel, Orange-Scented, 161
Syrups
  Earl Grey Tea, 208
  Ginger, 40
  Lime, 297
  Mint, 99
  Sage, 330
  Simple, 339
Szechuan Peppercorn Anglaise, 164
Szechuan Pepper Ice Cream, 63,
    313–14

T

Tangerine Sorbet, 284
Tapioca, 275
  Parfait, 87
  Sauce, 86–87
Tarragon Leaves, Crystallized, 147

Tart Dough
  Basic Sweet, 332
  Chocolate, 333
Tarts
  Apple Croustade, *212,* 213–14
  **Banana, with White Chocolate
    Cream and Passion Fruit
    Sauce,** *220,* 221–23
  **Caramelized Pineapple-Pecan,
    with Brown Butter Ice
    Cream,** *238,* 239–41
  **Carrot Cake, with Cream
    Cheese Ice Cream,
    Honey-Carrot Emulsion,
    Orange Blossom
    Meringue, and Fried
    Carrots,** *224,* 225–27
  **Fromage Blanc Soufflé, with
    Blueberry Marmalade and
    Fromage Blanc Sorbet
    with Cumin,** 228–30, *229*
  **Lucas Carton Fig, with
    Caramelized Figs,** 218–
    19, *219*
  **Mascarpone, with Roasted
    Figs and Mascarpone Ice
    Cream,** 231–33, *232*
  **Mediterranean Fennel, filled
    with Anise Cream and
    Candied Fennel,** *234,*
    235–37
  **Peach Streusel Upside-Down,
    with Lemon Thyme Ice
    Cream,** *246,* 247–49
  **Red Wine, with Sangria Prunes
    and Poached Pear in
    Vanilla Syrup,** 257–59,
    258
  **Traditional Apple Tarte Tatin
    with Banana Chips and
    Banana–Rum Raisin Ice
    Cream,** 254–56, *255*
  **Warm Chocolate, with
    Raspberries, Cacao Nib
    Crunch, and Gianduja Ice
    Cream,** *242,* 243–45

  **Warm Honey, with Candied
    Orange and Honey-
    Nougat Ice Cream,**
    250–53, *251*
  **Warm Lemon, with Fresh
    Raspberries, Lemon-Basil
    Sherbet, and Basil Oil,**
    215–16, *217*
  **Warm Ricotta, with Citrus-
    Mint Salad,** *310,* 311–12
Tart Shells, 215
Tart Shells, Chocolate, 244
Tomato(es)
  -Basil Sorbet, 324
  Chips, 281–82
  Oven-Dried, 326
  -Raisin Sauce, 326
  and Red Berry Gazpacho, 282
  and Strawberry Jam, 98
  Yellow, Sorbet, 281
**Trompe l'Oeil Phyllo Pears with
    Walnut Cream and Poire
    William Crème Anglaise,**
    91–93, *93*
Truffle Garnish, 65
Tuiles
  Cacao Nib–Espresso, 152
  Chocolate Pastry Cream, 22–23
  Fruit, 338
  Lemon, 216
  Orange, 339
  Parmesan, 312
  Passion Fruit, 57–58
  Plum, 50
  Rings, Orange, 300–301
  Rounds, Croustine, 35
  Spiced, 109–10
  Strawberry, 278
  Vanilla, 338–39

V

**Vacherin à la Minute with Licorice
    and Farm Strawberry
    Sorbet,** *14,* 15–16

Vanilla
  Bean Garnish, 82
  beans, about, 7
  Chantilly, 146
  Crème Brûlée, 203–4
  Ice Cream, 340
  Ice Cream Stick, 272
  Pastry Cream, 341
  -Prune Ice Cream, 78
  Tuiles, 338–39

W

Wafers
  Crispy, 120–21
  Hazelnut, 187–88
Walnut(s)
  Cake, 327–29
  Crumble, 330
  Pastry Cream, 92
Watermelon Soup, 295
White Chocolate
  Cream, 221
  Ganache Citron, 172
  Rice Crispy, 124
  Rice Crispy Disks, 175
  Rose Mousse, 123
White Pepper Ice Cream, 321
Wine
  Cassis Port Sauce, 139
  Poached Cherries, 54
  Port Sauce, 65
  Red, –Poached Dates, 322
  Red, Sauce, 233
  **Red, Tart with Sangria Prunes
    and Poached Pear in
    Vanilla Syrup,** 257–59,
    258
  Sangria Prunes, 77, 102–3, 258

Y

**Yogurt Cake with Sautéed
    Cherries and Candied
    Pistachios,** 52–53